FOUNDATIONS
FOR
PURPOSEFUL
CHURCH
ADMINISTRATION

FOUNDATIONS ✝ FOR PURPOSEFUL CHURCH ADMINISTRATION

ALVIN J. LINDGREN

ABINGDON PRESS ■ NASHVILLE

FOUNDATIONS FOR PURPOSEFUL CHURCH ADMINISTRATION

Copyright © 1965 by Abingdon Press

14th Printing 1986

ISBN 0-687-13339-4

Library of Congress Catalog Card Number: 65-16459

MANUFACTURED BY THE PARTHENON PRESS AT
NASHVILLE, TENNESSEE, UNITED STATES OF AMERICA

TO MY FAMILY
   Alma, my wife
   Patricia
   Judith
   James
   John
   Dianne

■ ■ ■ PREFACE

The insights of this book are largely the result of this author's experience in churches where he has had administrative responsibility, either as a pastor or as a district superintendent. The experience of working with persons facing the concrete needs of the local church formed the testing laboratory out of which this theory of purposeful church administration emerged. To all these persons and churches I owe a debt of gratitude beyond my ability to articulate for the joy, the challenge, and the insights gained through this relationship.

I am also deeply indebted to the many students of Garrett Theological Seminary whose critical and challenging attitude in my church administration course caused me continually to reexamine my assumptions and to crystallize more sharply the concepts set forth here. The urging of these students encouraged me to put in writing this approach to purposeful church administration which they indicated they had found stimulating in the classroom and helpful in their student charges.

My wife and children deserve a special word of appreciation for their understanding patience while this book was being written piecemeal over vacation periods, weekends, and evenings.

There are three persons without whose assistance this book could not have been completed for publication at this time. Lester Scherer, a doctoral candidate at Northwestern University, rendered invaluable service in proofreading and assisting in revising the entire manuscript in its final rewriting for publication. I am also grateful to Miss Ardella Nelson for typing the first draft of the manuscript and to Mrs. Geoffrey L. Story, Jr., for meeting the typing deadline for the final draft. I am also greatly indebted to Richard Deems, a former student, for preparing the index.

Although indebted to all these persons and more, I must assume full responsibility for the concepts set forth. It is my hope that this book will throw sufficient new light on an old subject to serve as a directional guide for the beginning pastor and to be helpful and welcomed as well by the experienced church administrator. It is even hoped that any disagreement with the concepts set forth will lead to a reexamination of the field and that a more effective approach of enabling the church to fulfill its mission will emerge.

ALVIN J. LINDGREN

■■■ CONTENTS

INTRODUCTION 13

CHAPTER I   CHURCH ADMINISTRATION AND THE
             CONTEMPORARY SCENE 15
      A. The Increase of Administrative Activities in the
         Life of the Church
      B. A Common Image of the Pastor as Administrator
      C. Two Basic Approaches to Church Administration
         Today

CHAPTER II   CHURCH ADMINISTRATION AND THE
             NATURE OF THE CHURCH 22
      A. Administration, by Definition, Requires a Clear
         Understanding of the Purpose of the Church
      B. Biblical Precedent Relates Church Administra-
         tion to the Nature of the Church
      C. Contemporary Pressures Require the Church to
         Define Its Nature
      D. Possible Approaches to Defining the Nature of the
         Church

CHAPTER III   THE NATURE AND MISSION OF THE CHURCH 38

     A. The Church as God's Chosen Community

     B. The Church as the Body of Christ

     C. The Church as a Fellowship of Redemptive Love

CHAPTER IV   A CONCEPT OF PURPOSEFUL CHURCH ADMINISTRATION 60

     A. A Definition of Purposeful Church Administration

     B. Purposeful Church Administration Rests upon a God-Centered, Person-Oriented Polarity Principle

     C. Steps in the Administrative Process

     D. Goals and Principles of Purposeful Church Administration

CHAPTER V   BUILD A SPIRITUAL FOUNDATION THROUGH WORSHIP AND STUDY 89

     A. The Importance of This Principle

     B. Begin with the Church Administrator

     C. Worship Must Be Kept Central and Vital in the Life of the Church

     D. Study Is Required of the Whole Church if It Is to Understand and Fulfill Its Mission

     E. The Relationship of Worship and Study to the Life of the Church as a Whole

CHAPTER VI   ESTABLISH REDEMPTIVE INTERPERSONAL RELATIONSHIPS 121

     A. The Importance of Redemptive Interpersonal Relationships

     B. The Pastor Must Be a Mature Person

C. The Implications of Personality Dynamics for Church Administration

D. The Pastor's Relationship with Persons

E. Establishing Redemptive Interpersonal Relationships Between Church Members

CHAPTER VII   PROVIDE FOR THE CREATIVE FUNCTIONING OF SMALL GROUPS IN THE CHURCH 153

A. The Importance and Use of Small Groups in the Church

B. A Definition of Group Dynamics

C. Principles of Group Dynamics

D. Opportunities for Growth Through Committee Relationships

E. New Life Through Study and Fellowship Groups

CHAPTER VIII   EQUIP LAYMEN FOR LEADERSHIP AND SERVICE IN THE CHURCH'S MINISTRY TO THE WORLD 181

A. The Necessity and Significance of Lay Service and Witness

B. Dimensions of the Lay Ministry

C. How May Laymen Be Equipped for Christian Service?

CHAPTER IX   STRENGTHEN THE CHURCH BY COORDINATED COMPREHENSIVE PLANNING 226

A. The Necessity and Value of Comprehensive Planning

B. An Approach to Long-range Planning in the Congregation

C. The Place of Annual Planning in the Local Church

D. A Continual Coordination of Plans

CHAPTER X   UTILIZE ALL AVAILABLE RESOURCES 255
            A. The Importance of This Principle
            B. Sharing Denominational Resources
            C. Sharing Interdenominational and Ecumenical
                Resources
            D. Relating Community Resources to the Church
            E. Keeping Abreast in Related Fields
            F. Conclusion

APPENDIX A 280

APPENDIX B 283

INDEX OF SUBJECTS AND AUTHORS 291

INDEX OF SCRIPTURAL PASSAGES 301

■ ■ ■ INTRODUCTION

This is not a book *about* church administration but a guiding statement *for* church administrators. The focus is upon preparing the minister to *be* a church administrator by interpreting what church administration is, the foundations on which it rests, and the prerequisites for leadership in this field. This book is written both for the theological student and for the experienced minister. For the latter, it is hoped that a new perspective may be offered here which will provide a happy alternative to the often disheartening demands of his present situation.

The need for a new viewpoint for church administration was dramatized when a well-known but frustrated pastor said to me, "All I do is rush from one thing to another. I don't really know what I am doing or why I am doing it." The aims of this book are to help the church administrator discover what he ought to be doing, to understand why he is doing it, and to set forth the basic principles for moving toward the goal of equipping the church to fulfill her mission.

This volume attempts to present a clear statement of the goals of church administration and to erect signposts pointing toward those goals. Any attempt to mark every step of the journey is of course precluded by the essentially dynamic nature of the administrative task. Every administrator must be free to guide his particular congregation from its present place in the wilderness into the promised land of the church's true mission. At the same time, however, the administrator must know that the promised land is a reality and in what direction it lies. The struggles faced and the obstacles to be overcome must be accepted and wrestled with by those making the journey. No one else can do it. The strength acquired in making the journey is essential for the enjoyment of the promised land.

It will be strongly emphasized throughout that the basic foundation on which all church administration rests is a clear understanding of the Christian faith and of the mission of the church. Such an understanding is essential, because the sole objective of church administration is the realization of the church's purpose. This is precisely why there must always be a theological dimension to *church* administration, if it is to be worthy of its name. Biblical, historical, and theological studies *prescribe* the goals of church administration and *circumscribe* acceptable methodology in moving toward the goals. The primacy and validity of the theological dimension of church administration will be developed in the first four chapters. All that comes after that will assume its validity and will be developed within that context.

The person of the church administrator will be our primary concern throughout. He will be introduced to a *God-centered* view of the administrative task, resting on a biblical-theological concept of the nature and mission of the church. He will also be confronted with the premise that church administration must be *person-oriented,* since the church's mission is to make known God's love to all men. Church administration must seek to become a discipline of the Holy Spirit for making the love of God a reality in the lives of persons, individually and socially. This means that there will be a dynamic, living quality about church administration, properly understood. By the very fact that it is held to be a work of and under the Spirit, the administrative task, as it is lifted up in these pages, is seen to be complex and difficult. The primary concern in every chapter is to prepare the person called to chief responsibility for that task.

CHAPTER I

CHURCH ADMINISTRATION
AND THE
CONTEMPORARY SCENE

A. The Increase of Administrative Activities in the Life of the Church

There is a widespread feeling today that administration has become the proverbial camel's nose in the tent, crowding out the church's proper work and message. Some commentators have claimed that administrative concerns have become an ecclesiastical Frankenstein, threatening to strangle the spiritual life of the church and thereby to destroy it as a Christian institution. Whether or not one shares this dark view, one can hardly doubt that administrative endeavors are now calling for more and more of every pastor's time.

This fact is confirmed by recent studies of the American church. Samuel W. Blizzard, writing under the pointed title, "The Minister's Dilemma," reports on a study of theological school graduates serving in several denominations.[1] The ministers' own evaluation of their work indicated that 40 percent of their time was given to administrative work and 10 percent more to organizational activities, half their time thus being consumed in organizational responsibilities. More important, however, is the fact that these ministers generally resented these growing demands upon their time. They felt that they

15

had been called primarily to preach, teach, and do pastoral work, tasks which received a decreasing share of their working time.

The studies of Richard Niebuhr substantiate the conclusion that any current examination of the role of the minister will encounter a growing prominence of administrative responsibilities.[2] In fact, after tracing the changing role of the minister through the centuries, Niebuhr discerns an "emerging new conception of the ministry"[3] in our time, that of the "pastoral director."[4] Obviously such a concept lifts the administrative task to a central place in the work of the clergyman. At this point we are concerned with the idea of the pastoral director only as an indication that, for good or ill, more and more of the pastor's time is in fact devoted to administration.

Ministers are becoming increasingly restless over their role as "organization men" within the institutional framework of the church. There is a feeling on the part of many pastors that they are being forced into this pattern by the expectations of their parishioners, the demands of their community and denominational leaders, and the "materialistic success culture" which is the matrix of American church life. These and other factors have created an image of the "successful" minister, which exalts his executive function within the organization.

In attempting to live up to this success image, the pastor finds his life filled with many harried activities. Often the pastor is called upon to perform such a variety of poorly integrated functions that he justifiably asks, "Just what am I doing, and why?" Such a pastor is seeking meaning, purpose, and coherence in his work. One cannot refrain from adding that the snowballing of administrative demands in the local church is parallelled at the denominational level, where general church boards are becoming increasingly aggressive in initiating programs designed for uniform application in the congregations.

The tragedy of all this is not that some men resent it, but that many have consciously or unconsciously accepted it as normative, embracing uncritically the success criteria of the culture. Daniel Walker concludes, "That administrative duties dominate most ministers' lives, there can be little doubt."[5] He suggests that this fact is

16

clearly revealed by asking a pastor casually, "How are things going?" The reply will usually be in terms of attendance figures, new buildings, financial campaigns, or some new organization in the church. Walker also suggests that the simple task of trying to set a date for a meeting will reveal how organized every church is and how much of a pastor's time is given to administrative affairs. Most pastors will, when rejecting a date, mention a conflict with another meeting of some kind. Would these same pastors accept as equally valid excuses the need to study for Sunday's sermon or to visit in the homes of the congregation? The demands of these latter duties seem rather lame excuses beside the clear-cut reply, "I have another meeting then."

B. **A Common Image of the Pastor as Administrator**
"Church administration," as commonly understood today, would involve the pastor in a host of particular responsibilities, of which the following are examples.

1. Carrying out the numerous plans and programs in the life of the congregation with the efficiency of a skilled executive.

2. Attending many meetings outside the congregation, connected with denominational and community affairs.

3. Assuring the financial success of the church, including building funds and denominational assessments, as well as the local budget.

4. Maintaining a favorable public relations response within the congregation and community, both to the church as an institution and to himself as a leader.

5. Leading the church in building and property improvement ventures.

6. Running an efficient office with prompt correspondence, accurate records and statistics, prompt reports to superiors, frequent mailings, and an efficiently managed staff.

7. Cooperating with denominational officials in carrying out prescribed programs in his congregation and securing lay attendance at many meetings away from home.

8. Serving on denominational boards and giving leadership to projects beyond the congregation (e.g., summer camps).

9. Encouraging "activities" in the many organized groups of the congregation, including trying to surpass the activity level of the previous year in every group in the church.

10. Securing the right leadership to move any program rapidly and smoothly.

11. Functioning as a personnel expert in "handling opposition" within the congregation, so that it neither slows down the program nor "harms the church."

12. Mixing well with social, business, and community leaders.

Even this incomplete list of tasks assumed to be related to church administration reveals that the primary skills commonly demanded of the pastor today are those of the executive and public relations man. It should be obvious that this constellation of tasks and skills does not grow out of the heart of the Christian faith but is derived from another source. Is it any wonder that many pastors are weary of the fact that these "dishwashing chores," required for smooth institutional operation, now take fully half of their time?

These common, but unspoken assumptions about church administration are evidenced by comments of persons in supervisory positions in the church and by pastors evaluating their fellow pastors. In one denomination when three new administrative offices were filled, these comments were overheard following the announcement.[6] Notice the implied incompatibility between administrative skills and competence in traditional pastoral tasks.

"He is too much of a student to be a good administrator," suggesting that study and an understanding of Christian thought are irrelevant to good administration. "He is too good a preacher to be a district superintendent. He should be in a local church." "He is a pastor at heart, too concerned about hurting people to make administrative decisions"; thus sensitivity to the needs of persons disqualifies a man as an administrator. "He will fool around with spiritual life retreats and discussion groups, instead of promoting the causes of the church," spiritual vitality apparently being a side issue compared to keeping the wheels greased. "He is very systematic, well organized; he knows the importance of good public relations and has a friendly personality. He will put the church on the map, and every-

18

one will like him." At last we seem to have arrived at what is really important.

Confronted with such attitudes as these, pastors often make one of three unfortunate responses. Some have simply rebelled at all the "busy work," ignoring it as much as possible. Every effort is made to keep activities to a minimum. Such a pastor will almost take pride in the lack of organization within his parish and in the congregation's rejection of denominational programs. Of course, since no creative alternative is offered, effective work of any kind is blocked. A second response is aloofness; administration is a menial chore suitable for laymen, while the pastor is above it all. A pastor who responds in this way will ask for a lay administrator if he is in a large church. If his congregation is small, he will leave everything up to volunteers, offering neither guidance nor encouragement, while he engages himself with "spiritual matters." Thirdly, a man may conform to the pressures and set about perfecting the details of administrative procedures. He majors in the minor areas of church life and becomes an expert in carrying out organizational details and in publicizing his church and himself.

Obviously none of these three responses is adequate for the minister's dilemma. What is called for is neither hostility nor aloofness nor conformity, but rather a serious examination of what church administration really is or ought to be. In the light of such a study, all of the activities commonly associated with church administration today could and should be reexamined with an eye to integrity and spiritual relevance. It is this kind of examination that we are undertaking here.

C. Two Basic Approaches to Church Administration Today

There are basically two ways of approaching the work of administering the work of a congregation. One is to develop a complete program for every area of the life of the church, giving detailed prescriptions for the time schedule, leadership training, and promotion techniques required to execute the program. A second approach is to be aware of a set of administrative principles that can be adapted and applied to every kind of situation and problem.

Most books in the field are written from the first point of view. A completely developed program is presented in a given area of assumed need—finance, evangelism, education—with full instructions, timetable, and even suggested letters to participants and members. There are certain values in this way of doing things that should not be ignored.

1. Such an approach is nearly always born of experience in the life of the church and has been tested by the author or compiler and usually by others.

2. Specific resource material is offered to churches and pastors facing perplexing problems. Such material is particularly desired by pastors and local committees with little experience.

3. Assurance is given regarding anticipated results on the basis of the experience of other churches, often providing real motivation for action.

4. Such plans always produce much activity and sometimes proper results. If failure does result, the blame can be placed outside the local committee.

This fixed program approach, however, has serious drawbacks, which more than offset its advantages.

1. It does not and cannot take into account the considerable differences among local situations and personnel. No two churches ever come to any project from exactly the same starting point, as every pastor of a two-point circuit well knows.

2. It cannot take into account what happens to persons *as they participate* in the project, and this factor is of fundamental importance. (Churches have even split over details of a program in progress.) Serious adjustments or even abandonment of the program may be called for, but the call will almost certainly be ignored in plowing ahead to complete the schedule.

3. Fixed programs rob the local committee of initiative, both in diagnosing its ills and evolving a prescription for the cure. Involvement in the painful process of diagnosis and in perplexing decisions about prescription is normally an important, if not an essential, part of the cure for the ills of most churches.

4. It is fallacious to assume that there is one answer for the prob-

lems of every church. The author has observed this fact as the pastor of several congregations and through the observation of many other pastors over a dozen years in supervisory positions. The inescapable conclusion from this experience is that there is more than one "right" way to administer a congregation and to approach any given problem in the church. In fact differing attitudes and leadership abilities demand different approaches.

Because of these disadvantages of a fixed program perspective on church administration, especially when it is linked to a rigid time schedule, we are proposing to move from a different direction. We are going to seek to understand and to learn to apply certain basic administrative principles. These principles are proposed as a constant guide in various situations and in changing circumstances. If these principles are basically sound, they will not become obsolete, as fixed programs do.

Purposeful church administration cannot be program centered. Not only do differing situations call for flexible strategy, but programs must always be seen as means to certain ends. When primary emphasis is placed on programs, they too often become ends in themselves, focusing attention upon the execution of the project rather than upon the persons served. Paraphrasing Jesus' denunciation of the unbending sabbath laws, programs exist for persons and not persons for programs. The administrator must, therefore, recognize the uniqueness of every situation and work with a flexible set of principles, keeping the goals, both near and distant, clearly in mind.

■ ■ ■ Notes

1. Samuel Blizzard, "The Minister's Dilemma," in *The Christian Century*, April 25, 1956, pp. 508-10.

2. H. Richard Niebuhr, *The Purpose of the Church and Its Ministry* (New York: Harper & Row, 1956).

3. *Ibid.*, p. 52.

4. *Ibid.*, p. 80.

5. Daniel Walker, *The Human Problems of the Minister* (New York: Harper & Row, 1960), p. 53.

6. These quotations are of actual statements made by five contemporary ministers.

CHAPTER II

CHURCH ADMINISTRATION
AND THE
NATURE OF THE CHURCH

**A. Administration, by Definition, Requires a Clear Understanding
of the Purpose of the Church**

A discussion of church administration should begin with an
understanding of administration generally. "Administer" is derived
from the Latin, *administrare,* meaning literally, "to serve." This
Latin root is useful in correcting the shortcomings of much modern
church administration, since in considering the verb "to serve," we
have to ask, "To serve what?" The idea of administration cannot
stand alone; it needs a referent object for the administrator to act
upon. Administration, then, is not just activity, but *purposeful
activity,* its purpose being determined in the context of a particular
field of endeavor—business, education, church.

An administrator is thus more than an executive, that is one who
carries out plans that others have made. The administrator cannot
be one who is absorbed in the mechanics of operation for its own
sake; he must be one who is vitally concerned with the achievement
of purpose. His sole criterion for determining whether a project is a
legitimate administrative activity is, Will it further the desired pur-

pose? To express this central idea in a definition: *Administration is the task of discovering and clarifying the goals and purpose of the field it serves and of moving in a coherent, comprehensive manner toward their realization.* Such a definition suggests certain questions that any administrator must frequently ask: What end or goal is to be served? What means will help reach the goal? How can *all* available resources and leadership be utilized in a coordinated and comprehensive movement toward the goal?

This concept of administration as the achievement of purpose has several very important implications. First of all, it says something about the *qualifications of the administrator.* (a) He must be one who shares with his group a common understanding of its purposes and objectives. (b) He must have a comprehensive understanding of his field, so that he can determine what means will contribute to the achievement of these objectives. (c) He must be able to work well with other persons whose contributions are as essential as his own.

Secondly, our definition implies that *there is a uniqueness about each separate field of administration.* That means that administrative methods in various fields will differ markedly from each other. Purposes differ, as we have suggested, and the means employed must be consistent with the desired ends. Methods and techniques, therefore, will differ from field to field. Campbell, Corbally, and Ramseyer illustrate this point regarding educational administration.

Undoubtedly there is much to be learned from a transfer of knowledge from one field of administration to another. But in an attempt to get help from research in a related field, one could make a grave error by incorporating practices designed to accomplish a mission different from that of the public schools. Big business deals in the production of goods. It is prompted by the profit motive. . . . Education, on the other hand, promotes the enrichment of living. The strategies employed for the accomplishment of these various objectives may be quite different. . . . It is sufficient for our purposes at this time to point out that in some respects educational administration is unique.[1]

Every pastor should be eager to say the same thing about church administration, since no other institution has the same purpose or mission as the church. This means that the administrative approach of business or public education cannot be transferred to the church. For example, the treasurer of a business firm may not necessarily make a good chairman of a church, finance committee, since the goals of church finance are not to cut expenses to the bone in order to show a "profit," but to deepen the stewardship commitment of church members and to provide funds generously to enable the church to minister effectively in all areas of need. This is not to say that *some* administrative knowledge from other fields might not be useful; faithful stewardship, for instance, includes budget control and strict auditing But the *controlling goals of the church* will determine which procedures from other fields may be useful in serving the church.

A third implication is that adminstrative methods will not only differ from field to field, but *will vary in different situations within any one field.* Again taking public education as the example, although the overall purpose may be the same everywhere, the administrator must take into account the economic, cultural, and emotional setting of his particular community if his work is to be effective. Methods employed in an urban system necessarily differ from those in a rural consolidated school. Applying the point to the church, any pastor who has served a two-point circuit clearly recognizes that the approach to initiating and carrying out an every member canvass or a visitation evangelism project will often involve quite different approaches in the two congregations. The attitudes and feeling of the particular persons involved must be taken into account, if each congregation is to move closer to the desired goal. In short, the administrator must respect the dignity of persons *as they are,* not as he wishes they might be.

This dynamic concept of purposeful administration eliminates the static, fixed program, or "canned" approach to the work of the pastor. An architect does not prepare a project by pulling an old set of drawings from his file. If he is conscientious, he learns the needs, desires, and feelings of his clients and translates these into sketches and blueprints designed for them alone. Similarly, the pastor as administrator needs something different from a full file of programs to be pulled out and followed in one church after another. Too many ministries go stale simply because that is done. Programs exhumed from the file, like sermons preached from the "barrel," cut off all creativity and freeze a minister's effectiveness at the point where he began. It can truly be said of such a minister at the time of his retirement that he does not have forty years of experience, but two years of experience repeated twenty times. Church administration is dynamic interaction of persons, no two of whom are alike, and no one of whom remains the same as his life unfolds. A project is therefore evolved in the context of one congregation alone. It may never be appropriate for another group; indeed, it may not be repeatable in the group which developed it, even though it was effective the first time.

We have seen, then, that administration properly understood simply provides the means through which a group can fulfill its purpose. If we accept this major premise, then the discovery of the nature and purpose of the church is the necessary starting point for developing a useful concept of church administration. There is a determinative relationship between the nature and purpose of the church and the proper goals of the administrator's work in the church. He must know where he is going and why, before he can decide how to get there.

If some pastors and congregations have not seen the need for doing their biblical and theological homework before engaging in a project, it is because they have uncritically accepted goals and objectives dictated by a culture foreign to the gospel. Without thinking, they measure the effectiveness of their program by such standards as popular acclaim, large attendance, and a rising budget. Of this more will be said later. It is enough now to say that when these success standards of our materialistic culture are substituted for standards derived from the real nature and purpose of the church, Christ is betrayed and the gospel is emptied of its power.

B. Biblical Precedent Relates Church Administration to the Nature of the Church

There is unquestionably a biblical basis for grounding church administration in an understanding of the nature of the church. Taking Paul's ministry as the example, the apostle insisted upon making administrative decisions within the context of a comprehensive understanding of the Christian faith. In dealing with the church at Corinth Paul discovered that he could not answer their long list of administrative problems simply by prescribing a program for each one. For example, in I Corinthians we find such specific local church problems listed as: dissension over previous pastors (Paul, Apollos, Cephus), the inroads of culture upon the church (eating food offered to idols), division and dissension over the relative importance of various leadership roles in the church (speaking in tongues, teaching, healing, prophesying, etc.). In each case Paul says in effect, "Let the local church operate in such a way that it fits in with the character of the whole church, as it has been given in Christ."

In answering the question as to who was the most effective previous leader of the church (I Cor. 3:4), Paul does not cite the statistical record of each or enter into any kind of comparison of the leaders. Instead, he reminds the people of how God's gospel came to them in the first place. The gospel, he says, is God's gift through Christ, and all of the men in question were entrusted with it "as stewards of the mysteries of God" (I Cor. 4:1). In other words the question of ministerial effectiveness and loyalty needs to be seen from the perspective of the meaning of God's call to apostleship, that is, of the place of the minister in relation to the gospel and the church. Actually, the problem of dissension over these various leaders arises because of a lack of understanding of the nature of God's gift of the gospel to them through calling men to apostleship to be God's instruments. The solution to this administrative problem calls for a clear understanding of the Christian faith and church.

Paul likewise finds that he is unable to give a quick answer to the problem of whether or not Christians should eat meat offered to idols (I Cor. 8). This is a problem of cultural patterns being accepted by church members as harmless. Though the particular form of the problem no longer exists today, the basic problem of conforming to various cultural practices is ever present. Paul says this question of eating food offered to idols must be seen in the light of the whole Christian faith. Though eating may be all right for those who know that idols have no real existence and therefore no effect on the food, other Christians may not only be offended if some of their brethren so eat, but their eating of such food may actually become a stumbling block in the relationship of others to Christ. Calling attention to the responsibilities of Christian love, Paul warns, "Take care lest this liberty of yours somehow become a stumbling-block to the weak" (I Cor. 8:9). One's own Christian freedom must always be seen in the light of one's responsibilities to his fellow men. "Therefore, if food is a cause of my brother's falling, I will never eat meat, lest I cause my brother to fall" (I Cor. 8:13). In dealing with the similar larger problem of Christian freedom in another connection, Paul indicates Christian love is the broad context out of which any specific decision must be made, and he tells the Christians in Galatia, "Bear one another's burdens, and so fulfil the law of Christ" (Gal. 6:2). In handling this administrative problem of eating meat offered to idols, Paul again demonstrates the necessity of grounding administrative decisions in an understanding of the Christian gospel.

Similarly, the problem of the relative merits of speaking in tongues, the gift of healing, prophecy, and other spiritual gifts called forth from Paul a detailed explanation of the nature of the church as the body of Christ and the resulting emphasis that Christ is the head of the body and all members of the body are to use whatever gifts are given to them to serve Christ (I Cor. 12). Paul refused to deal with each individual gift apart from its relationship to what the church ought to be as the body of Christ. This consideration then led him into his unforgettable chapter on the nature and importance of love within that body (I Cor. 13).

Thus Paul, early in the history of the Christian church, insisted that answers to specific administrative problems can be properly given only as they are seen in the perspectives of what the gospel is and what the church ought to be. This New Testament pattern should be followed today by church administrators. The fundamental question facing us is, "What is the nature of the Christian gospel and purpose of the church?" Only after this question is answered can wise decisions be made regarding specific questions and proposals.

C. Contemporary Pressures Require the Church to Define Its Nature

The contemporary church administrator faces many concrete decisions as to proper activities and programs to be encouraged or rejected in the life of the local church. His decisions will be reached by evaluating each as to whether or not the proposed activity (1) is in line with the objectives of the church as he understands it, and (2) would be effective in reaching the objectives. The first practical question confronting a church administrator is thus a clear understanding of what he is trying to do. He simply must have a clear knowledge of goals and objectives as a basis of determining acceptable programs and activities in the life of the local church.

If he believed the goals of the church were completely fluid to be determined by a majority vote in each congregation, then a knowledge of democratic procedures rather than a scriptural-theological study of the church would be the foundation for decisions in church administration.

Actually, it is assumed here, and will be elaborated in the next chapter, that the local church is not self-determining of its nature and mission. The church derives its character from its head, Jesus Christ, and there is a givenness about the church which each administrator *and* local church seeks to understand. The nature of God and the Christian gospel has *already* determined the goals and objectives toward which the church should be moving as it seeks to fulfill its mission. This fact requires of every administrator and congregation a serious study of the nature and mission of the church. Such a study is necessary to keep the church from accommodating herself to cultural patterns and expectations and thus actually ceasing to be the church and thereby losing her own uniqueness. The tragedy of cultural accommodation by the church has been well stated by Robert Raines in a penetrating analysis of why the contemporary church has lost its relevancy.

The church has accommodated herself to the cultural climate. The church is no longer changing culture, but is being changed by culture. . . .

[The church] is usually content to grow in physical stature and in favor with its immediate environment. . . .

The church becomes the mouthpiece of the people instead of the voice of God. The church, which is meant to be at tension with the customs and traditions of every culture, changes her protective coloring like a chameleon to suit the environment she is in. . . .

And the judgment is clear; the world pays little attention to the church. . . . The world believes it has tamed and domesticated the church and can keep her busily occupied in cultivating her own garden. The world has pulled the teeth of the church and no longer listens to her enfeebled message.[2]

A few examples may clarify Raines's conclusion. The state may seek to transform the church into a political tool to bless all its endeavors and seek to silence all criticism of governmental policies. Our day has witnessed many such attempts with varying degrees of success. Various economic interests may seek to determine the message and program of the church, in order to enhance their own positions of power and profit. The lures of economic advantages and the threats of economic reprisals succeed all too often in shaping church life. Ecclesiastical power may also be exerted to divert the church from its real purpose. Those in authority may become so engrossed in preserving the church as an institution, as well as their own positions in it, that the mission of the church is forgotten or violated. The Crusades of the Middle Ages, the sale of indulgences in the sixteenth century, the coldness of the English church in the eighteenth century, and the difficulties encountered in effecting denominational mergers today all testify to the powerful pressures of ecclesiastical institutionalism. Not only groups but individuals may seek to reshape the church after their own desires. Certain lay persons, entrenched in power, come to look upon the local church as a personal possession, blocking all change and perpetuating ineffective or unchristian practices. Some ministers continually refer to "my church" in their conversation and mean it literally. They dominate everything from routine handling of money to designing a new building. They try to use the church to win admiration for themselves as gifted leaders. Against such a host of groups and individuals seeking to pocket the church for their own ends, the only effective procedure is to determine what the church really is and what is its true mission in the world.

Defining the nature and purpose of the church is an intensely personal matter for the minister, since the concept of ministry emerges directly from the concept of the church. Contemporary confusion about the former is the result of vagueness about the latter. The expectations of various parishioners and ecclesiastical authorities differ so sharply from one another that the pastor can establish and maintain his integrity only by developing a clear-cut, viable concept of the church and its ministry.

Out of such an understanding the pastor may define certain goals toward which the church should be moving. The work of a particular congregation and the minister's part in that work become clear only in the light of definite goals or objectives. Furthermore, the means, as well as the ends of church life, emerge from a clear understanding of the church's task. More precisely, certain means may be judged inappropriate in view of the given character of Christ's church. Means must be consistent with the desired goal, or else they will destroy access to the goal. The evaluation of all church activities, both current and proposed, is the constant inescapable responsibility of every church administrator. The following questions might well guide such an evaluation.

1. What are the goals toward which the activity is supposedly moving?

2. Are these goals in harmony with the nature and mission of the church?

3. Will the activity actually contribute to achieving the goals?

4. Is the activity in conflict with any other equally valid project of the congregation?

5. Are sufficient personnel and resources available to carry out the activity? Or will the congregation be overburdened by it?

6. Will all the techniques employed bear examination in the light of the gospel?

7. Is there a danger that this activity, as a means to an end, will become an end in itself, thus obscuring the real goal by its very "success"?

8. Are there other more basic goals that require prior attention?

Each of these questions can be answered only in the light of a comprehensive understanding of what the church is and ought to do.

As an example of bringing a proposed project under this kind of scrutiny, suppose someone from Church Attendance, Inc., came to the pastor's study with a surefire proposal for doubling church attendance. Can the pastor assume that, if the promised result can really be produced, the proposal should automatically be accepted? Suppose that the proposal was to issue a hundred trading stamps to everyone in attendance and to hold a drawing for a one-hundred-dollar cash prize for someone in the "lucky pew" on ten unspecified Sundays through the year. Such a fantastic plan would undoubtedly increase attendance, perhaps even double it, but any sane pastor would reject the proposal. The grounds for rejection is not that the plan is bizarre. Preaching the gospel was bizarre when Peter began speaking on Pentecost; and the church is called to do many strange things in fulfilling her mission. No, the problem is that ends and means are confused here. Attendance at the public worship of God is a means toward the end of acknowledging God's sovereignty, praising him for his undeserved love, and seeking his will. Encouraging attendance for material gain would make worship impossible. The means proposed would betray the real end.

Unhappily for the minister, most evaluations of proposed projects are not as easy to make as the one just presented. Nevertheless, the process is the same. It always calls for examination to discover whether the activity is consistent with and contributory to the task which God has given to his church.

We are saying that the very content of the gospel predetermines the vehicles which are suitable for carrying it. Church administration is to seek to provide usable instruments (organization and programs) through which the Holy Spirit can work.[3] This can only be done when there is a basic understanding of what the church really is. Such an understanding becomes the yardstick for measuring the validity of any proposed activity in the life of the church. Only a clear concept of the nature of the church can keep administrative programs in their proper places. Effectiveness ought not to be confused with mere activity. Achievement of God's purpose, not activism, is the sole concern of church administration.

Beyond the local scene, experience has led the ecumenical church to an awareness of the necessity of examining the basic nature of the church before any real agreements on administration programs can be reached. It is interesting to note that in the ecumenical movement, early attempts were made to seek unity on an administrative and cooperative program level. Conferences on the "life and work of the church" soon revealed that administrative programs resulted from, and were implied in, prior assumptions about the nature and purpose of the church. The ecumenical movement today is now proceeding on the sound premise that unity of action must be found in examining the nature of the Christian faith and the Christian church and that all administrative expressions flow from a prior understanding of these fundamental concepts.

D. Possible Approaches to Defining the Nature of the Church

Before attempting to set forth the nature and mission of the church, let it be clear that our concern is with a definition of what the church ought to be, its essential nature and purpose, rather than a description of what it now is, or for that matter what the church has been, either in church history or even in the New Testament. This does not mean that these descriptions are irrelevant, but that we must *begin* our quest for a definition of the church with the acknowledged assumptions that the church has a unique purpose and mission and was called into being by God's intention to serve his definite purpose. It will be our central objective, therefore, to seek to discover and set forth as precisely and succinctly as possible what God's intention was in calling the church into being.

In one sense such a study involves the whole of theology. Theologians agree that the treatment of any single doctrine has inferences from and implications for every other doctrine in the theological spectrum. Any doctrine of the nature of the church must be related to a doctrine of God, Christ, man, sin, and salvation. Of course we cannot deal with all of systematic theology here, but we must be aware of its essential wholeness.

Since we are seeking a norm to use as a standard of what the church ought to be, it is obvious that we cannot find our answer in any or all of the various studies currently being made to describe and analyze the Christian church as it actually is found in today's culture. We cannot equate what the contemporary church *is* with what it *ought* to be. Since we have concluded that by definition administration must be purposive and is concerned with moving toward the fulfillment of the nature of the church, any *description* of the contemporary church must be rejected as a norm. Much of the current bewilderment about the role of the minister and about the church in society arises precisely at this point. In trying to adapt to contemporary culture the church has blinded itself to its own distinctive nature and has confused culture's definition of success with the church's own definition.

This is not to say that careful studies of the church in today's world are not of significance to the church administrator. As a matter of fact, such studies are essential for church administration, but not to establish norms and goals. Such studies are necessary to enable the church to understand its own attempt to fulfill its mission in a given cultural situation. Since the church's goals must be realized in human society and in the lives of persons, all administration must begin with persons and culture where they are and move toward a predetermined goal.

Some recent studies have thrown new light on the value and significance of possessing a clear understanding of the human elements in the church. James Gustafson's penetrating insights clearly illustrate that since the church is composed of persons in a community, it shares certain common characteristics with all other human communities.[4] A knowledge of the characteristics of various communities and their functionings can enable the church to bring its divine purpose to bear more effectively on its own community life, also made up of human beings. The church can never be contained in a theological concept but must always be conceived of as persons in relationship to God and one another. The more clearly the church understands persons and interpersonal community relationships, the better it can penetrate the human situation to communicate clearly the gospel and thereby move toward the realization of its purpose.

Since the church must fulfill its mission through persons in community, such studies as Gustafson's have real value. Christians must indeed be "as wise as serpents" in understanding the ways of men, in order to reach them with the gospel. Furthermore, we may expect to find somewhere within that amorphous entity called "the contemporary church" more than one clue to what the church ought to be today. Throughout history the Holy Spirit has evidenced the fact that the church is not dead but alive and is, therefore, not rigid but responsive to the signs of the times. No norm should be so static, therefore, that it does not take into account the living voice of God in the church today. Nevertheless, we must be clear that description cannot be normative; what the church is too often has a slender or a hidden relationship to what the church is called to be.

We already have alluded to the fact that church history will not by itself give us a norm for indicating what the church ought to be. It does have much light, however, to throw upon the question, through both positive and negative experiences of the church through the centuries. How the church fathers interpreted both the scriptures and the essence of the church is of great importance. Though time and space will not permit any detailed treatment of the history of the church, one cannot refrain from indicating that any church administrator worthy of the name must be more than casually acquainted with the field. As we consider the nature of the church it will be necessary to turn to church history from time to time to illuminate how various norms were tested in experience in the life of the church. A knowledge of the past centuries of experience enables the student of church history to search with clearer vision for what the church ought to be.

Surely the testimony of church history supports the conclusion that the action and life of the church spring from and are implied by the *basic beliefs* of the church. This is seen very dramatically in the Reformation movement led by Luther, Calvin, and Zwingli, which challenged the concept of the church as an institution endowed with authority to dispense salvation through its priesthood and sacraments. Luther's concept of justification by grace through faith, with its related concepts of the priesthood of all believers and the authority of the scriptures, had a far-reaching influence on not only the doctrine of the church, but on the day-to-day lives of individual members of it. The Reformation movement and the later evangelical awakening under John Wesley illustrate how accepted ideas of what the church ought to be were challenged and changed. We must, therefore, conclude that though church history cannot of itself provide undisputed norms for the church, insights from historical studies are invaluable in shedding light upon the quest at hand.

We have suggested that a search for a normative definition of the church must go beyond a study of the church of today and yesterday. We come now to examine a third possible source for the desired norm, namely, the scriptures. Here, as elsewhere, the Bible is the source book of our Christian faith, the record of God's revelation of himself to man. The biblical record of God's dealings with man and his intention in calling the church to a definite task will be of primary concern for us in seeking to discover what the church ought to be. In other words, *the church ought to be whatever God intended it to be,* and we search the Scriptures to discover God's intention for the church. The *basic* source for a normative definition of the church is thus to be found in the Scriptures themselves, though the scriptures will point beyond themselves in defining the church dynamically and in relating the definition to the living Christ, the Holy Spirit, and the whole human community.

Church administration requires a serious and continuing exploration of the nature of the church as it is set forth in the Bible. Several authors have made significant contributions toward a scripture-based doctrine of the church. Some of the more helpful recent ones are cited in the notes.[5] In the following chapter some of the important biblical concepts about the nature of the church will be examined. These will form the presuppositions for defining and developing the foundations of purposeful church administration.

■ ■ ■ Notes

1. Roald Campbell *et al.*, *Introduction to Educational Administration* (Boston: Allyn & Bacon, Inc., 1958), p. 20.

2. Robert Raines, *New Life in the Church* (New York: Harper & Row, 1961), pp. 14, 15, 17. Used by permission.

3. One denomination avowedly expresses its goal as making the organizational aspects of its life avenues for the Holy Spirit in fulfilling the church's mission. "We reverently insist that a fundamental aim of Methodism is to make her organization an instrument for the development of the spiritual life. . . . We do now express the faith and hope that the prayerful observance of the spiritual intent of the DISCIPLINE may be to the people called Methodists a veritable means of grace." *Doctrines and Discipline of The Methodist Church* (Nashville: The Methodist Publishing House, 1964), pp. 1-2.

4. James M. Gustafson, *Treasure in Earthen Vessels; The Church as a Human Community* (New York: Harper & Row, 1961).

5. The following volumes will be helpful to those interested in pursuing a more serious study of the nature of the church.

Gustaf Aulén *et al.*, *Man's Disorder and God's Design*. The Amsterdam assembly series. A one-volume edition of four books. (New York: Harper & Brothers, 1948).

Albert E. Barnett, *The Church, Its Origin and Task* (Nashville: National Methodist Student Movement, 1960).

Ernest Best, *One Body in Christ* (London: S.P.C.K., 1955).

Robert McAfee Brown, *The Significance of the Church* (Philadelphia: The Westminster Press, 1956).

Howard Grimes, *The Church Redemptive* (Nashville: Abingdon Press, 1958).

James M. Gustafson, *Treasure in Earthen Vessels*.

Daniel Jenkins, *The Strangeness of the Church* (Garden City: Doubleday & Company, Inc., 1955).

Donald G. Miller, *The Nature and Mission of the Church* (Richmond: John Knox Press, 1957).

Paul Minear, *Images of the Church in the New Testament* (Philadelphia: The Westminster Press, 1960).

James E. L. Newbigin, *The Household of God* (New York: Friendship Press, 1954).

Niebuhr, *The Purpose of the Church and Its Ministry*.

D. T. Niles, *The Preacher's Calling to Be Servant* (New York: Harper & Brothers, 1959).

Raines, *New Life in the Church.*
Alan Richardson, *An Introduction to the Theology of the New Testament*
(New York: Harper & Row, 1959).
D. Elton Trueblood, *The Company of the Committed* (New York: Harper &
Row, 1961).

CHAPTER III

THE NATURE AND MISSION
OF THE CHURCH

Our aim in this chapter is to set forth as clearly and concisely as possible the nature and mission of the church as God intended it to be. For the purpose of clarity the most significant scriptural concepts related to understanding the basic nature and mission of the church will be summarized under three main headings.

A. The Church as God's Chosen Community (the central concept of the Old Testament).
B. The Church as the Body of Christ (the most comprehensive and significant concept of the New Testament).
C. The Church as a Fellowship of Redemptive Love (a common mission of both concepts).

It must be recognized at the outset that these categories are neither exhaustive nor mutually exclusive. Each concept does have, however, a distinctive emphasis that must be recognized if the church is to be the church. One must also be aware of the fact that any attempt to define the church is not only very difficult but in a real sense presumptuous. The idea of the church is not only complex but is so identified with God's will and purpose that no finite human mind is capable of comprehending it fully. This fact, however, does not lessen our responsibility to seek to discover what God intended the church to be—what it indeed ought to be.

A. The Church as God's Chosen Community

The Old Testament furnishes us with a record of the *origin* of the church in recounting God's relationship to Israel. The primary factor in this relationship between God and Israel is that God called Israel as his chosen community. Many interpretations are given to this idea in the Old Testament, but the concept of Israel as God's chosen community persists throughout. It is our intent to indicate that the origin of the church is to be found here, that the basic concepts involved are central to the very nature of the church, and that the fulfillment of the concept is found in the New Testament.

The concept of the church as God's chosen community involves three basic ideas: (1) The church is of God; (2) It was chosen for the purpose of making known God's love; and (3) From the outset the church was a community of persons, the people of God. Let us examine each of these ideas and their relationship.

The order for the reception of persons into one Protestant church begins, "Dearly beloved, *the Church is of God,* and will be preserved to the end of time." [1] This concept of the divine origin of the church is basic to the understanding of its nature. The church is not the result of man's decision or planning; it is not just another human institution; it is of God. "The church exists because God intended it to exist." [2]

"The historical root of the Church is in the covenant which Abraham and his children entered into with Yahweh their God." [3] God's call of Abraham and the covenant initiated with Israel at that time are continuous through Christ and the New Israel of the New Testament community. The Scriptures are clear that *God* called Abraham, and therefore *God* initiated the covenant. Abraham responded to God's command, "Go from your country and your kindred and your father's house to the land that I will show you. And I will make of you a great nation, and I will bless you, and make your name great, so that you will be a blessing" (Gen. 12:1-2). In

39

responding, Israel became God's chosen community. This concept of the church as God's chosen community was present in these early beginnings of the church, remained a central concern throughout the Old Testament, continued into the New Testament concept of the church, and is still basic today. Because of the significance of this concept in biblical and church history it deserves careful examination.

The idea of God calling out or choosing anyone is a very difficult concept for many to understand. It becomes meaningful only when we understand the basis and the purpose for which Israel was called. God did not choose Israel because she was powerful, good, religious, or in any way merited the choice. As the writer of Deuteronomy reminds Israel, "It was not because you were more in number than any other people that the Lord set his love upon you and chose you, for you were the fewest of all peoples; but it was because the Lord loves you" (Deut. 7:7-8a). The only reason for the choice of Israel was God's love, and that was unmerited. God's grace in effecting salvation is thus evident in the Old Testament as well as in the New. It is thus by God's *grace* that the church was initiated. It is out of God's *love* that the church is called into being, God's seeking to make possible a relationship between himself and man.

If Israel had been thus selected to receive God's love to the exclusion of all other nations, such a choice would indeed seem unfair. However, Israel was not called to a place of special privilege as her prophets constantly reminded her. Rather, Israel was called for a special responsibility. This is most clearly stated in Exod. 19:5-6a, "Now therefore, if you will obey my voice and keep my covenant, you shall be my own possession among all the peoples; *for all the earth is mine,* and *you shall be to me a kingdom of priests and a holy nation*" (italics mine). Israel's choice required first of all her obedience to God in keeping the covenant. The requirement of obedience is always upon those whom God calls. Furthermore, God's choice was for a purpose; Israel is to be a kingdom of priests through whom God's love for "all the earth" is to be made known. Just as the Levites were set apart as a priesthood within Israel, so the nation should be set apart as a priesthood to all the world. *Israel was chosen as the instrument of God's love.*

Though Israel neither fully understood nor obeyed God's call, she never doubted that she was chosen by God. She never forgot the mighty events of the exodus, the experience in the wilderness, the giving of the law on Sinai, the possession of the promised land, and the establishment of the kingdom. Israel clearly and consistently saw God's hand in her own history and, though often misinterpreting its meaning, she persistently held to the concept that she was God's chosen people. It is true that Israel too often sought to "transform the covenant into a contract, where they could negotiate as equals with God and boast of its blessings as rights which they had earned, and in so doing they turned it into a curse instead of a blessing." [4] Nevertheless, she was never left without a prophet to call her back to the covenant and the divine mission; such men as Hosea, Jeremiah, and the writers of Second Isaiah and Jonah.

Several factors combine to indicate a close and unbroken connection between this concept of Israel as God's chosen community in the Old Testament and the new Israel of the new covenant as the rightful successor.

The most striking affirmation in the NT that the Christian community is now the true . . . [Israel] is to be found in I Pet. 2:9f., where the author somewhat freely quotes Ex. 19.4-6 *and applies what was there said of Israel to the Christian Church:* "Ye are an elect race . . . , a royal priesthood . . . , a holy nation . . . , a people of possession . . . , that ye may shew forth the excellencies of him who called you out of darkness into his marvelous light." [5]

Alan Richardson goes on to comment:

The passage affirms that the Christian community is commissioned and enabled to perform the task of being the light of nations, which the Old Israel failed to become. Likewise the Church of Jesus Christ was in fact a royal priesthood (cf. Rev. 1.6; 5.10; 20.6), a consecrated nation, representing God to all the nations of the world and the needs of all the world to God. The missionary implication of God's call to Israel was now being realized through the witness of the Church. [6]

Other incidents recorded in the New Testament continue to link the old covenant and the new Israel as its rightful successor. It is significant that Jesus called twelve disciples, undoubtedly corresponding to the twelve tribes of Israel, indicating that he considered his task to be the establishment of a new community of Israel. In referring to Jesus as the Messiah the concept of the *new* community of Israel is also acknowledged. The New Testament account of the institution of the Lord's Supper also indicates that the old covenant had been superseded by the new in these words, "This cup is the new covenant in my blood" (I Cor. 11:25; cf. Matt. 26:29; Mark 14:24; Luke 22:20). To those present on the day of Pentecost the power of the Holy Spirit was so unmistakably manifest that there was no doubt about the establishment of a new covenant, and those there assembled were certain that *they were called of God* as his chosen people to witness to the living Christ and to take the gospel to all the world. The basic point is simply that the Christian church was called into being by God's intention and acts, recorded both in the Old and New Testaments.

An emphasis also needs to be placed upon the fact that from the outset this concept defines the church as a *community* of persons, to whom and through whom God's love is revealed. Few ideas are more clear in the Old Testament than that God's concern is for a community or nation. This is evidenced first by God's call not only to Abraham but also to his descendants who were to become a "great nation" (Gen. 12:2). God's concern from the beginning was not just for the individual person, though it included this; it was also for the nation. God's concern for the whole community of Israel is evidenced in leading Israel out of bondage, the establishment of the law, in guiding Israel through the wilderness and into the promised land, in the establishment of corporate worship and even the national kingdom itself. Even when many in Israel ignored or rebelled against God, his concern for the total community continued to be expressed through the witness of the prophets and a concern to provide a "saving remnant." The community aspect of the church is evidenced in laws dealing with interpersonal relationships within the community and in the occasionally recognized responsibility to witness as a community or nation concerning Yahweh (see Isaiah, Jeremiah, Jonah).

The importance of the church as a *community* is as basic to the New Testament concept of the church as to the Old Testament. From the outset the Christian church was a community of those who had experienced the presence of the risen Christ. From the very first, to be a Christian meant to belong to a community. Clarence Tucker Craig asserts, "We may say that the Christian Church was the community which had been constituted by God through the resurrection of Jesus." [7] Surely the New Testament accounts are clear that no one thought it possible to be a Christian "by himself," but only in relation to the fellowship of his brethren. The common bond of the community clearly was that all had received the gift of God's grace through the living Christ. This concept of the church as community is basic to any scriptural understanding of its nature. The purpose of God's calling the church into being is to *make known his love,* and this is to be done not just by priests or by individuals, but through the witness of the entire church community. The corporate nature of the church is clearly indicated in a passage such as Eph. 2:19, "So then you are no longer strangers and sojourners, but you are fellow citizens with the saints and members of the household of God." What better description of a chosen community could be given than "members of the household of God." No Christian stands alone. Each is a part of a fellowship, a household, a community.

In summary, to say that the church is "God's chosen people" means that it is initiated by God; that it is chosen for a purpose, that of making known God's love; and that the divine task belongs to all members of the chosen community. There are important implications here for church administration, to be explored later, implications which are determinative both of its goals and its methods.

B. The Church as the Body of Christ

Although the New Testament uses many images to describe the church,[8] the most significant one is that of "the body of Christ" (I Cor. 12, Eph. 4). This image is so rich in meaning that a full and adequate analysis cannot be made within the confines of one short

43

section. Nevertheless, an attempt must be made, because the concept
is fundamental to any proper understanding of what the church
ought to be. A summary will be set forth under four headings:

1. The Church Is Christ's Body; Christ Is the Head of the Church
2. The Corporate Unity of the Church
3. The Church as a Continuation of Christ's Ministry
4. The Church as a Living Organism

1. The Church Is Christ's Body; Christ Is the Head of the Church.

There is nothing in the concept of the church as Christ's body that
contradicts the idea of the church as God's chosen people. God's
revelation of himself and his love through Christ became the means
through which the Old Testament concept of the Church was fulfilled.

When we refer to the church as the body of Christ, the first and
most obvious implication is that Christ is head of the church. The
Christian church rests solidly on the convictions that Christ founded
the church, is its head, and his resurrected living presence continues
to direct the church. The early Christians' first credal formulation
was "Jesus is Lord" (Rom. 10:9, I Cor. 12:3, Phil. 2:11). This meant
that he was Lord of all life, as well as death, and assuredly Lord of
the church.

The nature of the Christian church, therefore, *has been determined* by Christ who is its head and by his gospel which it is called
to proclaim. This substantiates the Old Testament concept that the
church is of God. God, through Christ, has determined its nature
and mission. This means that there is a givenness about the church
that church administration must recognize and seek to fulfill. It is
impossible to read either I Cor. 12 or Eph. 4 without discovering that
the whole concept of the church as the body of Christ with its various
parts and divisions has unity and meaning solely because Christ
is the head of the body and all other parts are subservient to the head.

Many other New Testament references bring out this same meaning through the use of different figures of speech.[9] Paul's own
analogy of the church as *the bride of Christ* is given within the framework of the ancient world's assumption that the husband is head of

44

the household. This is made very clear by the writer of Ephesians. "Wives, be subject to your husbands, as to the Lord. For the husband is the head of the wife as Christ is the head of the church, his body, and is himself its Savior. As the church is subject to Christ, so let wives also be subject in everything to their husbands" (Eph. 5:22-24).

The writer of Ephesians also likens the church to the building of a temple wherein Christ is the *chief cornerstone:*

You are fellow citizens with the saints and members of the household of God, built upon the foundation of the apostles and prophets, Christ Jesus himself being the chief cornerstone, in whom the whole structure is joined together and grows into a holy temple in the Lord; in whom you also are built into it for a dwelling place of God in the spirit (Eph. 2:19-22).

The reference to Christ as the chief cornerstone clearly supports the concept of Christ as head of the church since the cornerstone is laid at the juncture of two walls dependent upon it for support; indeed they would collapse without it. So it is with the church's relationship to Christ.

A third related figure of speech referring to Christ as *the vine* is used in John's gospel to indicate the utter dependence of Jesus' followers upon him. It also bears other interesting similarities to the concept of the church as the body of Christ. "Abide in me, and I in you. As the branch cannot bear fruit by itself, unless it abides in the vine, neither can you, unless you abide in me. I am the vine, you are the branches" (John 15:4-5a). It is clear here that the source of the life of the branches is in the vine, and if cut off from the vine, the branch dies. The emphasis is unmistakably clear that Christ is the source of life for Christian disciples. Only in acknowledging dependence on Christ, in recognizing his lordship, can Christians live.

Albert E. Barnett, through his study of the origin of the church in the New Testament,[10] concludes not only that Christ is head of the Church but that "the church Originated with Jesus." [11] A strong case is presented to indicate that "the Church was implicit in the

45

ministry and message of Jesus and owed its beginning to him." Barnett insists, "Germinally, the Church existed in the fellowship and collaboration of Jesus and his first followers." [12] An interesting observation is offered to indicate not only that the origin of the church can be traced to the historical Jesus, but that the Christian church antedates Pentecost.

Jesus' message of the Kingdom created the Church. The idea that the Church originated at Pentecost is refuted by the fact that the Church was meeting when Pentecost happened (Acts 1:15; 2:1). The earliest Church was the community of those assembled around Jesus. They expected the Kingdom and proposed to live as though it had already supplanted the order of Time. . . .

Pentecost was the "birthday" of the Church, but not the day of its origin. Just as a baby begins its life and completes nine months of development prior to "birth," so the church antedated Pentecost. *It actually came to Pentecost with its basic character and mission determined.*[13]

Barnett is here indicating that the Christian church was founded by Jesus Christ, that its nature was determined by his life, gospel, death, and resurrection which the church is called to proclaim. The conclusion to be drawn is clear: The church is of God, and through Jesus Christ God has determined its nature and mission.

Lesslie Newbigin [14] rightly observes that the church "derives its character not from its membership but from its Head, not from those who join it but from Him who calls it into being." It is for this reason that we are seeking to discover what the church ought to be, what its basic nature is, by turning to the Scriptures rather than seeking to analyze the institution of the church in today's world. The *norm* for the church is to be found here rather than simply studying the church in history or in modern life. This means specifically that the church as well as the church administrator must give serious consideration to discovering what the lordship of Christ means, first of all for the church and then for all life. The church cannot be true to her nature apart from a meaningful acceptance of Christ as head of the church.

The church and its members must therefore study the Scriptures seriously and diligently to come to know as clearly as possible the nature of God's revelation as manifest in Jesus Christ. The study of the New Testament as the source of Jesus' life, teachings, death, and resurrection, and their effect on the early church is basic to the discovery of what the Christian church is called to be. This accounts for the fact that a renewed interest in the study of the Bible has been the initial spark igniting the major reform movements in the history of the church. It is no accident that Francis of Assisi, Martin Luther, John Huss, and John Wesley all found the inspiration for the renewal of the church through a study of the New Testament.

As the New Testament clearly indicates, the headship of Christ is acknowledged by a personal commitment to Christ as Lord. This experience of knowing the risen Christ whose spirit is God's power unto salvation is also a basic mark of a Christian. In her quest to discover what the church ought to be, the modern church cannot ignore an exploration into the meaning of the headship of Christ over the church. This will lead both to a careful examination of the New Testament and the meaning of personal commitment to Christ as Lord.

2. The Corporate Unity of the Church.

The metaphor of the church as the body of Christ also implies the existence of a corporate unity within the church. Paul alludes to the body with its varied functions and many separate parts, not to call attention to the diversity found within the body, but rather to emphasize its corporate unity (I Cor. 12). Speaking of the rivalry resulting from possession of different spiritual gifts, Paul insists that the church is a corporate entity, composed of believers united in accepting Christ as their head, but diversified in the various ways they serve him. The several gifts are likened to the several interdependent parts of one body.

The *interrelatedness* of the parts of the body is also pointed out by illustrating how every individual part is necessary for the body to function properly; and each is bound up with the other, so that all suffer when one functions improperly. It is the same with the church:

47

"The eye cannot say to the hand, 'I have no need of you,' nor again the head to the feet, 'I have no need of you.' If one member suffers, all suffer together; if one member is honored, all rejoice together. Now you are the body of Christ and individually members of it" (I Cor. 12:21, 26-27). The implications of this figure are often repeated in the pages of the New Testament: (1) All gifts or talents are from God, gifts of one Spirit; (2) All are to be used in serving Christ; (3) All are to be used for the common good (I Cor. 12:4-7; also Eph. 4:11-13).

This sense of corporate interdependence of each church member in relation to one another through Christ has been a characteristic of the church from the beginning. Ernest Best in a very scholarly study of the early church [15] concludes that not only the phrase "the body of Christ," but a much more common phrase of Paul which refers to members of the early church as being "in Christ" (this phrase "in Christ" is used 164 times in the New Testament) also denotes a corporate community relationship. Whenever anyone enters into a relationship of being "in Christ," according to strict New Testament standards, he also enters into a fellowship of the brethren who also are "in Christ" *and in whose fellowship the resurrected living Christ abides*. There is really no possibility of being "in Christ" in a completely individualistic relationship. This sense of community, fellowship with the brethren in Christ (*koinonia*), is an essential characteristic of the church in all times and places.

3. The Church as a Continuation of Christ's Ministry.

To refer to the church as the body of Christ is also to imply that it is the body (instrument or agency) through which the Spirit of the living Christ continues to work. As Alan Richardson puts it, "The Church is thus the means of Christ's work in the world; it is his hands and feet, his mouth and voice. As in his incarnate life, Christ had to have a body to proclaim his gospel and do his work, so in his resurrection life in this age he still needs a body to be the instrument of his gospel and of his work in the world." [16]

It is important to recognize both the necessity for an organized institutional structure, without which the church could not function, and also to remember that the institutional structure is not an end in itself nor is any specific structure "given" as the one perfect form of church organization in the New Testament. The church has had difficulty in keeping its perspective in relation to the importance of the organizational and institutional side of its life. Without some institutional structure the church cannot live, yet when primarily concerned about its institutional well-being the church betrays its basic purpose, which is literally to do Christ's work.

This is no new problem. From the time of God's covenant with Abraham and man's response through worship and tithes (Gen. 13:14), to the giving of the law and the development of priestly worship described in Exodus, a structured organization has been both a strength and a weakness of the church. Undoubtedly the priestly ceremonies and institutional regulations provided a cohesiveness and strength that played an essential role in Israel's survival, and thereby in the survival of her faith. Yet it was an overemphasis of the institutional laws and regulations that kept Israel from fulfilling her role as God's chosen community. Israel's prophets certainly saw the peril of priestly institutionalism as evidenced by these sharp words of Amos,

> I hate, I despise your feasts,
>   and I take no delight in your solemn assemblies. . . .
> Take away from me the noise of your songs;
>   to the melody of your harps I will not listen.
> But let justice roll down like waters,
>   and righteousness like an ever-flowing stream
>   (Amos 5:21, 23-24).

In the main, however, Israel sought refuge in observing her institutional laws and regulations. She seemed to feel that these observances would place her in a favored position.

Since Israel was unwilling to accept the role of a suffering servant portrayed by Second Isaiah (Isa. 53), "when the fulness of the time was come, God sent forth his Son" (Gal. 4:4, KJV). Jesus denounced the legalism of the institutional church of his day. He sought to involve men in a direct personal relationship with God and to free man from the tyranny of institutionalism. Jesus gave himself that men might come to know the love of God and accept this love for themselves and then witness to others. Though Jesus was at odds with the institutionalism of his day, it cannot be assumed he was against all structure and organization. In choosing twelve disciples and sending out the seventy, Jesus recognized that some form of organization was essential for the experience of witnessing and the propagation of the gospel. Whether or not Matt. 16:18 is regarded as an authentic saying of Jesus, "You are Peter and on this rock I will build my church, and the powers of death shall not prevail against it," the writer of the gospel saw the beginnings of an organized church at hand and believed this to be in accord with Jesus' intent.

The initiation of the sacrament of baptism and the frequent administration of the sacrament of the Lord's Supper in the early church indicated that some form of worship and organization was soon considered necessary. In Acts it is recorded that the twelve soon found it desirable to introduce some form of organization into the life of the church.

The twelve summoned the body of disciples and said, "It is not right that we should give up preaching the word of God to serve tables. Therefore, brethren, pick out from among you seven men of good repute, full of the Spirit and of wisdom, whom we may appoint to this duty. But we will devote ourselves to prayer and to the ministry of the word." And what they said pleased the whole multitude (Acts 6:2-5a).

However, examination of the New Testament church indicates no unified or single type of organization, though there is clear evidence of the existence of a growing institution. In the New Testament the structure is secondary though essential, existing only as a means to enable the church to perform its central mission.

We are suggesting that the necessity of some organizational structure be recognized so that the church can function as the body of Christ. Organization and ecclesiastical structure have a legitimate

50

and necessary place in the church, but must always remain a means through which God's love may be made manifest. Organizational structure is neither the essence of the church nor its end or purpose. Nevertheless, organization—rightly used—can channel the strength of the church so that it can more effectively witness to the world, can provide increased opportunities for worship and service, can assist in leading men to a relationship with God, and can provide a redemptive fellowship for the mutual strengthening of the church's members. Though the institutional aspect of the life of the church must always remain in this secondary position, it is necessary to provide some organizational framework through which the church may continue Christ's ministry.

To speak in contemporary terms, the church is to be the instrument through which Christ continues to work in the world today. In other words, the church is to become the living expression of Christ's spirit in our time and culture. This means that if the church is true to its nature, it must recognize that its central reason for being is to continue God's work of reconciling the world unto himself begun in Jesus Christ. If the church is to fulfill its nature, it must *be* the body in which the living word of God's love is found and Christ's work and ministry extended to today's world.

If the church is to *be* an extension of the ministry of Christ, and not simply to *proclaim* in words that Christ came to minister, then the church must recognize that it exists to *serve* (Matt. 20:27; 23:11; Mark 10:44). D. T. Niles points out the central place the concept of servanthood must play in the daily life of the church, both for the preacher and for the church.[17] He advances the thesis that men are not just called to preach, a functional task, but rather men are called to *be* preachers. The call to preach is really "a call to share in the continuing ministry of the risen and ascended Lord. The Lord is servant and we are his servants sent to serve the world, so that the preaching ministry *like every ministry of the church* is consequent on this servanthood or it declares itself illigitimate." [18] This same concept of ministering servanthood is true of the church as a whole and consequently the lay ministry of every member.

To be an extension of Christ's ministry—his very body—the

51

church must take seriously the responsibility of being a servant. In the synagogue Jesus applied to himself the words of Isaiah 61:

> The Spirit of the Lord is upon me,
> because he has anointed me to preach good news to the poor.
> He has sent me to proclaim release to the captives
> and recovering of sight to the blind,
> to set at liberty those who are oppressed (Luke 4:18) .

But he did not merely speak of God's love; he acted it out—in village streets, in the upper room, and on Calvary. The church—every member of it—is called to "go and do likewise."

4. The Church as a Living Organism.

One final concept needs to be included in discussing the church as the body of Christ. *The church is a living organism and not a static organization.* The church must be conceived as a living organism which grows and develops by transformation from within.

First of all the church is alive; as has been indicated, it is the body of the resurrected *living* Christ who *continues* to speak and act. The experience of the power of the Holy Spirit on the day of Pentecost convinced the early church not only that Christ was alive but that God continues to speak to the church. Neither God's voice nor witness is confined to the pages of the New Testament. It must be recognized that the church is God's living witness, and those with ears to hear and eyes to see may find evidence of God's voice speaking today in any church, in the World Council of Churches, or in the lives of dedicated Christians anywhere. Lesslie Newbigin has put it this way, "The nature of the Church is never to be finally defined in static terms, but only in terms of that to which it is going." [19] One must therefore think of the church in *dynamic, changing* terms.

Because the church as the body of Christ is alive, it is best described as an organism rather than organization. An institution may be static and stilted, perpetuating its traditions or present influence. A building may be expanded by adding bricks and boards to enlarge it. A body or living organism grows not by adding separate parts but through growth from within by multiplying cells. So the church as an organism grows by transformation from within as believers are made new creatures in Christ.[20] Daniel Jenkins comments, "The strange thing about the church is not that it grows old but that it seems to have discovered the secret of being born again." [21] This power of internal renewal has been at work in the church through the centuries, saving her just when men have despaired and given her up.

Whenever one is tempted to despair of the church, it is good to be reminded that the church, being the body of Christ, is a living organism, granted the power of renewal from within. From the time of the Old Testament concept of the "saving remnant," through the New Testament proclamation of the "new covenant" in Jesus' blood, to the witness of a Martin Luther in more recent times, God has renewed the church from within and has made himself known in unexpected ways and circumstances. God is still directing the church and may yet make known new ways to reach men meaningfully in the twentieth century. Though the gospel remains unchanged, the ways of proclaiming it effectively from age to age may change. The concept of the church as the body of Christ is a dynamic one, pointing beyond the New Testament and involving the ever-present activity of the Holy Spirit and the living Christ.

C. The Church as a Fellowship of Redemptive Love

We now come to a third concept of the nature of the church, implied by and found within the other two: The church as a fellowship of redemptive love. Unless this is realized in fact, the church does not exist in any real sense. Christianity is not *primarily* an idea, a creed, a form of worship, or an ecclesiastical institution. Christianity is basically concerned with the matter of *relationships*—God's relationship to man, man's relationship to God, and man's relationship to man. These are personal matters; they involve giving, communicating, and responding to love. The basic concern of the church is for *persons*. Christianity is God's self-giving love—as seen in Christ —expressing itself in the life of the church. Hence, the mission of the church is to provide the opportunity and atmosphere for God's

53

self-giving love to be experienced by persons within its fellowship and through them to be communicated to the world. Richard Niebuhr concludes, "No substitute can be found for the definition of the goal of the Church as the *increase among men of the love of God and neighbor.*" [22]

If the church is to seek to increase the love of God and neighbor among men it must have a clear understanding of what this task involves. Love has meaning only in relation to persons. Persons are the objects of God's love and of one another's love. The church must then of necessity be concerned with persons, but persons in relationship to one another and to God. Love is not simply an intellectual concept that can be profitably discussed apart from personal experience and involvement. Love is made meaningful by one's past experience and current involvement. Jesus was very clear that love of God is to be expressed in relationship to other persons.

God chose to become incarnate in Christ because a human being was the most effective channel through which to communicate meaningfully his overflowing love for man. Men saw the love of God in Christ, in his relationship to persons, and in his crucifixion. This experience of love in human form spoke clearly to man as to the nature of divine love. Jesus indicated, "He who has seen me has seen the Father" (John 14:9). Though Paul eloquently describes the nature of love in the thirteenth chapter of I Corinthians, its meaning is made much clearer when it is observed in the person of Christ hanging on the cross and continuing to pray for forgiveness for those who nailed him there. Unquestionably, the meaning of divine love is most clearly seen in the person of Jesus Christ. Jesus spoke with authority not because of any external position given to him by men nor because of the newness or the logic of the truths he uttered. His authority was an inner authority springing from his understanding love for all whose lives he touched. Because they see in the crucified Christ God's love for all men "while we were yet sinners," men are able to see and accept the love of God as a heavenly father. Many others had talked and written of a God of love, but only when such love was experienced in human form as seen in the person of Christ did it become meaningful and real.

Jesus called his disciples to express this love of God through their love for one another. "By this all men will know that you are my disciples, if you have love for one another" (John 13:35). This love is to be expressed by a life of service. Not only individual Christians, but the church community is to accept the role of a servant, bearing in love the burdens of the world. Only as men experience love in their relationship with others can they accept and understand God's love for them. Likewise, once having received the overwhelming experience of God's love and forgiveness in one's own life, man must express his gratitude and love in his own relationships with all other men.

The Christian church, then, must *be* a loving fellowship. No man can either become or remain a Christian by himself. To be baptized into Christ is to become a part of "the brethren" (Rom. 16:14; I Cor. 8:12; Gal. 6:1; Col. 4:15). The importance of fellowship in the early church is evident throughout the New Testament. "You are no longer strangers and sojourners, but you are fellow citizens with the saints and members of the household of God" (Eph. 2:19). Paul tells why this fellowship of the saints is so important: "I long to see you, that I may impart to you some spiritual gift to strengthen you, that is, that we may be *mutually encouraged by each other's faith,* both yours and mine" (Rom. 1:11-12, italics mine). The fellowship of Christians strengthens the faith of those involved. It is a redemptive fellowship.

We see also that the meaning of fellowship in the early church involves much more than simply enjoying one another's company socially. It is a particular kind of fellowship, a fellowship of redemptive love. Too often in the modern church the word fellowship is used in a very shallow way to denote a self-centered mutual admiration society. This is not at all the meaning given to the word in its New Testament usage. The Greek word that has been translated "fellowship" is *koinonia.* It is found in the familiar benediction, "The grace of the Lord Jesus Christ and the love of God and the fellowship [*koinonia*] of the Holy Spirit be with you all" (II Cor. 13:14). Obviously in this context, *koinonia* refers to fellowship with the triune God, the Father, Son, and Holy Spirit. Thus the *source*

55

of the fellowship is God and the relationship of the person to God through the Holy Spirit. This sharply distinguishes it from all other types of fellowship. However, the fellowship is not only a God-man relationship; it is also between all those who share or participate in this "fellowship" with God. The early Christians were in fellowship with one another *because* they shared a relationship to the living Christ and his Spirit. The unifying bond and source of the fellowship is not the mutual attraction of persons for one another but their common experience of the presence of the living Christ in their lives.

As a college student, I once had an experience of fellowship in the New Testament sense of *koinonia*. At a student conference I was the only American Christian in a group of men in a dormitory style sleeping room. I had never met any of the group previously. Within a few minutes I felt a kinship with them deeper than I had experienced in a semester of residence in a college dormitory. All of the group were Christian students, and this sharing of a common commitment to Christ bound us immediately to one another. That experience helped me to understand the quality of fellowship in the New Testament church, which knew no barriers. All who were "in Christ" were a part of the fellowship, Jew or Greek, bond or free. Even time itself was no barrier, for the "communion of the saints" extended beyond the visible earthly church. The early church believed that this fellowship was indissoluble and that absolutely nothing could separate them from the love of God, or from one another (Rom. 8:35-39).

Participation in that kind of fellowship is for the purpose of both receiving the love of God and witnessing to it. The basis of all Christian fellowship is a common experience of God's love, which is then shared. Love is of such a nature that when it is shared it increases rather than decreases. In thus sharing with one another their own experiences of God's love, each person is strengthened in his own love of God and also his love for others. Hence this fellowship, being rooted and grounded in Christian love, is a redemptive experience, binding those involved closer to God and to one another. It is also redemptive in another way. Christian love cannot be experienced in a man's life without sending him forth as a witness to give this love to others. "Evangelism . . . is one beggar telling another beggar where to get food." [23] Christian fellowship thus binds the church together *as a witnessing community to minister to the world*. It sends forth the individual members to transmit the meaning of Christian love in all their relationships in their daily lives. Thus, a triple ministry results when the church actually becomes a fellowship of redemptive love: (1) Church members strengthen one another's faith; (2) The unity of the fellowship enables the church to be a ministering community to the world; and (3) Each person is strengthened to be a witness for Christ as he goes about his vocation and daily tasks. The fellowship is redemptive in that the love of God and neighbor is increased through it.

This concept of the church as a fellowship of redemptive love is closely related to an important New Testament concept of the priesthood of all believers. In writing to the early church (composed almost entirely of lay members) the writer of I Peter deals with the question of how Christians may "grow up to salvation" (I Pet. 2:2). He urges them (both the lay and ministerial members), "Like living stones be yourselves built into a spiritual house, to be a holy priesthood. . . . *That you may declare the wonderful deeds* of him who called you out of darkness into his marvelous light" (I Pet. 2:5, 9). The entire church is to be a fellowship of redemptive love, a ministering community. To say that every man is a priest does not simply mean that he is his own priest, but that he is his neighbor's priest as well, responsible for declaring the wonderful deeds of God.

The church is to be a fellowship of redeeming love in the deepest sense of the word. At the same time the fellowship of Christian love is furthering and strengthening the redemption of the individual members of the fellowship, these same persons are called to be God's instruments to redeem the world, both in the corporate ministry of the church and in the daily secular life of its members. Redemption is not a completed fact but a continuing experience. It has a point of beginning but no ending.

The church then is not to be thought of just as a community of the redeemed; it is rather a community *being* redeemed, and that is a vastly different thing. Strange as it may seem, this community in the process of being redeemed is at the same time a fellowship through which the redemptive love of God is expressed to redeem others. "The problem of how an unholy concourse of sinful men can be in truth the Body of Christ [the church] is the same as the problem of how a sinful man can at the same time be accepted as a child of God." [24] Those being redeemed must become involved in witnessing and redeeming others as a necessary condition of their own redemption. This is what it means to be a Christian. It is for this reason that if the church is to be the church it must be a fellowship of redemptive love.

This chapter is written on the assumption that church administration is the attempt to move in a coherent and comprehensive manner toward the realization of the goals and purposes of the church. To achieve this goal requires that the first and most basic concern of the church administrator is to have a clear understanding of the nature and purpose of the church. For this reason we have sought to outline in some detail the basic concepts involved in understanding the nature of the church as *God's chosen community, the body of Christ,* and as *a fellowship of redemptive love.* These conclusions will become the basis for the development of an understanding of church administration as a means to enable the church to move toward the achievement of its nature and the fulfillment of its mission.

■ ■ ■ Notes

1. *The Book of Worship for Church and Home* (Nashville: The Methodist Publishing House, 1965), p. 12.
2. William E. Hordern, "The Nature of the Church," an address delivered at Garrett Theological Seminary, September 8, 1959.
3. Jenkins, *The Strangeness of the Church,* p. 25.
4. *Ibid.,* p. 30.
5. Richardson, *An Introduction to the Theology of the New Testament,* p. 271. Italics mine.
6. *Ibid.*

7. Clarence T. Craig, in *Man's Disorder and God's Design*, p. 35.

8. See Minear, *Images of the Church in the New Testament*.

9. See Jenkins, *The Strangeness of the Church*, pp. 56-57.

10. Barnett, *The Church, Its Origin and Task*, pp. 9-43.

11. *Ibid.*, p. 25.

12. *Ibid.*, p. 25-26.

13. *Ibid.*, p. 36. Italics mine.

14. Newbigin, *The Household of God*, p. 21.

15. Best, *One Body in Christ*.

16. Richardson, *An Introduction to the Theology of the New Testament*, p. 256.

17. Niles, *The Preacher's Calling to Be Servant*.

18. *Ibid.*, p. 36.

19. Newbigin, *The Household of God*, p. 18.

20. Craig, in *Man's Disorder and God's Design*, pp. 39-42. These concepts are set forth and developed fully in a scholarly manner in this chapter.

21. Jenkins, *The Strangeness of the Church*, p. 14.

22. Niebuhr, *The Purpose of the Church and Its Ministry*, p. 31.

23. D. T. Niles, *That They May Have Life* (New York: Harper & Row, 1951), p. 96.

24. Newbigin, *The Household of God*, p. 23.

CHAPTER IV

A CONCEPT OF PURPOSEFUL
CHURCH ADMINISTRATION

A. A Definition of Purposeful Church Administration

Having considered the meaning of administration and the nature of the church, we are now ready to put the two words together and attempt a definition of church administration. We have chosen to add the adjective "purposeful" to church administration both to illuminate the content of the definition and to indicate that restricting church administration to organizational, executive, and promotional matters is not acceptable.

Purposeful church administration is the involvement of the church in the discovery of her nature and mission and in moving in a coherent and comprehensive manner toward providing such experiences as will enable the church to utilize all her resources and personnel in the fulfillment of her mission of making known God's love for all men.

This definition of church administration has within it three distinct elements that need to be identified clearly.

(1) The overarching concern of church administration is the fulfillment of purpose, to "let the church be the church." It is obvious that the concept of the church actually held by the administrator will determine the goals he will strive for, as well as the methods he

will consider acceptable in seeking to reach them. One of the constant responsibilities of the church administrator is to keep from confusing immediate means with ultimate ends. Principle rather than expediency is the basis for purposeful church administration.

(2) This definition of church administration is *comprehensive,* viewing the administrative task as concerned with every aspect of church life and seeking to coordinate every experience toward one unified purpose. Administration cannot be confined to the organizational, program, and promotional aspects of church life. Worship, preaching, pastoral care, and every other experience within the church must be seen as interrelated parts of one whole. Each one must be viewed in relation to its contribution toward the church's mission. Conversely, no activity is to be considered an end in itself (e.g., preaching, evangelistic outreach, finance), but *each is to be an avenue of ministering to the needs of persons,* as those needs are defined by the gospel.

(3) Finally, this definition *involves all members of the church in administrative responsibilities.* Administration is not the concern only of the pastor and a few "key" laymen. The whole congregation must understand the nature and mission of the church and must be involved individually and corporately in making known God's love, so that the congregation can fulfill its mission.

B. Purposeful Church Administration Rests upon a God-Centered, Person-Oriented Polarity Principle

The nature of the church is such that any valid approach to church administration must rest on a God-centered, person-oriented polarity principle. Like a battery, with positive and negative poles that must be connected to release its power, church administration that is purposeful must be both God-centered and person-oriented. Church administration can be effective and obedient only as it is carried on in the field of force between these two poles. To be God-*centered* is to acknowledge God as the source and life of the church's mission. To be person-*oriented* is to recognize that "God so loved the *world*" that he sent his own son to make known his love for all men. The church is, therefore, not primarily a concept or an institution but a *ministry to persons*. Being person-oriented is never to be confused with being person-centered, which would be to take the desires (even the whims) of people as the norm of administration. Church administration can be faithful and effective only as it is carried on in the field of force between these two poles, each of which will now be examined in some detail.

1. Purposeful Church Administration Must Be God-Centered.

Since the church is of God, there are certain characteristics that are intrinsic to its very nature, that men must accept and cannot change by congregational vote or denominational pronouncement. If the church is not God-centered, it falls into one of a long list of idolatries. It may become institution-centered, as it did in the Middle Ages, or program-centered or pastor-centered, as many churches do today. There is no end to the list of false centers possible to a congregation once the God-center is ignored; race and social class are two prominent ones in the current scene. Positively, what does it mean in daily parish life to administer a congregation with God at the center?

a. The church exists to please God rather than man. Practically, this means that the standard of judgment or measurement for any "successful" venture in the church is lifted to a high plane. Sermons that please and delight the hearers but never sound a prophetic or disturbing note are doomed for an F on God's report card, even though those who hear them may award them an A+. Crowded sanctuaries on Sunday and many well-attended meetings during the week may indicate an active church but not necessarily an effective one. Whether or not anything happens to relate persons vitally to God or strengthen them spiritually is more important in God-centered administration than attendance statistics or neatly executed programs by committees.

A God-centered church will seek to lift up the lordship of Christ in all areas of life. Such a church will be concerned to discover what this might mean in difficult areas, such as racial and social concerns. It will be more concerned about keeping its witness *Christian* than in the public relations or financial effect of its decisions. Such a church will look for God's plumb line against which it can measure itself, resisting the temptation to be so conformed to its culture that it cannot be distinguished from the culture itself.

b. A careful study of the Scriptures is essential in a God-centered approach to church administration. One of the chief concerns of the administrator will be to involve the church membership in a clear understanding of the Christian faith. The means of achieving this may vary from parish to parish, but will probably involve some combination of a serious study of the Scriptures by the minister, vital preaching from the pulpit, a strong Christian education emphasis throughout the church, special Bible study classes, prayer and fellowship groups, careful pastoral care, and well-chosen opportunities for lay witnessing and service. A concern for a clear understanding of the faith and the experiencing of a vital commitment to it will constantly be in the forefront of a God-centered church. This will be a concern of the life of every auxiliary group in the church. It is precisely at this point that the church gains its sense of direction.

c. The establishment of a vital personal relationship to God is basic. The Christian faith involves more than having an intellectual understanding of the nature of God. It also entails a personal commitment to God and a personal acceptance of Christ as Lord and Savior. If church administration is to be God-centered, then this requirement must be paramount. Beginning with the minister, a meaningful personal commitment to Christ is essential. Such a vital commitment, expressed through action, is of equal importance for every member. The church will attempt to establish and enrich such personal commitment in many ways, among which will be a concern for vital worship, both public and private, small *koinonia* groups, continuous pastoral care and counseling, well-chosen service opportunities, as well as missionary and evangelistic outreach *experiences.* Christian commitment must be made and *kept* meaningful. Christian commitment must be viewed as an ongoing experience that has a beginning but no ending.

d. Missions and evangelism are seen as fulfillments of the church's purpose. In examining the nature of the church it became clear that God called the church into being because of his love for all men. The reason and meaning of the Incarnation are found in God's love for all men and his desire to seek and to save the lost. The risen Christ sent his disciples "into all the world." The Scriptures are very clear that the church is not called to be a group of cloistered "saints" withdrawn from the world, but a fellowship of those who will go forth to serve the world. The church administrator is thus not to conceive his role as that of serving the *institution* of the church, but rather he is to train and lead the church in serving the community and the world. Missions and evangelism involve lay witnessing and are bound up with the very nature of the gospel and the mission of the church. God-centered church administration seeks to involve the whole church in understanding and *participating* in this its mission. The realization of this goal is directly related to the three previous goals discussed above, and most of the suggestions previously made would be contributory to a resultant missionary and evangelistic outreach. The importance of the responsibility of lay witnessing through each member *being* Christian in his daily vocation and social contacts are basic here, as is the witness of personal stewardship in the area of financial giving. Specific means and methods of achieving these ends will be discussed later.

2. Church Administration Must Be Person-Oriented.

Although the first thing that needs to be said about the church is that it is *of* God, the second thing that needs to be recognized is that is is *for* men. Our study of the nature of the church made it clear that God's purpose for the church is to be fulfilled in and through persons. All aspects of the life of the church derive their significance from their contribution toward enabling persons to understand and accept the love of God. The experiences of the church, recorded in the Old and New Testaments and repeated often in the centuries of Christian history, indicate how very difficult it is for the church to remember that persons are and must remain her central concern.

In the Old Testament we read of Israel's preoccupation with her place among the nations and with the sacrificial cultus, both to the detriment of her ministry to Jews and gentiles alike. In the New Testament we find Jesus' harshest words reserved for the keepers and promoters of the minutiae of the law. "The sabbath was made for man, not man for the sabbath" (Mark 2:27). Israel's nationhood, her temple worship, and her law were all gifts of God for revealing and maintaining the living knowledge of his love. But God's purpose was betrayed, as these institutions became ends in themselves. In the Christian era such concerns as ecclesiastical authority, institutional structure, credal statements, ritualistic form, political influence, and materialistic wealth have often become substitutes for the church's proper concern for persons and their relationship to God in Christ.

Furthermore, God in showing his love for persons has *used* persons to speak and act out his revelation. Throughout the Old Testament God seems to be able to speak most clearly when the message is brought through the witness of a person. Perhaps this is natural since love is a matter of interpersonal relationship. Even an imperfect experience of love may speak more clearly of what the love of God is like than abstract concepts either written or spoken. It is not surprising, therefore, that God used a series of personal spokesmen in the Old Testament to proclaim his message. The accounts of these spokesmen for God throb with successes and failures as each in turn experiences God in his own way and seeks to relate his own experience to his fellow men. As one enters into the experiences of Hosea, Jeremiah, or Second Isaiah, something of the meaning of God's love for man unquestionably breaks through.

Finally, God became man in order that he might meaningfully make known to man the nature and depth of his love, even knowing that this would involve the acceptance of the cross. Only in this way could God's unending love for man be seen in its full dimension by man, and man's own sin be revealed in its true perspective. It is significant that Christ, instead of leaving a written record of his teachings, commissioned his followers to be his witnesses, recognizing that *only through these persons* could the meaning of God's love, revealed through his crucifixion and resurrection, be transmitted to the world. Hence, the members of this chosen community who have experienced the love of God through the presence of the living Christ in their own lives are called upon to make known God's love to the rest of the world. Therefore, the very nature of the church is

65

such that all persons making up its fellowship are involved, as a condition of membership, in participating in a witnessing community. This concept will be developed in much greater detail later. It is sufficient here to indicate that persons are of central concern for the church, not only because they are the object of God's concern but because they are the means through whom God's love is to be transmitted to others.

In a person-oriented approach to church administration, it is imperative that persons become the central concern of the church. Persons and their needs thus become the raw material of church administration. What happens to persons (or what does not happen) in the life of the church is of prime importance. Here is a measurement to be applied to all areas of church life. The church must never forget that the object of its every activity is a concern for what happens to persons. This standard of judgment is to be applied to worship, preaching, education, committee meetings, programs, auxiliary subgroups within the church, the pastoral ministry, and every other kind of experience within the life of the church. Whenever the church ceases to be person-oriented, it is to that extent untrue to its nature in addition to being irrelevant.

Perhaps the meaning of person-oriented church administration may be illuminated further by indicating its application in some practical areas of parish life.

a. Programs and activities are kept in their proper perspective. First of all, this principle makes it very clear that programs exist to serve persons and not persons to serve programs. What happens to persons is more important than what happens to programs. In fact, the only reason for having *any* program is the contribution it can make to enrich the lives of the persons touched by it. In our day, when the church is besieged with programs in every area of its life as the answer to all problems, we need the perspective to be gained in a person-oriented approach to church administration. Busyness normally does not result in a redemptive experience for persons. Carrying out a program does not mean persons have been really "reached." A person-oriented approach adds a needed depth dimension to the organizational program area of the life of the church.

b. **A person-oriented approach underscores the importance of personal relationships as a means of communicating the gospel.** A gospel of love is best communicated through a person-to-person relationship. The Incarnation is ample endorsement of this principle. Love has meaning only as experienced by a person and that meaning is best communicated in interpersonal relationships. This has tremendous implications for church administration. Who the pastor *is* as a person is of more importance than what he does (functionally) or says (verbally). He communicates his interpretation of the gospel in every relationship he has, whether it be in personal counseling, a committee meeting, preaching from the pulpit, a social contact, or functioning as a presiding officer in a meeting, not to mention his social and personal contacts in his nonprofessional roles.

Since the gospel is transmitted most effectively in interpersonal relationships, there are revolutionary concepts for church administration relative to lay participation in the life of the church. Committee meetings could be an experience of redemptive growth. Small *koinonia* fellowship groups could be more transforming than the old mass revival meeting. Evangelism may take place anywhere, any time, when two or more persons meet at work, home, in a committee meeting, or at a social occasion.

If persons are the most effective means for communicating love, then surely an administrator must seek to enlist and train all members of the church to become a ministering community to their own culture and community. Here is a clue as to how the church must permeate the secular world. The power of a person-to-person contact of a Christian in his daily work and life is tremendous. Perhaps society is to be redeemed not by the *institution* of the church but by the witness of church members acting and witnessing as Christian persons in their daily "secular," social, and vocational life, where the decisions that change the world are actually made.

c. **This concept lifts up the importance of pastoral care and interpersonal relationships in the life of the church.** In any concept of person-oriented church administration the importance of the ministry through pastoral care is obvious. In a pastoral relationship there is a significant opportunity for the pastor to have a face-to-face, one-to-one relationship with persons. Here is an unparallelled opportunity for a meaningful interpretation to be given to Christian love and understanding through a close personal *relationship*. This is true whether the pastor is engaged in a regular pastoral call, a crisis situation relative to illness, death, or great anxiety, or a long-term counseling situation. Through the *relationship* established between pastor and person will flow an interpretation of the meaning of Christian love and faith, whether these terms are ever mentioned in the conversation or not. Here the "language of relationship" [1] speaks loud and clear in communicating the meaning of the Christian gospel. In the best sense of the term, the missionary and evangelistic outreach of the church may be served through the relationships established in pastoral work.[2] This can happen only when pastoral care is given with the well-being of each person *as a person* in mind, and all else is seen as secondary, a by-product of the pastoral relationship established. It is indeed a serious sin (because it counterfeits a real concern for persons) for any pastor to seek to exploit pastoral care simply as a means of "building up" the institution of the church.

There is a necessary relationship that needs to be very carefully and cautiously drawn between pastoral care and person-oriented preaching. Through the experience of pastoral care the pastor will come to an understanding of his congregation and community. He will come to know his people as they really are, the kind of world in which they actually live, and the kind of language they understand. This will provide a clue as to the religious maturity or immaturity of those to whom he preaches, thus contributing to genuinely person-oriented sermons. However, a stern word of caution is in order against any reference from the pulpit, however veiled, to any personal conversation or situation relating to experiences and confidences disclosed in any pastoral contact.

One further practical application of this principle is evident in lifting up the importance for church administration of adequate preparation of the minister in the field of pastoral care. Such preparation must include an adequate understanding of the Christian gospel, a clear insight into personality dynamics, self-insight of the pastor into his own personal strengths and weaknesses, and supervised clinical experience in ministering to persons. Without such training it would be impossible to carry forward a person-oriented administration.

d. Alertness to redemptive opportunities in group meetings. An additional word is appropriate here underscoring the importance of interpersonal relationships among laymen in the life of the church. The administrator must constantly be alert as to what is happening (or not happening) to persons as they attend the various meetings of the church. Are these interpersonal contacts strengthening them as persons and deepening their faith? Is a redemptive and growing experience challenging persons to new life as they participate in the face-to-face encounters of the program life of the church? Group activities can be renewing and invigorating.[3] A wise administrator will know how to work toward effective and enriching group experiences in the life of the church. This subject will be discussed in detail later;[4] suffice it here to point out that person-oriented administration calls for an intelligent concern for what happens to persons in the program and group life of the church.

We have here set forth in broad outline what is involved in a polarity concept of church administration that is God-centered and person-oriented and have suggested a few of the implications of this concept in the practical day-to-day life of the church. Many of these concepts will be developed more fully in later chapters.

C. Steps in the Administrative Process

There is one other aspect of our definition of purposeful church administration that needs to be dealt with. The definition says,

Purposeful church administration is the involvement of the church in the discovery of her nature and mission and in moving in a coherent and comprehensive manner toward providing such experiences as will enable the church to utilize all her resources and personnel in the fulfillment of her mission of making known God's love for all men.

We have discussed in detail the nature of the church and her mission to persons, but have not dealt with what is involved in *"moving*

69

in a coherent and comprehensive manner" toward providing such experiences as will enable the church to fulfill her God-given mission.

To move in a coherent and comprehensive manner toward a goal or an objective implies much more than a knowledge of the goal of our striving. The selection of the specific means which will bring about the realization of the desired objective is also essential. In church administration, as in other forms of administration, the administrator must not only know where he wants to go but also how to get there. Whenever any group of persons is striving for a common goal, some organizational process is necessary to coordinate all the resources and leadership in such a way that each in fact does contribute toward moving in the direction of the common goal. The New Testament church soon discovered this fact and set up a simple form of division of labor for that purpose.[5] The larger the local church and the more complicated the cultural and social structure, the more necessary it becomes for the church administrator to have an understanding of this organizational process in order to coordinate all activities into a comprehensive movement toward the achievement of the basic purpose. We turn, then, to examine the administrative process whereby resources and actions are coordinated.

The church administrator is concerned with preaching, pastoral care, worship, Christian education, group meetings of all kinds, church board decisions, programs and commissions, lay witnessing, financial matters, the outreach of the church, community problems, personal relationships within the church and outside it, and a host of other matters. The church administrator seeks to bring coherence into this myriad of activities through linking each to a common purpose and relating them in a mutually supportive way to one another. For this reason it is imperative that the church administrator be familiar with the following steps in the administrative process, as applied to church administration:

1. Recognition of need
2. Planning
3. Organizing
4. Stimulating
5. Evaluating[6]

These steps in the administrative process have an ordered sequential requirement about them. They may be likened to the classic stages of personality development set forth in *Childhood and Society* by Erik Erikson in that they involve a dynamic coexistence and continuation through all stages. Effective administration requires that they be taken in sequence, the second step being added to the first, the third to the first and second, and so on. If one step is omitted or improperly taken, deficiencies in administration will appear later in the process, and that step will have to be given corrective attention.

Before examining each step in the process it needs to be said also that the dynamic principle of involvement of as many affected persons as possible is a common requirement of each step. The more effective and widespread the actual involvement of affected persons in step one, the more likely it is that step two will be taken satisfactorily, and so on to the conclusion of the process. This dynamic common denominator of involvement is essential to the proper functioning of the administrative process.

These steps are the technical working tools with which any administrator ought to be familiar, forming as they do the framework within which decisions are made and action initiated toward fulfilling the mission of the church relative to any particular situation. In applying these steps in the administrative process it must be constantly kept in mind that *the standard of acceptability for every idea and suggestion will be determined by the nature of the church and the God-centered, person-oriented concept of church administration previously described.*

1. Recognition of Need.

The first step in the administrative process is the recognition that some real need *related to the central purpose of the group* exists. Whenever the administrator thinks he sees a need to be met, his first concern is to evaluate the validity of the suggested need. The preceding discussion of God-centered, person-oriented administration will serve as a standard against which any supposed need of the church can be measured. The wise administrator will also involve the most concerned group of laymen of the church in a preliminary evaluation of the need. If the proposed need seems valid, the next concern of the administrator will be how to secure a recognition and an awareness of this need on the part of the particular group responsible for this area of church life and finally by the church at large.

Let us be crystal clear that we are referring to a recognition that some area in the life of the church is not measuring up to Christian standards and therefore needs attention. We are *not* referring to some proposed plan or program designed to answer a supposed need not yet acknowledged. As used here, an awareness of need is *not* a proposed answer, but *the prior need or concern* for which some program might be an answer. For example, evidences of need calling for attention might include poor stewardship, spiritual shallowness, ineffective Christian education, indifference to missions or to evangelism. The first step in the administrative process is to awaken the church to the fact that there is a problem area about which they should be concerned. The *first* step is *not* selling the church on a program to answer some assumed need, even though the need proves to be a real one. Before trying to solve any need with any program, it is necessary that the need itself be clearly understood and recognized. Unless there is such a clear and common recognition of the basic need to be met, any proposal of a plan or program will seem as pointless as scratching where there is no itch.

It is precisely at this point that church administration procedures often break down by pushing some program as an answer to a need that has not yet been felt. To try to get a church to accept an every member canvass it thinks it does not need is like trying to get a man to wear an overcoat in August. The more you tell him about the quality of the coat and its ability to keep him warm, the less interested he becomes because he is warm enough already. The first step in getting a church to accept an every member canvass is to make the people aware of how poor their Christian stewardship is and how limited their church program is because of the need to pinch pennies. Of course, this will come about through exposing them not just to the negative facts of the current situation but by exposing them to the meaning of Christian commitment and the mission of the church, that is by showing what the congregation might do with greater resources.

How may a congregation come to recognize a need? Let us briefly outline a few basic suggestions.

a. The more clearly the church understands its central purpose, the more likely it is to recognize any specific need related to that purpose. Concretely, this means that the pastor who clearly and consistently holds before his people the real meaning of the Christian faith and the nature of the church through worship, preaching, Christian education, fellowship, and pastoral care will find that many members will readily recognize the specific needs of the church. The soundest approach to awakening a congregation to any concrete need is to strengthen the overall spiritual condition of each of the members. Every church has a few laymen of vision who understand and are committed to the Christian gospel. They can always be counted on to recognize any matter about which the church should be concerned and give of themselves and their substance to meet all such needs. Because of their deep understanding and commitment to the Christian gospel they do not need high pressure promotional sales pitches to enlist their support. No amount of publicity and promotion of individual specific needs of the church can produce as effective and long-lasting results as a clear understanding and commitment to the Christian faith itself.

This means that the wise church administrator, seeking a sensitivity on the part of laymen in recognizing any basic needs of the church, will give his constant attention to the spiritual condition of the members of his church.

b. The closer any need is to the central purpose of the church the clearer and more widespread is likely to be the recognition of it. Conversely, the more marginal the need in relation to the purpose of the church, the more difficult it will be to secure widespread recognition of it as a need. A widely recognized basic need is usually cared for at once. If the church heating plant breaks down in January, little time usually needs to be spent discussing whether or not to replace it. On the other hand, a proposal to buy a solid gold zipper for the pastor's robe or a Cadillac for the janitor's use would be immediately rejected as being unrelated to the needs or basic work of the church. The principle is clear, the more basic the need the easier it is to get widespread recognition of it. This means the church administrator must carefully evaluate all causes claiming to be basic needs of the church to see whether or not they really qualify as such. A church may dissipate its energy promoting secondary or false needs.

c. There is no substitute to a firsthand exposure to basic need as a means of helping people to recognize it. Those who teach, or parents who visit the primary class which meets in the furnace room, are acutely aware of the need for more adequate facilities for Christian education. The objective of securing a common recognition of need is always advanced by a firsthand exposure of as large a proportion of the total congregation as possible to a firsthand experience or observation of the situation under consideration.

Dramatic ways of action may be used to bring out the existence of some area about which the church ought to be concerned but is currently indifferent. Martin Luther King uses this approach effectively in the area of civil rights by confronting the nation in an inescapable fashion with problems demanding attention. Such a firsthand demonstration of need in a dramatic fashion will often give a quality of urgency and inescapability to a need that cannot be achieved in any other way.

d. A careful study of any area of proposed need with a widespread presentation of the findings of the material presented will often be of great assistance in leading to a recognition of a need. Such studies are often real eye-openers for some and will usually succeed in injecting the proposed need into discussion by the total group, whether or not there is an immediate inclination to agree with the findings. This is usually a helpful step whether or not it is an immediately decisive one.

e. Widespread discussion across the church is often an effective means of awakening an awareness of a need. Full discussion is of course required in the church board or any pertinent committee. But it is also helpful to involve the whole membership in such discussion on all major matters. This may be done through neighborhood family unit groups of about ten families each.[7] One church asked such groups to "dream out loud" about what they hoped their church would be like ten years hence and was astounded at the vision of the members. Church family nights with discussions and group buzz sessions have also been used to stimulate congregational discussion. It is important on such occasions to have all reports, studies, and facts fully and clearly presented, so that informed discussion can take place.

f. Probably the least desirable method of trying to get approval of a given need as being basic is to prepare, publicize, and promote some specific plan to answer some need not yet recognized (i.e., the every member canvass, a new educational building, a visitation evangelism program). The temptation is ever before the church administrator to see a need so clearly himself that he gets carried away in preparing some specific plan to meet what to him is an obvious need and then to go forth to sell the church board on the plan (answer) before they even realize there is any problem (need).

It should be underscored that the first step in the administrative process, then, is to secure a common recognition that there is some legitimate need or area of concern which the church ought to face. This is of basic importance, first because of the concept of the church as a ministering community, and secondly for the very practical reason that sooner or later the whole church must be involved in and respond to whatever program is evolved to answer the need. If the membership is not involved at the outset in recognizing the need, it may refuse to participate when the time comes to carry out the plan.

2. Planning.

The second step in the administrative process is planning precisely how the recognized need will be met. Although effective planning calls for final plans to be worked out by a small committee, at the outset opportunity should be given for *as many persons as possible* to make suggestions. The very nature of planning makes it advisable to secure every possible suggestion and recognize every possible obstacle before settling on any definite plan. "Consideration must be given to the possible alternatives. The consequences of each alternative course of action need weighing." [8] Since the congregation is a community of priests, the ideas and insights of all are needed, to allow the people to evolve the best possible plans and strategies for *their* ministry.

Experience in recent years has led many congregations to recognize the principle of maximum involvement in planning, even in such a mundane matter as budget making. The time when the budget could be drawn up by a small committee, or even by one man, is quickly passing. It is now commonly recognized that the church budget represents the resources needed to carry out the "work of ministry" in a particular place. This fact implies that the program of the church ought to be agreed upon *first*, and then the budget is drawn up in such a way that the program is adequately financed. (If the financial response is inadequate, the church program must of course be reevaluated.) Obviously, the shaping of the congregation's work for a given year is not the responsibility of the finance committee but of the whole church. In many congregations in recent years, all members have had the opportunity to participate in program planning, at some level, before the budget is framed. Some churches have simply sent out questionnaires, asking the people to indicate what they feel the church should do in various program areas. Other congregations have used the more satisfactory method of holding neighborhood discussion sessions, where the people can pinpoint and discuss ways of improving the church's ministry and then pass on their suggestions to a compiling committee. Such general involvement in program planning has resulted in marked increases in financial support for these programs when they have been translated into budget askings later.

If people have been involved in a vision of a need in their church, experience indicates that they are quite likely to come up with some very constructive suggestions in planning to answer that need. Furthermore, those involved in *making* plans are likely to be more interested in *carrying them out* later.

The following characteristics of the planning step should be kept in mind.

a. It must begin with a clear statement (widely distributed) of the problem as it has been recognized and defined by the congregation. Any vagueness at this point will result in hours of wasted time in the subsequent planning process.

b. Planning must be based on *facts,* the soundest and most revealing set of facts that can be obtained. Research of various kinds may be required, such as searching past records to discover trends which clarify the present situation confronting the congregation. Church figures may need to be compared with community studies of similar or related factors (such as population mobility), in order to interpret the facts properly. Sometimes a church will need expert assistance in the technical matters of research and interpretation. A consultation with an architect, organ builder, or city planner at the proper time can clarify alternatives for further consideration by groups in the church.

c. Planning involves projecting one's thoughts from the present to the future, from the known to the unknown. That process requires the exploring of every possible avenue of approach to the problem in an effort to discover *every conceivable* solution, so that the *best* solution can be reached. Each proposal must be openly and honestly discussed with an eye to the difficulties that each might entail. Here we see that the *consecrated imagination* is an essential planning tool. If the imaginations of many persons are at work from the beginning, it is likely that all major obstacles and objections will be quickly isolated for consideration, and that the necessary ideas and resources will be brought forth.

d. Finally, after the fact-finding and consulting are complete, and after the imaginations of many persons have ranged far and wide over the alternative courses, the proposals and suggestions must be narrowed down. This is the task of a small planning group, all members of which have been *thoroughly* involved in the process up to this point. Some sort of rough consensus will normally have evolved by this time; upon that consensus the small group can build a definite plan, outlining the steps to be taken in reaching the commonly accepted goal. This final aspect of the planning step will involve interaction between the planning committee and the church board or the congregation or both. The result is a clearly defined plan which large numbers of members will understand and recognize as their own, since it was hammered out through their actual participation. Plans developed in this way will bear much fruit in the later steps of the administrative process.

3. Organizing.

The third step in the administrative process is organizing the congregation to coordinate all activities in preparing to carry out the plan. This organizing step requires both a knowledge of all the details involved in the plan and a full understanding of the relationship of the particular plan to the basic purpose of the church. The actual degree and type of organization will vary widely according to the project, as for instance between establishing a *koinonia* group and building an educational wing. Certain key words suggest different aspects of the organizing step.

a. What? The first organizational decision is *what* needs to be done to actualize the plan? What is the best way to confront the entire membership with the matter at hand? The answer may involve one event or a series of coordinated activities, such as preaching, group meetings, and lay visitation. The *plan* already developed states the goals and general direction of the project; the details of *organization* are necessary to provide the many highway signs required for a sure journey to the goal. In projects requiring a high degree of organization, such matters as the following must be decided early:

Number of committees needed and the exact responsibilities of each.

The executive and supervisory arrangement; the "chain of command."

Methods (Christian ones) for recruiting persons for committee work and other tasks.

The amount and type of training required for the various workers.

The means to be used in presenting the matter to the whole congregation: mailing materials, special meetings, visitation, etc.

b. When? When should the plan be put into operation? Timing is important to the effectiveness of the project. Either undue haste or delay can be detrimental. Several questions arise in establishing the timing. Are there other projects that should be completed before introducing this new one? Is this project commonly recognized as so urgent that it should be undertaken at once? How much time is needed to prepare adequately to undertake the project? How long will it take to complete it? Once the basic timing is worked out, each event within the project must be scheduled with an eye to avoiding conflicts and to integrating the project within the total life of the congregation.

c. Who? The question of who should carry out the several responsibilities needs early and careful consideration. The best plan can be ruined by incompetent personnel or a shortage of manpower. No aspect of the organizational process deserves more attention than the selection and use of personnel. The number of committees and workers should be determined realistically in accordance with the work required and the persons available. The committees and the executive structure should be set up in such a way that both duplication of labors and multiple assignments are eliminated. The actual selection of persons to serve should be determined by the general committee in charge of the project, whose members will fit the types of jobs to the personal talents available.

d. Follow through. Many a fine plan has gone unrealized because no one gave attention to *following through* to completion a project well begun. Experience indicates that in a long project there will inevitably be some persons who cannot complete their responsibilities, owing to illness, family emergencies, or just generally growing weary in well doing. From the beginning some plans must be made to cover these eventualities. The best precaution, of course, is not to assign anyone too heavy a load. In the every member canvass, for instance, some churches train separate "follow-up" teams, who take over after the initial visitation. In any case, some thought must be given from the beginning to the problems of replacement of workers and the reassignment of tasks.

79

e. Accurate records. Just a word should be injected here about the importance of recording all procedures carefully—time schedules, committee membership and responsibilities, training sessions, etc. Often these records consist simply of copies of the job analyses, instructions, and other communications, which will normally be sent to the several leaders and workers. All of these materials should be carefully compiled and labeled. They are essential for later evaluation and for orienting new persons in case it is necessary to change leaders in the middle of a project.

4. Stimulating [9] *and Implementing.*

Following the completion of the plan of organization, the time arrives to begin actually carrying out the project. The administrator plays a significant role in the various ways he stimulates response to an activity already planned and organized.

Some administrators may exert considerable pressure upon those in charge of the program to produce results. Such an attempt to be a "big operator" is the least desirable of all methods for stimulating response, since it focuses on the operation and results of the *program* and ignores or minimizes a concern for the growth of the persons involved. Other administrators will rely almost entirely upon a rational approach to stimulate action. They will confront the congregation with facts and logic in the belief that these will provide the necessary motivation. They rely on the old adage that facts speak for themselves. Certainly all stimulation to action must have a rational foundation, but many an administrator has discovered that facts alone do not produce deep motivation. How often has a minister had the facts on his side, but the congregation has remained immovable.

Unquestionably the administrator's personal relationship to the persons involved is a key factor in stimulating them to action. "Stimulating members of an organization to action is as complex as human personality itself. What seems to be effective in the administrator's relationship with one person may not be effective with the second. There is no cookbook procedure or 'never fail' recipe for stimulation." [10] There is little doubt, however, that the degree of acceptance the administrator has by the persons involved in any program is important. Persons respond to a leader in whom they have confidence on the basis of their personal day-to-day relationships with him.

The administrator must also be aware that clear and effective communication is a vital factor in stimulating members to action. Faulty and hazy communication can be a stumbling block that may prevent the best idea from becoming a reality. "Communication needs to be of three kinds: down, up, and across." [11] The administrator must communicate to those *under* his leadership in such a manner that they can both understand and accept his message. Likewise communication must be loud and clear as it comes *up* to the administrator from those "on the firing line." The administrator must be an understanding listener. It is entirely possible that as many good programs are "saved" by understanding listening on the part of the administrator as by effective speaking. Stimulation to action likewise involves clear communication *across* the board in widespread member-to-member-to-pastor conversations.

Let us seek to apply these principles of stimulating action in a congregation by suggesting certain points that demand the attention of the administrator.

a. It is important to secure all workers early and to arrange adequate training for them. Every effort should be made to see that there is no breakdown at this level. This matter is of sufficient importance that the minister may well give of his personal time to the recruitment and training of workers. If difficulty is encountered in recruitment or training of workers, it is unlikely that the plan can be carried to a successful conclusion. Experience indicates that it is wise to recruit workers through personal face-to-face calling. It is also important to recruit about 10 percent more workers than are actually needed. Some will fall by the wayside and others will be needed for follow through responsibilities. The *quality of instruction* given to prepare workers for their responsibilities is of utmost significance. Careful planning should precede the training sessions and the best possible leadership and materials should be secured. Training that deals only with superficial mechanical trivia will repel capable persons. It is absolutely essential for all persons involved to see the relationship of what they are doing to the central mission of the church.

b. **Clear communication with all workers is vital.** Make sure all persons clearly understand their particular responsibilities and the meeting dates affecting them and the amount of time they will be expected to give. This should be done by letters written to each person and followed by a discussion within each committee.

c. **On the job supervision is called for in executing any plan.** The coordination of the various stages of any project demands that the administrator know exactly what is happening everywhere all the time. He must, therefore, maintain personal contact with workers and leaders. Some persons will need encouraging, a few will drop by the wayside and need to be replaced, while others will do much more than is expected. Supervision is also important because unexpected problems are often encountered and decisions must be made about how they should be handled. It may well be that in some circumstances even major changes in the original plan may be called for. For example, a church-wide activity in a rural church may need to be rescheduled if an unexpected rainy season has postponed spring sowing until the week of the event. A sensitive rural pastor would "hear" what his people are really saying as they complain about the late spring and propose a change in the church's timetable.

d. **One aspect of stimulating action is keeping on the time schedule unless significant circumstances, such as that just cited, should make a change advisable.** Each separate aspect of the program is dependent on the preceding event being completed on schedule. The coordination of the time schedule is important; a delay at any given point may be serious later on.

e. **Keeping the congregation informed is always a stimulant to action.** Both the workers and the members ought to know how things are going. If it is truly their plan, they will be interested, and honest reports will stimulate renewed interest and response. A reluctant but necessary word of caution is called for here. All information given must be accurate and complete. Confidence can easily be destroyed by careless, incomplete, or inaccurate reports. All reports made should be filed and used later in evaluating the effectiveness of the project.

5. *Evaluating.*

A final step in the administrative process is evaluating the work. This is a final step only for purposes of discussion. The other steps in the administrative process are to be taken chronologically in the order named (i.e., recognizing a need, planning, organizing, stimulating). Evaluation, however, is a continuing process, taking place simultaneously within each step of the administrative process. As every idea is considered it is evaluated in relation to its contribution to the fulfillment of the mission of the church as well as to its feasibility for the local situation. As planning takes place and detailed organizational structure is developed, evaluation is constantly made by all the persons involved. Even the willingness or unwillingness of persons to work in the project is a form of evaluation. All expressions of concurrent evaluation should be encouraged. The more persons involved in the evaluation process throughout the project, the more effective the project is likely to be.

In addition to a continuous evaluation of each project as it moves through the various steps in the administrative process, there should also be a separate evaluation made at the completion of the project. Each separate committee should have its own evaluation session, and the general committee (including all committee chairmen) should work out an overall evaluation of the experience. Complete honesty and frankness are the order of the day here. Careful notes should be kept of these sessions and filed for future reference in the master folder containing all project records. Real growth in grace for all participants can result from these evaluation sessions.

Continual evaluation of all aspects of church life is one of the fundamental responsibilities of the administrator. Armed with a clear understanding of the nature of the church and the resultant concept of church administration as God-centered and person-oriented, he can measure every proposal as to its acceptability. He can also help bring the whole congregation to a sensitivity which will enable them to make sound judgments about ways and means. Conversely, periods of evaluation provide important opportunities for leading people to greater understanding of the nature of the church and its mission.

D. Goals and Principles of Purposeful Church Administration

Just what is the church administrator trying to achieve? What does he hope will happen as a result of all his efforts? In other words, what are his goals? They are, as we have seen, implied by his understanding of the church and of church administration. Here we will identify them clearly and then go on to set forth the principles that will make possible the realization of these goals. The goals are as follows:

1. *To secure understanding of and commitment to the Christian faith.* Leading the congregation toward an ever-deepening commitment to Christ is the all-inclusive objective of church administration. Only as this is done can Christians become conscious of their unique nature and function as a ministering community. It is this central concern that sets off church administration from all other kinds of administration. Every experience and activity in the life of the church is to be evaluated on the basis of whether or not it contributes to this goal.

2. *To coordinate all experiences and activities so that they are mutually supportive of one another, as well as of the common mission of the church.* Church administration should seek to make every committee, every auxiliary group, every corner of the congregation aware of the common goal toward which the church is moving. Furthermore, the activities of the several groups must not only contribute to the proper goal, but must support one another, avoiding the duplication and conflict so often encountered.

3. *To see every aspect of church life as an opportunity to minister to persons.* Administration is not merely a means of "getting the work done" but a means through which persons can be served by having

84

their lives enriched in Christ. The church administrator must never forget that persons and their needs are the raw material of his work.

4. *To understand the surrounding culture and to communicate effectively to it.* God's love is for all men. The church must find ways of communicating its message meaningfully to the culture in which it finds itself. Though the church must always remain true to its message and mission, the vehicles appropriate to effective witness will vary from culture to culture.

5. *To involve all members of the church in the work of a ministering community.* God does not intend for laymen to be spectators while clergy "do" the work of the church. When a person receives the love of God, he is impelled to share it. Church administration, therefore, has a predetermined objective to provide opportunities for every member to minister to the congregation and the surrounding community. Richard Niebuhr says of the pastor,

His first function is that of building or "edifying" the church; he is concerned in everything he does to bring into being a people of God who as a Church will serve the purpose of the Church in the local community and the world. . . . For the church is becoming the minister and its "minister" is its servant, directing it in its service.[12]

It is clear from this statement that laymen are not merely to *play* at witnessing in order to feel religious. They *are* the witnesses—in places where no clergymen could ever find entrance, places where the world-changing decisions of business, labor, government, and education are being made. If the administrator ignores this most significant social fact, he betrays his calling.

The goals just outlined will be realized only by a proper understanding and application of certain basic principles. These principles identify broad areas of method, by which the administrator may lead the congregation from where it is to where it ought to be. Attention must be given to each of these principles, in proper relationship to the others, in order to work in any particular aspect of church life.

Perhaps an example from the field of music will illustrate the function of these principles. To become a good performing musician a person must recognize certain principles upon which all musical achievement rests: reading musical notation, learning the time and pitch value of each symbol, translating the written notes into the manipulations of the instrument to be played, securing a good teacher, practicing regularly and critically. These fundamentals are essential to all professional performance. Yet they allow a full range of freedom as to the instrument chosen, the type of music played, and the interpretation of any selection. But these options have no meaning apart from the prior mastery of the basic principles.

In a similar way one cannot become a good church administrator merely by obtaining "recordings" of someone else's programs, even if they should happen to be masterpieces. Only by mastering the principles involved in the day-to-day *development* of such programs can the church administrator work toward developing the approach that is precisely suited to his situation.

The remaining six chapters of this book will be given to developing the following basic principles:

1. Building a spiritual foundation through worship and study.

2. Establishing redemptive interpersonal relationships.

3. Providing for the creative functioning of small groups in the church.

4. Equipping laymen for leadership and service in the church's ministry to the world.

5. Strengthening the church by coordinated, comprehensive planning.

6. Utilizing all available resources.

These principles form the operational framework of purposeful church administration.

As a postscript to this chapter, it may be helpful to represent the definition with which the chapter opened, together with subsequent points of clarification, in the following diagram.[13]

Purposeful   Church   Administration

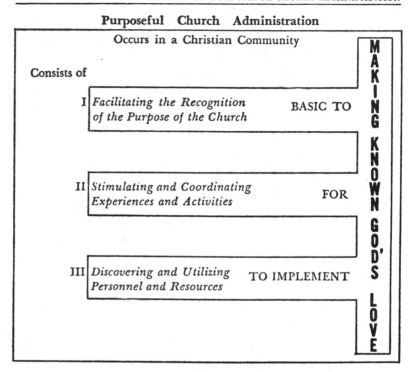

Purposeful church administration is the involvement of the church in the discovery of her nature and mission and in moving in a coherent and comprehensive manner toward providing such experiences as will enable the church to utilize all her resources and personnel in the fulfillment of her mission of making known God's love for all men.

■ ■ ■ Notes

1. Reuel Howe, *Man's Need and God's Action* (Greenwich: Seabury Press, 1953), p. 73. An illuminating discussion on "the language of relationships" is to be found in pages 65-76.

2. Paul Rountree Clifford, *The Pastoral Calling* (Manhasset, N. Y.: Channel Press, 1961). See this work for a detailed treatment of the meaning of shepherding as the dominant pastoral role in a parish.

3. John L. Casteel (ed.), *Spiritual Renewal Through Personal Groups* (New York: Association Press, 1957). Raines, *New Life in the Church*. The above volumes deal helpfully with the establishment of redemptive relationships within the church.

4. See Chapter VII of this volume.

5. See Acts 6:1-8 (the choosing of seven deacons); I Tim. 3; Tit. 1:7-9; also Mark 6:7.

6. This particular combination of components are the author's own, but each component is drawn from one of the standard lists in the field of administration. See Campbell, *et al.*, *Introduction to Educational Administration*, pp. 174-79, for an historical review of the origin and definition of the administrative process.

7. See Chapter VI, pp. 147-50 for a full discussion of neighborhood family unit groups in connection with establishing redemptive interpersonal relationships within the life of the church.

8. Campbell, *et al.*, *Introduction to Educational Administration*, p. 180.

9. *Ibid.*, p. 182. I am indebted to the writers for this particular term, as well as for certain concepts elaborating its meaning.

10. *Ibid.*

11. *Ibid.*, pp. 182-83.

12. Niebuhr, *The Purpose of the Church and Its Ministry*, pp. 82-83.

13. The *format* of the diagram presented was conceived as a result of a study of a similar diagram of educational administration found in Campbell *et al.*, *Introduction to Educational Administration*, p. 68. The *content* of the diagram setting forth the definition of church administration, however, is the author's own.

CHAPTER V

BUILD A SPIRITUAL FOUNDATION
THROUGH WORSHIP AND STUDY

A. The Importance of This Principle

A basic principle refers to that which can never be forgotten or neglected if any venture is to be brought to its intended conclusion. We are now ready to identify and examine six areas of concern that are so fundamental that they must be regarded as basic principles of church administration. They are the vehicles the church administrator will use to move the church from where it is to where it ought to be. Since church administration was defined as involving the church in the discovery of her nature and mission, and its uniqueness identified with its theological dimension of being God-centered, the first basic principle is the undergirding of the church by making worship and study the spiritual foundation stones on which all else rests. It is only through meaningful worship and a study of the Christian faith that the church can gain an understanding of her nature and mission.

Until the church administrator develops a worshiping congregation and an inquiring, studying fellowship deeply committed to Christ, he cannot hope to succeed in other aspects of the life of the church. He cannot succeed, that is, in leading the church toward fulfilling its mission of making known God's love to all men. Without such vital worship and study, it is of course possible for a church to become a great modern institution with impressive buildings, a popular gathering place on Sunday morning and at other times, a community center with many social fellowship activities—but not to be an authentic Christian church. The church's sense of direction, her motivation for action, and her goals and standards rest on the foundation of worship and study by the whole membership.

Where worship results in a deep commitment to Christ, and when meaningful study results in an understanding of the Christian faith, every area of the life of the church is strengthened. The areas of lay witnessing and evangelism, of missionary vision and response, of stewardship, of social concern and sensitivity, as well as the quality of Christian education—all will be enriched or impoverished in direct ratio to the vitality of the worship and study life of the church.

B. Begin with the Church Administrator

Since church administration is not only God-centered but person-oriented, the personal integrity of the administrator is intimately related to the fulfillment of each administrative principle. The nature and quality of his relationships with his parishioners is a matter of primary importance in his effort to communicate the Christian faith. Two basic observations about effective communication between the minister and the people are in order. First, the deeper his understanding of persons and the closer his pastoral relationshsip to them, the more effective he will be in speaking to them meaningfully. Second, the nearer the minister personifies the message of the Christian faith in his relationships, the more receptive the people will be to that message and to his leadership.

The person of the minister is a potent agent by which the Christian faith moves either toward clarity or confusion in people's minds. A lay committee once said to the writer,

Any visiting pastoral relations committee would conclude that our minister preaches as fine a sermon as any minister in the state. We would agree with them if we could listen only to the *words* he speaks on Sunday morning. If he could only be locked up from Sunday to Sunday, so we didn't have to see what kind of person he really is, he could preach helpfully to us. Knowing what we do about his personal life, it doesn't matter very much what words he utters in prayers and sermons; they are nullified by the self-centered person he is.

1. A Vital Personal Worship Experience Is Essential for the Minister.

The minister must not only know about God, he also must know God as one with whom he has a living relationship. Prayer and personal daily worship must be so much a part of his own life that he may speak with the authority of experience when he seeks to deepen the devotional life of others.

Many a minister rationalizes his neglect of devotional discipline with the thought that he is studying the Scriptures regularly in preparation for sermons and is constantly preparing or selecting prayers for worship services. Such a minister is likely to be so busy discovering the proper scriptural scalpel to remove the splinter from a church member's eyes, that he becomes unaware of the log in his own eye. Daily prayer and personal Bible study are easily put off by the pressure of many other duties which fill all the available hours. A wise retired minister once reminded me at a very crucial time in my own ministry, "Whenever *any* minister becomes too busy for daily prayer and personal Bible study, he is just too busy." To allow one's daily period of private worship to be crowded out by other demands is similar to driving off on a trip across the desert with a nearly empty gas tank. Only a meaningful and vital experience of the presence of God is sufficient for the task; and, like bread, every man's peace with God must be made fresh daily.

2. Continual Study Is Required of the Minister Administrator.

If the administrator is to lead the church into an increasing understanding of the Christian faith, then his own insights into the meaning of the gospel must be clear and continually growing. This demands rigorous and regular study. If the church administrator believes that it is essential for the whole church to engage in a constant quest for clear insights into the Christian faith, he can set no lower standard for himself. Every minister must give himself to continuing study. Indeed, a theological education is successful only if it succeeds in introducing the student to various fields of Christian knowledge so provocatively that he desires to explore them further. In fact, the basic goal of theological education is to provide each student with the tools and methods of research and with the motivation to carry on fruitful independent study throughout his lifetime.

Most ministers will find sufficient motivation for study within the local parish if they are alert to it. Relevant preaching demands long hours of regular disciplined study. Bible study classes or special courses on Christian beliefs require serious preparation. Opportunities to speak to "outsiders" on the campus, in the business world, in the field of labor, or in political circles should challenge the best of ministers, if the responsibility for clear communication is taken seriously. Problems encountered through the minister's relationship to persons in pastoral calling or counseling experiences should also spur him to disciplined study. When the people discover the real contribution their minister brings to them as a result of his own study life, they will both respect his study hours and respond expectantly to his invitation to participate in study experiences.

Regular study is related to the minister's time schedule; that is to his continual decisions about what are the most important concerns of the Christian faith to which he will give himself. Every pastor will experience pressures to become involved beyond the total number of hours available in the week. These pressures will include innumerable local church needs, community meetings and problems, persons needing pastoral care, denominational meetings to attend, enterprises seeking leadership, causes seeking a champion, and the needs of the minister's own family—not to mention his own personal needs. Since these needs vary from one community-church-pastor combination to another, no set time schedule is suitable for every minister. Let us be very clear at this point, however: The time schedule actually kept by any minister is an accurate gauge of what he *really* believes to be important, else he would not so spend his time and energy. This will be denied by many, who say that the pressure of community expectations or ecclesiastical authority forces them to be involved in programs, meetings, and trivia which they detest. However, in giving in to such pressures, they really are revealing that professional advancement and personal acceptance actually are their most compelling goals, rather than that of leading the church toward the fulfillment of its mission. With due recognition for both the intensity and density of the many pressures on the minister, he alone ultimately must choose that to which he will give his time, and he is responsible for his choice.

Applied to the point at hand, this means that, no matter how numerous other demands on the minister may become, nothing should rob him of regular study hours, without which he cannot effectively preach, teach, counsel, visit, or function as a minister. Most ministers find twenty to twenty-four hours every week a minimum amount of time for such study. One group of local church *lay leaders* were concerned about the use of their pastors' time. After meeting and discussing the problem for a full day, they urged each congregation to "encourage the local pastor to become truly a spiritual physician, protecting his time from stenographic and errand-boy efforts, that he may more fully work and study and create in the realm of the spirit."

They further said,

We recommend, insofar as is practical in the opinion of the local pastor, as an ideal daily and weekly schedule of work the following:

    a. That five mornings a week be given for study and meditation and creative effort.

    b. That four afternoons and four evenings a week be given for pastoral calling and committee work (and office and organizational detail).

    c. That Sunday be given over entirely for church activities.

    d. That one day and two evenings a week be taken as the pastor's day of rest. (For those who care to figure the hourly effort of such an activity schedule, it would result as follows: (a) $22\frac{1}{2}$ hours, or $4\frac{1}{2} \times 5$ days, in study, preparation of sermons and reading related to problems, counseling, etc.; (b) 24 hours, or 6 hours by 4 days, to be given to pastoral calling, committee activity, etc.; (c) Sunday, a total of 12 hours, 9 a.m. to 9 p.m. This totals $58\frac{1}{2}$ hours per week, and it is all difficult, hard work. Also, it is highly probable the above listing is figured on a minimum basis; most pastors will spend more time in each area listed. This represents a ten-hour, six-day week) .[1]

Circumstances and individual differences may demand that different hours of the day be used to achieve these ends, but there is essential realism in recognizing that the ministry calls for long hours of work and that regular and serious study demands a high proportion of the pastor's time.

Only a minister who has disciplined himself in his own study habits will be prepared and able to involve the whole church in a serious and continuing inquiry into the nature of the Christian faith. This will be true because:

a) He must have a clear understanding of the faith himself.

b) Only then will he be aware of the value and necessity of study and of the teaching ministry.

c) His preaching and personal contacts will be enriched so as to create an interest and a desire in others to explore the Christian faith.

d) He will be able to suggest resources for study to meet the particular requests as they arise, whether from groups or individuals.

e) He will inspire and attract competent teachers and leaders to accept their responsibility to serve the church in this manner.

We would again underscore the fact that if the church is to be undergirded by building a spiritual foundation through worship and study, the place to *begin* is with the minister.

C. Worship Must Be Kept Central and Vital in the Life of the Church

1. Corporate Public Worship Is Basic to the Life of the Church.

Christian worship is a unique activity of the church. No other institution in society assembles for the primary purpose of worshiping God as revealed in Jesus Christ. Other groups in society may share certain activities with the church, such as education, fellowship, so-

94

cial service, and character building, but the church alone calls men to worship the God of Jesus Christ as Creator and Redeemer. The church administrator, therefore, has a stewardship to see that worship remains central and meaningful in the life of the church. He must resist all pressures to hide worship in the shadow of a mountain of other activities. Likewise, he should resist any temptation to alter the service of worship to suit personal desires or for dramatic effect, thereby changing and adulterating the basic character of worship.

Worship involves a conscious acknowledgment of a vital relationship between God and the individual. Man gratefully acknowledges that God is his Creator, that his own strength and abilities are insufficient, and that he must turn to God for his salvation. "The Christian does not worship to get something for himself, but to remind himself and testify to the community that God is the author of life and we are his creatures." [2]

When we enter into such a relationship with God and experience his acceptance of us, our sense of awe of the Almighty is deepened, we become more sensitive and receptive to the leading of his Holy Spirit, and we receive enlightenment and power to become living witnesses of his way. Vital worship is thus the mainspring and source of the church's power.

Worship must be a significant experience for the *whole* church. Worship must never become merely a form or a practice habitually observed or, even worse, an opportunity for the minister to "perform" by throwing the spotlight on himself as he leads the worship service. The worship service can easily become perfunctory for minister and congregation alike. All the proper forms and words can be used, but the vital relationship to God can be missing. This experience is not unlike the place of love in some marriages. A couple may go through all the outward forms of expressing love for years and yet not experience the relationship of meaningful love. They may live together, kiss one another good-bye daily, even have sexual intercourse, and yet not enter into a real love relationship. Some members of every congregation and even some ministers have this identical type of experience in relation to worship.

2. The Minister's Responsibility for Corporate Worship.

The minister must do all in his power to enable every person to have a meaningful worship experience. He must remember, however, as John Irwin reminds us, "In public worship it is the people who do the worshiping. The minister cannot worship for them. It is his function to provide the form and select the materials so that *they* may perform *their* worship." [3]

It is one thing to experience the presence of God; it is quite another to enable others to share in the experience. The minister must be a student of worship; he must know something of its biblical roots and of its development in the history of the church. He must be aware of the wealth of worship resources available from the past and present that may enrich our worship today. Reading in this field should be a part of every minister's study program. [4]

It is important for the minister to be clear in his objectives as he structures the pattern of worship for the Sunday morning service. Many Protestant services are based upon the pattern revealed in Isa. 6:1-8. This pattern suggests at least four steps in worship:

a) Praise and adoration.

b) Confession.

c) Renewal or communion.

d) Dedication or commitment.

Many rich resources for worship are to be found in denominational worship manuals. Every minister should be thoroughly familiar with the material of his own denomination and also that of other churches. I have found it helpful to keep a file of contemporary worship material, selected from current periodicals or services of worship where helpful liturgical resources were used. Constant alertness to resources for worship is as important as alertness for sermon themes. Poorly or carelessly planned worship services may be precisely the reason why worship lacks meaning to many congregations. Though the minister cannot worship for his people, careful planning of the worship service and the selection of materials can do much to create conditions conducive to their own lively participation.

Great care should be used in the selection of Scripture readings, especially since in the typical congregation the Sunday readings are the only passages heard or read by the majority of worshipers. Surveys have indicated that no more than one third of all church members read the Bible in private. (Some ministers follow a lectionary in their selection of Scripture, to insure that the whole message of the Bible be periodically set forth to the congregation.) A similar point applies to the use of prayers in the worship service. For the majority of the congregation, these are the only prayers they say or hear. Careful preparation of the pastoral prayer is as basic as careful preparation of the sermon. Each week this will be the high moment of the service for some persons. Whether they are read or not, all pastoral prayers should be prepared in advance, and every liturgical prayer should be selected with the needs of the particular congregation in mind.

No discussion of the selection of material for use in the worship services can ignore the importance of the proper use of church music. It cannot be ignored partly because of the practical difficulties surrounding the weekly use of music in the Sunday service. The quality of the singing of the choir or congregation may be very poor or the selections of the organist unsuitable for worship. The congregation may feel that they cannot worship because the hymns selected are unfamiliar to them. Then, too, there is the matter of securing good musical leadership, and, the other side of the coin, retiring inadequate musicians. This is enough to suggest that the minister as worship leader must be prepared to give attention to the proper place of music in worship and the selection of materials and music leadership in the church. Some of the elements of his administration in the area might be listed as follows:

a.) The minister must acquire a basic understanding of church music and its relationship to worship. Blessed is the minister who has had a good course in this field during his seminary days. An excellent book in this field is Lovelace and Rice, *Music and Worship in the Church*.[5] This book contains not only sound theory but also valuable lists of suitable hymns for various age groups and helpful lists of solos and anthems.

b) A music committee needs to be carefully selected in the local church and trained to function to provide the best possible music program for the church.

c) The minister should encourage and support the music leadership of his church. Words of appreciation for work well done always are in order. The lines of communication between the minister and the organist and the choir director must be kept open.

d) Hymns for the worship service must be selected carefully as to the suitability of both the tune and words to express the desired experience and message.

e) Some program of familiarizing the congregation with good hymns in worship may be undertaken, beginning with the organist and choir. A hymn-of-the-month program may be utilized in the worship service itself. Here, a hymn may be introduced as an organ prelude or offertory with a brief written description in the bulletin the first Sunday. The choir may sing it the second Sunday as a special number, and it may be sung by the congregation the next Sunday. Other suggestions for familiarizing the congregation with good hymns will be found in Lovelace and Rice.

f) The selection of hymns for use in the church school should be such that the children will become familiar with many hymns found in the church hymnal. They will thus be acquainted with the hymns used in the worship service by the time they become members of the church. The hymnal itself ought to be used in the youth and adult divisions of the church school. This will do much to improve congregational singing in the years ahead.

g) The minister should plan his preaching in advance, so that sermon and worship themes can be given to the director of music to enable him to select appropriate choir anthems in sufficient time for the choir to rehearse them.

Moving now to preaching, it is important to keep in mind that the sermon, unlike any other address, takes place within the context of worship. Its purpose is to communicate the gospel to man in his concrete situation. The hearer must recognize that God is speaking through the message, that God is speaking to him personally, and that God is calling him to decision and action in his specific situation. Preaching thus has an awesome dimension to it that no minister can ignore. The sermon unquestionably and rightfully holds a central place in worship. Every sermon theme must therefore be selected with great care and developed with genuine thoroughness and understanding. It must not only set forth God's message clearly, but also must reach the hearer at his point of need, so that God not only speaks, but speaks to *him*.

Good preaching not only is a necessity for vital worship, but lays the groundwork for many other aspects of parish life. The depth of a congregation's understanding of the Christian faith is largely dependent on the quality of preaching that the people hear. The receptivity of a minister's teaching ministry through special courses is affected by his preaching. If the minister's preaching reflects understanding and real love of both God and man, then many doors will open in his pastoral ministry. Both the quality and quantity of volunteer leadership that comes forth to assume responsibility in the church will be a reflection of the preaching done in the pulpit.

3. The Sacraments Must Be Duly Administered.

In worship, the word of God comes to man as clearly through the sacraments as through the spoken or preached word. The minister is obligated to administer the sacraments in such a way that the people may worship through them as truly as through the usual order of worship. The attitudes of various congregations may differ widely at this point, not only in different denominations but within any given denomination. Some churches view the sacraments lightly, and attendance drops markedly when they are administered. In other cases the reverse is true. It is the minister's responsibility to do everything possible to make the sacraments a meaningful worshipful experience in every congregation. Aspects of this responsibility include the following points:

a) Every minister must clarify his own theological interpretation of both baptism and the Lord's Supper.

b) The meaning of the sacraments should be shared with the congregation through the pulpit, through discussion groups, in personal conversations, and through the distribution of literature. All new members should be instructed in the meaning of the sacraments.

99

c) All youths and adults to be baptized and the parents of children to be baptized should be fully instructed as to the meaning of the sacrament and of the vows they are assuming in relationship to it.

d) The church members need to be reminded periodically of the responsibility they assume as the body of Christ and as the household of faith into whose fellowship those being baptized are received.

e) The minister must prepare himself for the administration of the sacrament as thoroughly as he would to lead the usual worship service. Unfortunately, some ministers schedule the sacrament of the Lord's Supper as a "fill-in" when they are too busy to prepare a sermon, as for instance on the first Sunday after vacation.

f) Be sure that the elements for the Lord's Supper are in readiness and all the mechanical details arranged, such as ushering, music, lights, candles, and instructions for coming to the table and receiving the elements.

g) Use the ritual of your denomination, following the instructions carefully. Read the ritual clearly and with meaning. The minister should maintain an attitude of reverence and worship personally throughout the service.

h) Even though the communion meditation is brief, it should be prepared as carefully and thoroughly as a full-length sermon.

i) Announce the Communion service in advance and urge your people to prepare themselves for it.

j) The administration of the Lord's Supper should be provided regularly to the sick and shut-in.

The minister who seeks to follow the above suggestions will find that he is moving in the direction of a more effective worship experience in the life of the congregation through the use of the sacraments.

4. The Leadership of Each Service of Worship Is Important.

The leadership of the service of worship is as important as the planning of the service itself. The leader must come to the service prepared in spirit as well as having prepared the materials to be used in the service. His dress and manner must not call attention to himself. Loud ties, brilliant Argyll socks, and unshined shoes may detract the worshiper's attention from God's presence and focus it upon the person of the minister. All materials used in the service should be read over aloud before the service, until the minister understands them well enough to convey their meaning clearly to the congregation. Need it be said that all mechanical details should be thoroughly checked ahead of time (the lighting, availability of hymnal, Bible, finding of scripture passage, proper location of offering plates, functioning of ushers, etc.). Although these responsibilities may be delegated, the minister should make certain of the arrangements before every service. The manner in which the minister leads the service can do much in making the congregation aware of the presence of God. To illustrate this negatively, the minister whose concern for the number attending the service leads him to count the congregation during the anthem or offertory, is behaving in a manner that hinders rather than assists the worship of the congregation. The spirit of worship is best communicated through the person and manner of the worship leader.

5. Enlarging the Congregation's Understanding of Worship.

Since the minister cannot worship for people, it is imperative that the congregation grow in their own understanding of worship and in their participation in it. One of the concerns of the church administrator as a leader of worship is how to maintain a continually deepening appreciation of the necessity of worship throughout the church. Three suggestions will be offered here as to how an enlarging concept of worship might be developed.

a. **Through constantly lifting up the universal need for regular worship.** If a vital worship experience is held to be essential for all Christians, then let the church say so clearly to all new members at the time of their uniting with the church. The centrality of worship in Christian experience needs to be discussed carefully with each group of new members previous to their acceptance of the membership vows. Testimony from other members is the most effective manner of presenting this matter. It is important that the emphasis not be placed on church attendance for its own sake. Members are not to be pressed to attend services merely to keep a vow, but rather helped to discover that spiritual renewal through worship is as vital for the Christian life as food is for the physical body. All members-in-training should be part of the worshiping congregation throughout the training period and should discuss with the minister and with one another their own experiences in worship. The testimonies of pastors who have provided this kind of preparation give encouraging evidence that the worship life of a church can be strengthened markedly in this manner.

A similar lifting up of the importance of worship needs to be made to nonattending church members. Since they are not involved in training classes, a different approach must be found to achieve the same end. Pastoral calling often is the means of reopening the door of worship to these persons. At other times, lay calling to invite inactive members to renew their participation in worship, say, for a special series of Sundays such as Lent, may be all that is needed. A personal testimony of the value of worship given to a friend during a normal business or social contact may stimulate a response to return to public worship. Some ministers find it helpful to refer to the centrality of worship periodically in sermons.

A vital and meaningful service of worship is its own best testimony. Careful preparation for each service must be combined with a challenging sermon to make every service as effective as human diligence can make it. When people find spiritual nourishment and renewal in worship, they will come again, will tell their neighbor where they have found spiritual food, and will often bring him with them.[6]

b. Through a functioning worship committee of laymen. The task of enlarging the congregation's understanding of worship is too great for any minister to undertake by himself. He will need the assistance of laymen to increase the congregation's intelligent participation and to help them accept changes in the order of worship. For these reasons, most ministers will want to establish a worship committee. In fact, several committees which often exist independently might be combined into one large coordinating worship committee.

Such a committee might include the committees on ushers, music, flower arranging, greeters, communion stewards, and the altar committee. Actually, each of these groups can fulfill its particular function only if it shares a common understanding of worship with the others and with the minister. Even though the minister is in charge of the worship life of the church, such a coordinating committee could enrich the worship of most congregations, for the following reasons:

1. This group of laymen who are functioning through independent committees need a common understanding of the meaning, purpose, and practice of worship if their individual contributions are to produce a unified worship experience. The pastor can best meet this educational need by training a single committee.

2. The pattern of worship and the significance of each item in it need to be understood by everyone involved in the service. Concerns for better music, improved ushering, etc., are not isolated matters but are a part of the whole service. Only a worship committee can keep each of these areas in its proper perspective.

3. The music program can best be strengthened when seen as an integral part of the service. The committee can encourage the use of suitable music in Sunday services, at weddings, and at funerals more effectively than the pastor can by himself.

4. Such a committee can aid greatly in interpreting the objectives of worship to the congregation. The several members of the committee will be members of most of the auxiliary groups of the church. Whenever questions arise in these groups about worship, informed committee members can interpret the objectives of worship on the spot.

5. Worship committee members also can keep the pastor and one another informed as to the effectiveness of the present worship service by reporting the reactions of members of the congregation. This

103

process will pinpoint the aspects of the service that need discussion, interpretation, or change.

6. A worship committee may be of assistance to the trustees and the memorial committee by coordinating and clarifying all needs for sanctuary and chancel equipment, so that all purchases or gifts may be consistent with the accepted objectives of worship.

c. **Through training laymen as leaders of worship.** The church is responsible for training all persons in positions of leadership, and leaders of worship are no exception. Too often when a layman is asked to lead in worship, either no help is offered, or he is handed a book containing "prepared" or "canned" worship services. If such material is to be used effectively or if the leader is encouraged to develop or select worship material independently, some understanding of the objectives and methods of worship leadership is required. As different persons receive training over the years, it will add significantly to the congregation's understanding of worship. As in the case of other kinds of leadership training, there are rich dividends awaiting the congregation that makes this investment of time.

D. Study Is Required of the Whole Church if It Is to Understand and Fulfill Its Mission

1. The Teaching Ministry Is Implied by the Very Nature of Christianity.

The necessity of every Christian's being both student ("disciple") and teacher ("apostle") is grounded in the example and commission of Jesus. The New Testament is abundantly clear; the call to teach is as basic as the call to preach. Indeed, the two are as inseparable as two sides of one coin. New disciples must be taught the meaning of their commitment. The whole church must be taught its basic nature and mission before it can witness effectively. The whole world needs to be taught the good news of the gospel. The church administrator is called to a teaching task which he cannot escape. He fulfills this task in two ways: first, by exercising a direct teaching ministry and, second, by teaching laymen to teach each other. Let us look at each of these roles in turn.

104

2. The Administrator's Responsibility as a Teacher.

a. Through the pulpit. Although preaching is usually defined as proclaiming the gospel, it also provides one of the minister's most important direct teaching opportunities. The faith must be explained and applied as well as proclaimed. More adults depend upon the pulpit to increase their scriptural knowledge than upon any other single source. This being the case, no minister ought to take the teaching role of the ministry lightly. Since most of his hearers are at least nominally committed to Christ, the preacher fulfills an essential teaching task as he clarifies for them the implications of the gospel.

Series of sermons lend themselves well to the ends of teaching. Series on basic beliefs, the Beatitudes, the Lord's Prayer, or particular books of the Bible are examples of fruitful possibilities. One value of a sermon series is that it often stimulates individual Bible reading and study during the series, especially when such participation is explicitly encouraged. Sermon series may also lead to personal discussions and the raising of questions during pastoral calls made at that time.

The teaching opportunities of the pulpit are not to be neglected. Contemporary congregations need enlightenment on scriptural truths. Here the minister may reach his largest single audience with Christian teaching.

b. Through training for church membership. The minister functions directly as a teacher in preparing persons for church membership. Few teachers have classes more receptive to learning than the pastor's membership class. If this opportunity is used wisely, it can transform the whole congregation over a period of a few years. The enthusiasm, commitment, and leadership of alert and dedicated new members can do more to awaken a slumbering congregation than anything I know. Usually, there are different approaches to membership training for youth and for adults. Let us look at each briefly.

Youths are received into the church at various ages, usually between the sixth and ninth grades in school, with the seventh or eighth grade being the most common. The pastor should make personal calls on all eligible youths and their families. It should be made clear that attendance at class sessions does not automatically lead to church membership. A personal commitment to Christ is a prerequisite for membership. It is important to visit with the parents about the nature of the class, about its requirements, and about their part in the training process. Many times one or both parents may be reached at this time to accept Christ as Lord and to be enrolled in an adult membership class. This evangelistic opportunity ought not be overlooked.

The length of training and the nature of the class vary considerably. Each denomination has one or more suggested approaches to youth membersheip training. For example, the author has used a training period of thirty-two weekly hour-and-a-half sessions, beginning in September and continuing to Pentecost Sunday. Saturday mornings are often the most acceptable time for class sessions. The purpose of the class is to discover the meaning of being a Christian and of belonging to a Christian church. The requirements of the class need to be carefully explained at the outset. The group is in training for church membership. The young people must begin by seeking to understand commitment to the Christian faith "from the inside," by seeking to live, think, and act as a Christian and as a church member. Just as training for football involves practicing exactly as one expects to play the game so must it be in training for church membership. Each class member is asked to accept the following requirements as items of self-imposed discipline:

1. Regular attendance at all class sessions.

2. The completing of all assignments for class preparation.

3. Daily devotions—personal prayer and Bible reading.

4. Regular worship in church on Sunday and attendance at church school.

5. Acts of service to the church and to other persons.

6. Using offering envelopes as training for regular giving to the church.

7. Writing the life of Jesus in your own words.

8. Promising not to join the church unless you can accept Jesus Christ as Lord.

The content of the class sessions must take into account the material being covered in the church school currently as well as previously. The church school teachers involved must be apprised of what the pastor is doing each week in the membership class, so that membership class material does not compete with or duplicate church school sessions. A good place to begin is to explore with the youths their past and present contacts with the church and to interpret their meaning. Then the class can reach out to consider the relationship of the local church to the denomination, thence to other denominations, and on to a study of church history and of Jesus' life and teachings. This may be followed by an interpretation of how we got our Bible and how we are to regard and use it. Basic Christian beliefs may then be discussed. Finally the class will want to examine the vows taken by each member and to explore their meaning.

Pentecost is a singularly appropriate day to unite with the church. The entire service should be planned to make this a meaningful event for both the class and the church, including a sermon directed toward the meaning of church membership and Christian commitment.

One of the important values of a long period of training is the close relationship the pastor can develop with each member of the class. For many, this is their first close association with a minister, and for all it is the most sustained relationship they may ever have. A bridge of understanding and concern can be built that will open many doors of future ministry to these youth. This experience offers unparalleled opportunity to witness to the meaning of Christian faith. Many a young man first considers the ministry as his vocational call because of this initial experience shared with his pastor.

Adult membership training is equally important, but must of necessity be discussed more briefly. All adults uniting with the church on confession of faith should be required to have membership training. Adult members transferring from another church will need certain portions of the course, and all should have the section dealing

107

with the life and program of the local church. The number of sessions usually varies from two to twelve, with four to six sessions probably being the most common. The requirements of a commitment to Christ as Lord and of membership in the church need to be forthrightly stated and thoroughly discussed by the group. A capable layman makes the best leader of such a discussion.

It is of utmost importance that the minister be clear as to the objective of adult membership training. Adult membership training seeks to *initiate* or *confirm* a commitment to Christ and to enlist adults in a *continuing quest* for the meaning of his Lordship for all life. The Christian commits himself not only to accept Christ as Lord but to seek diligently to discover what this means in every area of his life. The adult membership class does not seek to impart complete knowledge of the Scriptures or a full course in Christian theology. The basic objective is a recognition of a relationship to Christ that involves a continuing *lifelong quest*. Laymen who exemplify service to Christ ought to have a part in setting forth the challenge of church membership. The objective is to introduce new members to the church in such a way that they are eager to enter into the great adventure of Christian fellowship.[7]

Nowhere is it more true than with membership training that we reap what we sow. The pastor who takes his teaching opportunity of membership training seriously can lift the vision of his whole congregation in five years, but he who shirks his responsibility will compound existing lethargy. The new member eagerly knocking at the door of the church is fertile ground, and if good seed is sown, the harvest will be a hundredfold.

c. **Through special courses.** The church administrator has a wonderful opportunity to exercise a teaching ministry by periodically offering special short-term courses and by serving as a teacher in study projects sponsored by established church groups. Any minister who does not offer one or two short courses of six to twelve weeks each year is passing by an important opportunity to lay the foundation for the kind of vision and understanding required of lay Christians if they are to assume the responsibilities expected of them in the contemporary church.

Experience has indicated that the subject matter of these short-term courses can profitably be centered in Bible study or basic Christian beliefs. Harold Bosley offered such courses each fall for several years at First Methodist Church, Evanston, Illinois, with increasing interest and response. It usually is wise to do a depth study of a limited content area rather than general surveys of broad areas. For example, it is more fruitful to study I Corinthians for six or eight weeks than all the letters of Paul, or to study one gospel rather than all four gospels. This is equally true in examining basic Christian beliefs. A depth study of Christology, the Holy Spirit, or eternal life is more rewarding than a hop, skip, and jump over the Apostles' Creed. There may be specific circumstances where a broad survey course is called for in a given year, but over a ten-year period a church will profit more from ten depth studies than from ten survey courses.

Few experiences will be more rewarding than the teaching of such courses. It is a joy to discover the thrill of seeing new insights come to laymen in these classes. More than this, one never ceases to be amazed at the insights the laymen contribute to enrich the meaning of a particular passage for their minister. Teaching involves two-way communication, and every preacher needs to be involved in such a dialogue. People cannot ask questions or talk back when the sermon is in progress. In classroom discussion the atmosphere is, or should be, different. If a point is not stated clearly enough to be understood, the teacher is stopped by a question. This discipline of having to speak so that he is understood, though often disturbing, is one of the most valuable aspects of the teaching experience for the preacher. It should sharpen his ability to communicate more relevantly and effectively from the pulpit. Discussion is always a requirement of good teaching. Not only do class members insist on clarification but will go on to disagree many times with the point made. The exploration of disagreements usually is helpful to class members and teacher alike. Real encouragement should be given to free expression of opinion, including doubts and disagreements. In such circumstances a minister may come to know the real spiritual I. Q. of his congregation, and this can be of great value in all his relationships with them as preacher, teacher, and pastor. The results of these classes will be evident over the years as the local church grapples with what its own responsibilities and what its mission ought to be. The vision and insight gained will become evident in concrete local decisions that will follow. As Paul knew, administrative decisions and actions must rest on an interpretation of the Christian faith. These study classes are the foundation upon which the church's program for tomorrow will be erected. If no such foundation is built, the program will rest upon sand.

One other opportunity for a direct teaching experience needs to be considered briefly. Many churches are discovering the values of a retreat period for the official board and all officers of the church. Such retreats are often a combination of worship, study, and fellowship. The teaching opportunity of such retreats is invaluable, and the minister who sees them merely as a time for organizational program building has missed the mark. Here is an opportunity for church leaders to share intimately in worship and study, examining the foundations of their faith. For example, a theme might be selected for the retreat, such as "The Mission of the Church." All members might be asked to read the six chapters of Ephesians before coming to the retreat. The devotional periods could lift up the nature and mission of the church, and the study periods could be chapter-and-verse discussions of the book. Much creative work is being done in this area, and every minister ought seriously to consider such an approach with his people.

3. Christian Education Is Needed by the Whole Church.

a. The goal and scope of Christian education must be clearly understood. The goal of Christian education is to seek a personal commitment to Christ as Lord, and then to grow in understanding the implications of this commitment as the circumstances of life impinge upon persons and society, calling for decision and action. It is this goal of commitment and growth in Christ that makes Christian education unique among all educational endeavors. The church administrator must keep this goal clearly before all who work in the educational life of the church.

110

Though the Christian faith calls for a complete commitment to Jesus Christ as Lord as an entrance requirement, it would be erroneous to assume every Christian could or should know all of the possibilities as to where this commitment might lead in the future. This means that one element in every commitment to Christ is an obligation to continuous study and exploration toward an increasing understanding of the Christian faith. The Christian education activities of any church ought to be accurately described as "the church at study."

The scope of Christian education in the local church includes all persons related to the local church and its constituency. It becomes obvious at once that the magnitude of the responsibility for Christian education is beyond ability of any minister to fulfill alone and that many lay Christians must be engaged in the church's teaching ministry. Because of this fact, the Sunday school has developed largely as a layman's movement. Within Protestantism, the priesthood of all believers has found functional expression most completely in the area of Christian education.

One very important value in using lay teachers needs to be kept in mind. Learning takes place through the experience of teaching. Nearly every teacher will testify that in the process of preparing and conducting class sessions, he learns more than the members of the class. Thus the proper training of teachers provides the church with an opportunity to deepen the insights and increase the vision of a large group of Christian leaders in the church.

b. **The minister's relationship to Christian education in the local church.** The cost of failure in the educational task should be apparent to every minister. A minister once said to me:

This church is paying the penalty for a weak program of Christian education over the years. Most adult members lack both an understanding of and an interest in the scriptures. They are biblical illiterates and, even worse, they don't care. This lack of Christian understanding is evident throughout the leadership of the church. The committee chairmen and board members lack vision because they do not really understand what being Christian means or what the mission of the church really is.

111

Not knowing where they are going, these leaders hesitate to start on any journey at all, and so the church does nothing. Our church cannot sing many of the historic hymns of the church because the church school uses its own song book, even in the youth and adult departments, and consequently, nearly all the hymns in the hymnal are unfamiliar. Perhaps, worst of all, our youth go away to college, the armed services, or out into life, not knowing what they believe. Unless something can be done to break this cycle by revitalizing our Christian education program now, the pastor of this church twenty years from now will be facing the same problems that confront me today.

This agonizing testimony clearly lifts up the necessity for every minister to be concerned about the Christian education program of the local church.

(1) *An adequate structure for comprehensive and continuous Christian education.*

A wise administrator will not only welcome a lay board of Christian education with whom he may work but will do everything possible to assist this board in fulfilling its vital function in the life of the church. The minister's enthusiastic leadership in setting up a board of Christian education and in securing the most capable and qualified persons to serve on it is the first step in providing a sound approach to Christian education in the local church. Most denominations give guidance as to the personnel and organization of such a group. The pastor should be familiar with and follow the pattern of his denomination.

Once the group is established, it is important that it share with the pastor a common understanding as to the basic goals and objectives of Christian education. There will never be agreement on methodology, program, curriculum materials, space and equipment needs, or teaching personnel, without a common agreement on goals. The proper functioning of a board of Christian education involves much more than meeting regularly. Activity must never be confused with effectiveness. A clear channel of communication must be established between the minister and the commission on Christian education, both as to what *is* going on and what *ought*

112

to be going on. A sound program of Christian education requires conscientious attention by the minister no matter how capable his lay coworkers may be.

(2) *The pastor's relationship to the board of Christian education.*

(a) If an effective board is to exist, it must be staffed with capable leaders, who in turn must secure qualified teachers for all educational endeavors. The pastor's role in securing educational leadership for the church is to acquaint responsible persons with current and future needs, to make the leadership talent file available to the board, and to help evaluate the qualifications of each candidate. Throughout the process of selection as well as in the final vote, those chosen must be the committee's choice and not just the pastor's, nor that of any other particular person. Finally, in some instances, the pastor *may* team up with a layman to make a recruiting call on a potential leader.

Experience suggests the following guides for securing the best possible leadership in Christian education for the church, either as members of the board or as teachers.

1. Begin early to anticipate future personnel needs.

2. Consider only committed Christians and those who are open to continued growth through additional training.

3. Gather accurate data about past training and service of all persons considered.

4. Make face-to-face personal visits on prospective leaders early, in teams of two.

5. Have a definite limitation of tenure for board members (three or four years), and elect teachers for one year at a time, with everyone subject to reelection each year.

6. In the initial interview offer adequate and early training opportunities.

7. Be sure each person understands *why* his job exists and exactly *what* his responsibilities are.

8. The pastor must not usurp responsibilities given to laymen (i.e., function as chairman of meetings, take over responsibilities

113

that ought to belong to the church school superintendent or make decisions that belong to the board of education).

9. The pastor's personal interest in Christian education and in persons working in the field will strengthen the work. (This may be expressed by participation in meetings of the committee and in personal comments to workers.)

10. A carefully planned installation service for all Christian education workers, which seeks to deepen the commitment of each worker, is of great value.

(b) The pastor and the board must seek a common understanding of the goals and methods of Christian education. If such an understanding is not achieved, confusion and conflict will undermine the effectiveness of the Christian education program.

A *process* of open, fully shared searching for objectives is an indispensable first step. This search will continue over a period of time and may take the form of trying to answer the simple and practical question, "What do we want to happen to those who go through our church school?" Another layman put it, "What are we trying to do with those who do come?" In this particular local church, the committee of Christian education spent one full year of monthly meetings discussing the question, with several smaller subcommittee meetings held as well.[8] The following list of objectives resulted from the exploration.

The goals and objectives of Christian education are:

1. To foster in growing persons a consciousness of *God* as a reality in human experience and a sense of their personal relationship to him.

2. To present the life and teachings of *Jesus* so that a growing understanding and appreciation of him will lead to an acceptance of him as Savior and Lord.

3. To teach the Christian way of life in such a way that there will be a continuous development of *Christlike character*.

4. To provide a growing understanding of the *Bible* as a revelation of God and his relationship to man, so that the truths of the scriptures become an effective guide to present experience.

5. To develop a meaningful relationship to the *church* that will not only provide an understanding of particular denominations, but will lead each person to active participation in the church through membership.

6. To provide opportunities for communion with God through meaningful *worship* experiences that will be a prelude to the corporate worship of the church and the cultivation of a personal devotional life.

7. To provide opportunities to understand and experience the Christian faith embodied in the concepts of the fatherhood of God and the brotherhood of man, so that *in all relationships with others* Christian love and concern will be expressed in daily life.

8. To develop a growing appreciation of the meaning and importance of the *Christian family,* and to prepare each person to participate in and contribute constructively to its life.

9. To attain these goals by *reaching each person* meaningfully at his maturity level with particular concern for his individuality and his specific needs.

More important than the final statement of goals was the process of full discussion that produced a thorough understanding of them. The statement, or an equivalent one, could have been distributed at the first meeting and perhaps adopted by vote, but an understanding of such goals could come only after the personal involvement of board members in working them out.

After wrestling with their own understanding of these goals, this group felt the need to consult authorities in the field. They then turned to the published goals of their denomination and the National Council of Churches as well. Outside resources are always needed to supplement or alter initial opinions. They will be more helpful, however, if the particular group applies its own insights first. The pastor should be ready with suggested resource materials.

Following the acceptance of these general goals, each department of the church school worked out in detail the meaning of the goals for their particular age group, including the kind of experiences needed in that age group for the achievement of each goal, the teaching methods best suited for the realization of the goals, and the type of facilities and equipment needed for each class to realize its goals.

(c) The pastor should have a firsthand acquaintance with the educational program of the local church. The educational work of the church is and must be largely carried out by laymen. The minister will not be able to visit every educational endeavor in the church. It is important, however, that he be well acquainted with the educational work that is done, and is aware of its strengths and weaknesses. The pastor's attendance at board of education meetings will enable him to keep abreast of what is going on, to participate in any policy changes, to encourage others by his own interest, and to bring any insights he may have for improving the educational work of the church. The minister cannot attend all subgroup meetings in the church, but the scope of Christian education is so broad in the number of persons it touches and so fundamental to the life of the church, that this particular group deserves his personal attention.

The pastor's attendance at board meetings may help broaden their perspective to consider and coordinate all educational endeavors of the church, and not just the Sunday church school. Educational ventures beyond the Sunday session of the church school should include a school of missions, daily vacation Bible school, summer camping projects, special weekday groups and classes, choirs, church library, and programs or study groups of the various organizations of the church (women, men, young adults, youth, etc.). By developing these and other educational opportunities, the pastor and board can extend the teaching ministry of the church to every age and interest group.

If the minister is to enter intelligently into the discussions of the board of education, he must have firsthand knowledge of the church school. This is becoming more and more difficult to achieve since many pastors are either on a circuit or hold two or more worship services in a station church. This situation is removing the minister even farther from the educational life of the church and from contact with the children of the church. Some way must be found to deal with this problem.

The board of education and the pastor need to discuss the desirability and feasibility of the attendance of the pastor at the church school sessions occasionally. One circuit church did so and concluded their pastor ought to visit the church school in each church two or three times a year. They asked the church board to request the pulpit committee to find someone to fill the pulpit on those Sundays. They cited the following reasons for their request.

1. The minister can be of little help in improving a church school he has never seen. The church ought to utilize his training and skill in Christian education.

2. A visit to the church school enables the minister to observe the teachers in action so that he can form a basis for evaluating the quality of work done and suggest possible improvements.

3. Such a visit will let those in the church school know the pastor is interested in this aspect of the life of the church. This is especially important to the children and is of significance to the teachers as well.

4. It is important for the minister to observe the use of the physical facilities during the church school hour.

This church board accepted the request and secured the names of nearby retired preachers and lay speakers who could supply the pulpit on these occasions. Every church ought to work out a way for their pastor to attend church school occasionally.

(d) The minister should encourage adequate training opportunities for teachers. The surest way to improve the church school is to secure adequately trained teachers by providing a continuous program of teacher training. The minister will best serve this effort by offering encouragement and resources rather than by assuming direct responsibility for teacher training, although in some circumstances he may lead a teacher training course.

A few specific ways in which teacher training may be encouraged by the minister are:

1. Manifest a continuous interest and concern for it.

2. Bring information to the board of education about all opportunities for training beyond the local church, such as:

a) A cooperative training school sponsored by several churches in the community.

b) District leadership training schools of the denomination.

c) Laboratory schools, which offer the best possible type of teacher training.

d) Observation schools.

e) Correspondence courses offered by some denominations, sometimes as a supplement to class courses.

3. Guide the board in setting up a suitable program of teacher training in the congregation. Local training opportunities might include:

a) A series of evening sessions for training teachers.

b) New teachers observing or assisting experienced teachers before assuming responsibility.

c) Training in regular departmental meetings or at workers' conferences.

d) Training regular teachers on a series of Sunday mornings while substitutes take their classes.

e) Inviting denominational authorities to hold an observation or laboratory school in your church.

f) Inviting a denominational Christian education staff person to visit your church.

g) Departmental planning for new units.

h) Personal help for individual teachers as requested.

The church budget should provide adequate funds for leadership training. It is doubtful whether money can be invested anywhere more fruitfully than in the training of leadership. The education commission budget that provides for church school literature but not for teacher training is shortsighted.

E. The Relationship of Worship and Study to the Life of the Church as a Whole

It has been the thesis of this chapter that basic to the achievement of the mission of the church in making known God's love to all men is the involvement of the whole church in meaningful worship and in a vital study of the Christian faith.

118

When worship and study in the church are neglected or done inadequately, there will be clear signs of weakness throughout the church.

1. There will be a lack of concern for the evangelistic and missionary outreach of the local church toward its own community as well as the world.

2. The stewardship response in both leadership and financial support will lag.

3. Study groups, prayer groups, and all other spiritual ventures will fail to get a response.

4. The goals and standards for measuring the success of church activities will become more and more identical with those of contemporary culture.

5. The church will neglect its prophetic witness, becoming more concerned about community opinion than about the requirements for making a Christian witness.

6. The church may lose its perspective on the *whole* gospel through overemphasizing a single concern.

When Christian worship and study are vital in the personal experience of church members, there will also be clear signs of this throughout the church:

1. There will be eagerness and desire for further exploration of the meaning of Christian commitment (through prayer and study groups and in other ways).

2. Weaknesses in the various organizations and programs of the church will be recognized and changed.

3. A sense of Christian concern will emerge, involving the church in meeting the needs of the local community and in expressing a concern for making a Christian witness to the world through missions.

4. Church members will more readily accept leadership responsibilities and respond more generously to the financial needs of the church.

5. Laymen will be interested in working with the pastor and one another in developing and carrying out programs that focus the Christian gospel sharply on contemporary needs.

119

Just as surely the accurate use of mathematics is basic to the scientist, so is the building of a spiritual foundation in the church through worship and study basic to the church administrator. If this basic principle is neglected, the church cannot and will not understand its mission and, hence, can never achieve it.

■ ■ ■ **Notes**

1. Adopted by the district lay leaders of the Omaha District of The Methodist Church, January 7, 1958. Used by permission of Richard W. Miller.

2. John C. Irwin in *Field Education Manual,* ed. by Alvin J. Lindgren and Charles H. Ellzey (Evanston, Ill.: Garrett Theological Seminary, 1963), p. 23.

3. *Ibid.*

4. Helpful books in this area include:

Raymond Abba, *Principles of Christian Worship* (New York: Oxford University Press, 1957).

Pehr Edwall *et al., Ways of Worship* (New York: Harper & Brothers, 1951).

Thomas S. Garrett, *Christian Worship* (New York: Oxford University Press, 1961).

Oscar Hardman, *History of Christian Worship* (Nashville: Cokesbury Press, 1937).

George P. Hedley, *Christian Worship* (New York: The Macmillan Co., 1953).

Ilion T. Jones, *Historical Approach to Evangelical Worship* (Nashville: Abingdon Press, 1954).

Nathaniel Micklem (ed.), *Christian Worship* (New York: Oxford University Press, 1936).

Willard Sperry, *Reality in Worship* (New York: The Macmillan Co., 1925).

Bard Thompson, *Liturgies of the Western Church* (paper, Meridian Books edition; New York: World Publishing Co., 1961).

Evelyn Underhill, *Worship* (paper, Torchbooks edition; New York: Harper & Row, 1937).

5. Austin C. Lovelace and W. C. Rice, *Music and Worship in the Church* (Nashville: Abingdon Press, 1960).

6. A paraphrase of D. T. Niles's definition of evangelism as "One beggar telling another beggar where to get food."

7. Raines, *New Life in the Church.* See pp. 103-24 for a detailed discussion of a six-session period of membership training, using laymen in the training process.

8. The Covenant Methodist Church, Evanston, Illinois.

CHAPTER VI

ESTABLISH REDEMPTIVE INTERPERSONAL RELATIONSHIPS

A. The Importance of Redemptive Interpersonal Relationships

God-centered, person-oriented church administration must be concerned about redemptive interpersonal relationships, since persons and their needs are the raw material of administration. Persons are not only the object of God's love, but also the means through whom the living Christ is made known today. The Scriptures are clear that love for God is to be shown through love for persons. The New Testament testifies to the validity of personal relationships as a means of witnessing to the Christian faith and of strengthening it. Paul does not hesitate to suggest that his personal visits might increase the faith of others, and he admits quickly that his relationships with others in the church have been a source of strength to him. God's treasure (love) is lodged in the earthen vessel of Christian persons, who are to act in such a way that his love is influential in all relationships. Church administration, therefore, is *necessarily* concerned with the relationship of persons with one another.

Personality is *formed* through our relationships with others; it is *deformed* through personal relationships of a negative nature and is *reformed* or transformed by the grace of God acting through creative relationships with persons. These simple facts have staggering implications. If the church is to be a fellowship of redemptive love in actual fact, the experience of redemption must take place on the level of interpersonal relationships. The Christian community must constantly strive to provide the atmosphere of Christian love and supportive fellowship that is conducive to the formation of Christian personality. The church must also offer the quality of relationship that will be strengthening and accepting to the deformed personality, who may thus be reformed and transformed through such relationships.

Redemptive interpersonal relationships must take place on three levels: between pastor and people, among the members themselves, and finally between church members (including the pastor) and the community. Persons must be seen not only as the object of God's concern but also as the means through whom God works in transforming others. In this context personal relationships become a necessary concern of church administration, and every effort must be made to see that such relationships serve a redemptive purpose.

The basic necessity for such a point of view was pointed out clearly twenty-five years ago by Richard H. Edwards in his pioneering work, *A Person-Minded Ministry*.[1] More recently, Paul Johnson has focused attention on this point of view in his book, *Psychology of Pastoral Care*.[2] Johnson illuminates the implications of this concept by citing the following illustration. When a pastor is appointed to a new church, where is he to begin? He *could* begin by seeking to discover the *problem areas* of the church (budget, inadequate facilities, irregular board and committee meetings, faltering church organizations). He could work out a well-prepared *program* to improve each situation and persuade the chairman involved and a few loyal followers to "push ahead" in the program. Such an approach would keep a new pastor very busy working at his administrative tasks, as he promotes and executes these programs. Johnson rightly observes that such a *problem-centered approach* may be more *active* than *effective*. His time could easily be consumed by organizational details to the real neglect of his people.

Strange as it may seem, such a pastor may meet with his people many times while working on the problems of the church and yet never really be introduced to them as *persons*. Meeting people with his eyes on his problem, he may never see them as *persons*, but as allies or enemies in the solution to his problems. Such an approach may not only consume a lion's share of the pastor's time in dealing with programs, promotional techniques, and publicity material, but actually may reduce the pastor's capacity to love and understand persons as such. He may meet with people regularly, may call them by name and classify them for or against his program, without really "knowing" them or understanding their concerns as persons.

A person-oriented approach to church administration is thus to be preferred to a program- or problem-centered approach. Since this is the case, the church administrator is committed to a constant effort to establish redemptive interpersonal relationships throughout the parish.

Problems arise out of the basic needs and nature of persons. To deal with the problem and ignore the person is like taking aspirin to reduce the fever and ignoring the inflamed appendix which caused it. Problems in churches are symptomatic of the needs of persons. Their lack of vision, their dogmatic intolerance, their indifference, and their hostility and bitterness are expressions of deep personal needs. These attitudes are conditioned by past personal experiences heightened by varying degrees of emotional involvement. Therefore, in seeking to deal with any problem on a deep level, past and present personal relationships cannot be ignored.

In the area of interpersonal relations, many pastors have difficulty at two levels. Sometimes they cannot accept the full importance of redemptive relationships in the life of the church. They have come to believe that an active program is the sign of a successful church. They become insensitive to persons, overlooking their needs (or even consciously casting them aside), assuming that organizational promotion is what really counts. At a second level, a pastor may accept the need for redemptive relationships and yet be unable in practice to relate to persons, except superficially and perfunctorily.

Persons must be seen as ends not means; they are the ultimate reason for all programs and activities of the church. They must never be seen as tools for executing a program or as statistics to prove a successful ministry. A crucial question confronting the administrator is how interpersonal relationships within the church may be of sufficient depth and quality to be redemptive for individual persons. Let us begin to apply this concept by looking at the pastor and his relationships.

B. The Pastor Must Be a Mature Person

The quality and depth of the pastor's interpersonal relationships is a more important factor in the life of the church than is commonly supposed. Such relationships will affect the response of people to be more or less receptive to his preaching, more or less willing to become leaders, to support the church financially, or to accept new ideas. If the pastor's personal relationships are deep and positive, a significant avenue is open for the church to move toward the achievement of her mission of making known God's love. Conversely, if the pastor establishes only superficial or negative relationships, many doors are closed; persons will reject his leadership generally and may even reject the church itself, of which he is a symbol. In the author's judgment inability to relate to persons is the greatest single cause of ministerial ineffectiveness. Let us be perfectly clear that we are not suggesting that the pastor should seek to please everyone. The point is that in every personal relationship the pastor must evidence a genuine concern for persons, communicating a sincere desire to understand them, and offering Christian love through the relationship, even when differences of opinion are sharp.

The pastor must therefore be a mature person and possess a reasonable degree of self-understanding. He must be able to see himself realistically, recognizing his areas of weakness and of strength. The pastor who cannot acknowledge his own weaknesses, even to himself, will surely be unable to accept gracefully any criticism from others. Defensiveness becomes not only a barrier to "hearing" what is being said, but often is reflected in a hostile attitude toward persons, thus blocking any significant or deep personal relationships from developing.

There are many ways in which the pastor's own insecurity, im-

124

maturity, or hostility may prevent him from functioning helpfully in relation to persons. For example, there is the pastor who cannot relate to any person who praises his predecessor. Or again, there is the pastor who is so insecure that he resents the fact that a committee chairman holds a regularly scheduled meeting of the committee while the pastor is out of town. Or the insecure pastor may seek to run the church as a dictator, not only by being on hand at every meeting to exert his personal influence, but insisting that he personally select every leader and be involved in every activity. On the other hand, an insecure pastor may react by being a "jellyfish." Fearing criticism, he seeks to please everyone by agreeing with each person. He stands on both sides of every question. In such cases personal insecurities block any really helpful relationship with persons from developing and become stumbling blocks to the church realizing its mission.

An immature pastor may also cut himself off from any helpful continuing personal relationships by demonstrating his own lack of depth and understanding. The pastor who is overanxious, who always comes up with quick and easy answers, who continually exercises poor judgment, or who is given to emotional outbursts will, by his own actions, repel persons by creating the conditions which prevent significant personal relationships. Such immaturity can do untold damage to establishing any meaningful understanding or experience of Christian love in a parish.

The hostilities of the pastor may wreck his personal relationships. A bitter, hostile person never attracts other persons, since his mind is closed in many areas and his judgments are severely distorted. Hostility toward authority, toward a theological point of view, or toward a type of program may cause the pastor to caricature every person related to this particular area of hostility, thus creating a serious barrier to effective personal relationships.

Enough has been said to indicate that any pastor seriously concerned about redemptive interpersonal relationships in his congregation must be willing to take a long, honest look at himself. The person of the pastor is the most important single factor in establishing such relationships. He need not be perfect, but he must be aware of his limitations and capacities. He must be alert to every insight in his relationships that will help him to understand himself better. He must realize that the admission of weaknesses does not disqualify him. He has an important contribution to make in spite of them. Like Paul, he must recognize that he has not yet arrived but he must press on toward the mark.

One mark of a mature person is his ability to love persons, even though they are often not very lovable. The more unlovely they are, the more they are in need of love. The beginning of any personal relationship that is deep enough to effect change is the feeling of being understood, that someone really cares. Jesus is the incarnation of this quality. He communicated it to every person he met. Likewise, the pastor is called upon to possess this quality of mature love. This means he must not prejudge persons on the basis of their past deeds or of their present condition. George Bernard Shaw is reported to have said, "My tailor is the only man who understands me. He takes my measure anew each time we meet." The pastor must be ready to do exactly that in the realm of personal relationships. A concern for persons must be stronger than one's feelings about a point of view they may hold or about an act they may have committed. Every person must be valued as one for whom Christ died. Maturity in Christian love can accept no lower standard. Let us not forget that the experiencing of genuine love and understanding on a human level opens the door for accepting God's love on a divine level.

If persons and their needs really *are* the raw material of church administration, and if all programs and activities are to be designed and measured by their effect on persons, and if the object of pastoral care is personal renewal, it becomes imperative that the church administrator possess an understanding of personality dynamics. He must be aware of the factors that affect human behavior. This is essential first of all for his own mature self-understanding. It is further required in any attempt to effect change in persons through a relationship with them. Church administrators must always be conscious of the complexity and multiplicity of forces that contribute to every person's present condition. Ministers need not be professional psychologists or psychiatrists, but they must possess some understanding of the fundamental factors that shape personality and condition behavior. Good intentions are insufficient; the acquiring of certain knowledge and skills is required.

C. The Implications of Personality Dynamics for Church Administration

No attempt will be made to discuss in any detail the dynamics of the factors entering into the formation of human personality. For competent treatments of this complex subject, a selective bibliography is provided.[3] There are, however, certain conclusions that have particular relevance here, and these will be briefly noted, together with their implications for church administration. The pastor who is aware of these factors will be better equipped to establish positive interpersonal relationships and to provide the opportunity for the kind of experiences that will build positive relationships among church members.

1. Personality, Attitudes, and Feelings Are the Results of a Lifelong Multiplicity of Personal Experiences.

Emotional experiences of many years converge to condition present reactions and feelings of the moment. Every present reaction is called forth not simply by an immediate experience, proposal, or relationship, but results from all past experiences that may in some way be linked with the current situation in the mind of the person. These past associations usually are on the emotional and feeling level and are often so deep-seated as to be unconscious. In dealing with persons we must never forget that, although man is a rational being, he is never merely rational; he is also an emotional being, and his feelings are often more important in determining decisions than his intellect. In fact, it can be said that all behavior is emotionally conditioned.

All of this has pointed implications for the church administrator. An actual case study can best illustrate the point. A church had just experienced a serious financial deficit the previous year and had borrowed heavily to pay current bills. The finance committee had agreed to confront the official board with the facts and to propose an every member canvass for the coming year. Although such a canvass had not been held in over twenty years, the finance committee felt that the situation was so desperate that something radical had to be done. When the proposal was made, one of the most progressive young adults of the church quickly called for the floor to speak. As chairman of the membership and evangelism committee, he had led his committee in discovering and enrolling many children from a nearby substandard housing area in the church school, helping to break the barrier in getting some of the parents to attend church and in getting the church to accept them. In addition, he had urged the church to undertake two special missionary projects the year before, in spite of the difficult financial situation. Everyone expected him to back the every member canvass proposal. With trembling lips and drawn face, he said,

Before this proposal is discussed, I want to say that, as much as I love this church, I will feel compelled to withdraw my membership if you decide to initiate an every member canvass. I understand our financial situation; I also know what an every member canvass involves, and I will do all in my power to keep us from inflicting it on our people. There are other ways of getting people to give.

The board was stunned; the silence could have been cut with a knife. The chairman hardly knew how to proceed, so he turned to the pastor and inquired, "What do you think we should do now?" The pastor suggested that the matter be referred back to the finance committee to report back at a later date.

Here is a clear case of a momentary reaction being conditioned by feelings, attitudes, and experiences of the past. This is true of every person's reactions, but usually with much less intensity and is not as easily detected. The degree of emotional involvement here was evident in the drawn face, the trembling lips, the threat of withdrawal from the church, and the intense reaction to the proposal. The pastor recognized the necessity of seeking to understand why this layman felt that way before attempting to deal with his reac-

128

tions. Obviously no amount of logic about the soundness of the every member canvass or the financial needs of the church would be helpful in altering the man's feelings. Several months of pastoral calling produced a willingness to explore these strong feelings and finally resulted in an understanding of them. This young man's father had once made a pledge in an every member canvass he could not pay. The church pressed his father for payment, and he sold livestock he should have kept. Later, the father became finance chairman of the church, dropped the every member canvass, and successfully raised the budget without it for fifteen years. In the proposal to reestablish the every member canvass, this young man had "heard" (because of *his* past experiences) a rejection of his deceased father's leadership and a renewal of his family's unhappy experience with an every member canvass. Through a counseling relationship with the pastor, this young man gained sufficient insight to overcome his initial reaction. Several months later he did not object to an every member canvass, and five years later even served as canvass chairman.

The momentary reactions of every person are linked to a myriad of past experiences. There are inescapable implications in this fact for the church administrator, as this case clearly indicates. No person can be understood apart from his past, a fact which is too often ignored by administrators concerned about getting programs carried out. Even when a program is presented in an identical manner, no two persons or churches begin from exactly the same point, because of differing past experiences.

2. *Persons Cannot Be Understood Apart from Their Social and Group Relationships.*

No person can be fully understood unless we know something of the nature of the groups with which he has had intimate relationships. Personality is formed in relationships, with the family exerting the greatest influence because of the formative and primary nature of the relationship. To a lesser degree, because of the declining intimacy and intensity of contact, this is true of all other groups of which we are a part—schools, friends, churches, office or shop groups,

129

clubs, lodges, etc. Although each person is more than a sum total of the groups to which he is or has been related, because of his own personal response to them, no person can be understood apart from the groups of which he has been a part.

The church administrator is constantly confronted by persons in the church whose basic attitudes have been influenced by other cultural groups and who are seeking to import these alien behavior patterns into the church. The exact opposite—the conversion of the world and the transformation of secular groups—is the goal of the church. For this reason, it is important for the church administrator to be alert to the ways and means through which persons are influenced by groups. This is of such sufficient importance that the next chapter will be devoted to exploring the dynamics of groups.

The political and economic groups to which a person belongs may be determinative of the attitude he takes toward prophetic preaching or toward seeking to apply the gospel to contemporary issues. For instance, some church finance committees are operated by men who cannot really distinguish whether they are functioning as members of a church or the board of directors of a business corporation. If the church administrator is serious about understanding persons, he will have to get to know individual persons well enough to know the groups to which they are or have been related and to know something of the character of the groups themselves. It is even more important, however, to understand the nature and degree of relationship and the reaction of the person to the experience. Difficult as this may be, no person can really be understood apart from this knowledge.

3. *Every Person Has a Basic and Inescapable Need for Love and Understanding.*

The nature of persons is such that love and understanding are as basic to the personality structure as are food and drink to physical well-being. Every person needs and responds to love. The depth and nature of one's experience of love or hostility conditions one's ability to relate to other persons, as well as the manner and nature of such relationship. In any understanding of how personality is formed, deformed, or reformed it is necessary to take into account the experience and meaning of love in the relationship of this person to others.

Reuel Howe [4] points out one implication of this fact in the religious development of persons through recounting the relationship of an infant to its parents. Within the first year of life, an infant develops an attitude of trust (or lack of it) through his relationship with his parents as they care for him and his needs. This attitude of trust or love is obviously communicated more through relationships than verbally. This early *experienced relationship* makes possible a meaningful verbal communication of the nature of trust and love at a later time. The ability to accept the idea of a loving God is significantly preconditioned by this early relationship of trust and love between parent and child. The church must, therefore, be concerned about the Christian home and take seriously its responsibility for preparing youth for Christian marriage and parenthood. The significance of infant Baptism and the preparation of parents and the church at large for the responsibilities they assume in the baptismal vows thus takes on new proportions. The importance of experiencing love and understanding in the early years should also focus the concern of the church on the quality and nature of the Christian education program for these children.

Love and understanding are not only important in the formation of personality; they also are basic to its reformation and transformation. This is more than a psychological fact; it is also a religious reality. God is love, and through his love we are redeemed. This is the gospel acted out in the life, death, and resurrection of Jesus Christ. It is no accident that Paul places love at the pinnacle of Christian virtues. Christian love, the unreserved giving of oneself for the well-being of another, without concern for personal gain, is the greatest life-changing force in the universe. The relationships between pastor and members and among the members themselves should, therefore, be motivated by such love. If the transformation of persons is our aim, then love of the unlovable person in the congregation becomes essential. If on the other hand the achievement

131

of a certain program is our aim, then love will be submerged in the need to suppress opposition at all costs.

Love and understanding are communicated on their deepest level through a "language of relationship" [5] rather than through verbalization. This has implications for the outreach of the church into culture as well as for its internal affairs. The world can and has long ignored what the church may say about love, but it cannot ignore the practice and witness of loving service. As the church ponders its evangelistic and missionary outreach, it must come to terms realistically with this fact. What the church *is* as it relates to the world around it is as important as what the church *says*. A clear case in point is evident today in regard to segregation and racial brotherhood. The pronouncements of the social creeds of the churches make good reading, but the practice of the church too often betrays its pronouncements.

If the church is seriously concerned about reaching and transforming persons, it must reckon with the fact that every person has a basic need for love and understanding and act accordingly in its internal and external relationships.

4. No Person Can Be Understood Apart from the Goals and Values Toward Which He Strives.

Every person gives himself to those things in life that seem most important to him, the things which make life worthwhile. This is what Viktor Frankl refers to as the "willing to meaning" that surges up in every life. A person's interest is captured by his personal goals; he gives his time and energy toward their realization; they assume top priority in his scale of values. No person can be fully understood apart from a knowledge of his goals. One's goals may be focused in the business world, the farm, the family, personal pleasure, wealth, social acceptance, or some great cause or movement; but that to which a person gives himself becomes an essential aspect of understanding the person himself.

The pastor needs to know where his people really live and what the actual motivating factors directing their lives and their responses are. Pastoral calling thus becomes a *possible* treasure-house of important discoveries of the world of parishioners. Preaching can be more relevant and communication more clear when the real goals of the people are known. The kinds of church activities and experiences required are illuminated by a discovery of where people really live.

Many people "dress up" on Sunday for the worship service until they are hardly recognizable. The masquerade often goes on at a deeper level as persons seek to cover up their real goals and values. Before any significant understanding of persons takes place, the real motivating factors must be uncovered and recognized. Only when this is achieved can the church administrator communicate meaningfully to the person involved, challenge him to move from secondary to primary goals, and utilize his interests and talents for more noble ends.

5. Persons Are Capable of Change and Growth.

The final principle of personality dynamics with special implications for the church administrator that will be lifted out for consideration is a recognition of the fact that persons are capable of change and growth. This is easy to forget. First of all, everyone—the pastor included—is tempted to categorize or "pigeonhole" individuals on the basis of some previous contact. This person is then prejudged at some later date, the supposition being that he has not changed. Secondly, one must be careful lest he fall into the trap of supposing that, just because every person is conditioned by his past experiences, he is a prisoner of them with no capacity for personal reaction or change. As a matter of fact, the exact opposite is true. The whole purpose of understanding the past is to gain insight not only to understand the present but to change it. It is absolutely essential for the church administrator to bear in mind the fact that persons are capable of change and growth. If this is not true, it is pointless for the church to seek to reach persons for Christ or to seek to establish redemptive interpersonal relationships within the church. There are many causes and occasions for personal transformation.

Persons change through their relationship with other persons. A

133

relationship with other persons is the most effective life-changing force known. In the life of the church this is often seen in the relationship of church members to the pastor. There are countless examples of persons who have been changed through a relationship with their pastor in times of physical, emotional, or spiritual crisis. Pastoral counseling is simply a more extended and structured way of transforming a relationship between pastor and parishioner. The pastor, however, has no monopoly on transforming relationships. In one church the concern of a church school teacher for the well-being, education, and future of a youth in his class not only produced real growth and change in the youth but in the parents as well.

Persons change not only as a result of a one-to-one relationship but also through group relationships. The impact of Alcoholics Anonymous is a well-known example of a life-changing relationship with a group. A group of college students once spent a summer with a work camp project. This experience so changed them and deepened their Christian dedication that, for months afterward, their campus friends would remark, "Pardon me, but your enthusiasm is showing." Renewal in the church today is being found in many parishes through small groups gathering to explore common personal and Christian concerns. The impact of the group members upon each other is a thrilling story that is told by John Casteel in *Spiritual Renewal Through Small Groups* and by Robert Raines in *New Life in the Church.*

Persons also change through education and new ideas. The church school, the membership training classes, the various study and discussion groups in the church, the sermon—all seek to change persons by exposing them to a deeper understanding of the Christian faith and a fellowship experience with other Christians. There is no doubt that growth takes place through constant exposure to the meaning of the Christian faith. Understandings are not only enlarged, but commitments are deepened at the same time.

Persons change through participation and fellowship in the life of the church. The church makes its greatest impact on the persons who participate in its life and leadership. As they give them-

134

selves in witnessing to their faith and working with their fellow Christians, they grow both in their understanding of the faith and their commitment to it. Those who assume leadership responsibilities and prepare adequately to carry them out nearly always gain more than they give. Often the discovery is made that they can do many things they thought were impossible. Many a fine teacher was once sure he could never teach. One of the finest and most capable laymen in visitation evangelism I ever knew once spent a whole evening explaining that he could never visit with others about the claims of Christ because he just accepted him at forty-one years of age and didn't know enough about the Christian faith to talk to others about it. His new commitment was so strong, however, that it drove him to learn what was involved, and he was soon going out regularly to visit others. Because he understood life outside the church from recent personal experience, he could communicate with the "outsider" and understand his point of view. His own commitment was so meaningful that it was contagious. Through participation in the evangelistic outreach of the church, real change and growth took place in him. A strong word of caution needs to be given here, however, against the popular notion that simply giving everyone a job and putting him to work will make a good churchman and Christian of him. This does not always happen, and it is an unsuitable approach for many members. Careful judgment must be exercised.

D. The Pastor's Relationship with Persons

A person-oriented approach to church administration calls for the development of significant personal relationships between pastor and people. Many pastors underestimate the importance of these relationships and their influence on every area of the life of the church. The quality and depth of relationship developed between pastor and parishioner will be evidenced in the ability of the minister to function as a pastor in crisis and counseling situations, in the acceptance of leadership and stewardship responsibilities by the people, in their openness and receptivity in administrative and organizational affairs, and even in their reactions to

135

the preaching and worship leadership of the church. The plain fact is that the pastor's relationship to his people is one of the key factors in any congregation's ability to reach persons on a deep level of understanding in which the meaning of redemptive love is taken seriously.

The pastor must be aware of the fact that he is establishing his relationships with persons in everything he does, twenty-four hours a day. He cannot confine the impact of his personality to "on duty" hours. The manner of man he is as he lives among men is the chief ingredient in his relationships to others. His wholeness, maturity, integrity, real concern, competence, and commitment all help to determine the quality and depth of relationship he will be able to establish in any ministerial role. All this, however, does not free the pastor from specific and painstaking preparation for his ministry of pastoral care. This ministry includes pastoral calling, preparation for marriage and Baptism, crisis ministry, and counseling. Since it is not possible to discuss all these areas of pastoral care, we will confine ourselves in this section to an examination of the much-neglected and misunderstood ministry of pastoral calling.

1. Is Pastoral Calling Really Necessary?

In recent years, the time given to pastoral calling by the average minister has declined markedly. There are several reasons for this, not the least of which is the growing demand upon the pastor's time from administrative responsibilities discussed earlier. Pastoral calling has suffered also from changing social and cultural factors, such as the husband and wife both working and thereby making it difficult to find anyone at home, the rapid mobility of the population, and the nature of apartment housing projects in the inner city. Many pastors have frankly questioned the value of pastoral calling in relation to the time it consumes, especially since many pastoral calls are no more than shallow social visits. In addition, some pastors have focused their interest on theological ideas and concepts rather than in persons and, consequently, have simply stayed in the study rather than going to the people. Strange as it may seem, at the opposite extreme, pastoral calling has suffered because some have become interested in persons, but only those with sufficiently serious problems to bring them to the minister's office for extended counseling. These pastors feel that their time is better invested in counseling a few than in calling on the many.

Furthermore, certain misconceptions as to the nature and purpose of pastoral calling also have caused a decline in this type of ministry. For instance, a generation ago it was taught in the seminaries that "a home-calling pastor makes a church-going people." But pastoral calling must have a higher motivation than church attendance. Though increased church attendance may be a by-product of faithful pastoral calling, it is inadequate as a main goal. A person's motivation to worship must be deeper than the pastor's personal urging or expectation, or a sense of guilt that has been heightened by a pastoral call. Practically speaking, the larger the congregation becomes, the more impossible it becomes for the people to be called upon by the pastor to remind them to come to worship, much as a mother would remind a small boy daily to brush his teeth. The acceptance of church attendance as the main goal of pastoral calling may actually interfere with its primary function of ministering to the needs of persons. One pastor embarked on a series of "church attendance calls" one Lenten season. Verbatim reports of several of the calls were made for later analysis. Several calls revealed parishioners seeking to communicate deep personal needs to the pastor but he missed the clues. In one instance, a farm wife had just learned her husband had sold the farm and was moving the family to a new community. She was upset about what this adjustment would mean for the children. She wanted to talk about it, but the pastor cut her off with, "You will be here eight more weeks; come to church each Sunday and remember that the family that worships together stays together." In another instance, a mother twice mentioned her concern over the behavior of her high school son and was told, "Bring him to church with you each Sunday." Calling with a view to increasing church attendance interfered with ministering to the needs of persons in these situations.

Some laymen and a few pastors believe pastoral calling increases financial giving to the church. For this reason they are anxious for the pastor to call. One disillusioned pastor who had actually called from this motivation said to me, "I can now prove that calling doesn't pay." When I asked what he meant, he replied, "I have compared the financial receipts of the church the last six months when I did not call with the previous six months when I called regularly, and there is no difference." How tragic. Both those who call to increase attendance and those who call to increase the budget are looking at calling *as a technique to build up an institution rather than an opportunity to minister to the needs of persons.*

One other misconception as to the motive for pastoral calling needs to be noted. A minister once said to me, "If you want to be well liked, do a lot of calling on your people." To use calling as a means of building up personal popularity is to use a God-given opportunity for an ungodly selfish purpose. The pastor who has this end in view gets his just reward. People inevitably become aware of his self-centered shallowness and reject him for his lack of genuine concern for them.

In spite of all that has been said, I am convinced that regular pastoral calling is indispensable to an effective and useful ministry. It is necessary to pastor and people alike if the church is to succeed in achieving her mission of making God's love known to persons. For pastoral calling to be of value, however, it must have the proper objectives.

2. *Objectives of Pastoral Calling.*

Although differences in individual needs require that every pastoral call be unique, there are certain basic objectives that ought to guide every call.

First and foremost, the central purpose of the pastoral call is *to minister to persons.* The pastor must go because he loves and cares for persons. In my first placement interview with a district superintendent as a theological school graduate, I was taken aback by his opening question, "Do you love people?" While I gasped for air and groped for an answer, the wise superintendent said, "You will need to love people if you are going to be able to reach them and minister to them." If a pastoral call does not communicate the fact that the pastor cares, it will never be able to communicate God's abounding love. Paul Clifford has paraphrased a familiar New Testament passage, "Though I say all the right words, perform all the right actions, conduct all the services in the Prayer Book and have not love, I am a sounding brass and a clanging cymbal." [6] Without love, pastoral calling is in vain. This first objective of pastoral calling—to convey a concern for the person himself—is easily forgotten in a concern to promote the institution of the church, some special program, the popularity of the pastor himself, or in striving to hold a personal devotional service of prayer and Scripture to give the call a "religious" flavor.

A second objective of a pastoral call is *to get to know intimately the persons* or family involved. No pastor can adequately minister to the needs of his people until he knows them as persons, understands who they are, and where they really live—emotionally, culturally, and religiously. He cannot gain such knowledge of them apart from entering into their hearts and homes through pastoral calling. Only as the pastor really knows his people as persons can he preach to them relevantly, counsel with them wisely, minister to them helpfully in crises, and guide them into the kind of experiences in the life of the church that will mature their Christian faith. The minister may be ever so well equipped to minister to the needs of persons, but he cannot do so until he knows each one well enough to understand his particular need and, through this, collectively feel the pulse of the congregation as a whole. It has been well said, "This intimate and personal knowledge of his people is the foundation of his ministry to them." [7]

A third objective of pastoral calling is *to minister to the personal needs* of those called upon. Here the light, power, and love of the gospel are focused on a particular person or family. Pulpit generalizations are no longer in order. A face-to-face encounter requires personal attention, and here the frightening demands of pastoral calling become most clear. There is no place to hide, issues cannot be dodged, robes and pulpits cannot protect one from probing,

139

searching questions. In meeting personal needs in a face-to-face relationship any fuzziness in understanding the gospel, any wavering of personal commitment, any lack of genuine concern for persons will be laid bare.

If personal needs are to be met, they must first of all be recognized. This calls for an alertness on the part of the pastor. A sensitivity to recognize the emergence of some special concern or need must be developed by the pastor. Often, a person may very cautiously and indirectly point toward an area of concern; and, unless the trained ear catches the distress signal in the tone of voice, the facial expression, the expectant look or questioning inflection, the need may go by unrecognized. In every call, the pastor should listen not only for what is being said but also for the hidden clues to deeper need, the feelings being expressed, and the emotional overtones involved. Usually any indication of understanding or interest will elicit further conversation on the subject. The most common barrier to recognizing the needs of persons is the pastor's concern to discuss or promote the institutional program of the church.

Every call is unique and must begin where the person is. There are no stock approaches and answers that can be used even for similar problems. As in counseling, the response and relationship must develop out of the situation itself. "The gospel is not a theological pill, a panacea for all ills; it cannot be swallowed in equal dosages and produce the same result in everybody." [8] In each call attention must be focused on the person at hand and his unique needs.

It is important to remember that pastoral calling is but one aspect of a larger ongoing process of the total ministry of the church to the individual. There are some needs that can be handled during the call itself. Other needs will demand additional calls, or perhaps extended counseling sessions. Involvement in the life of the Christian community through participation in worship, study, and fellowship is essential if the full ministry of the church is to be appropriated. The pastor needs to see each call in its proper perspective, seeking to do neither too much nor too little in a given call.

Fourthly, every call *must convey God's love and the church's concern* for those called upon. The minister goes into every home as God's ambassador, and it should be made clear whom he represents. Although the minister may be a neighbor and a friend, he is more. The very presence of the minister symbolizes God's love and the church's concern to most people. He is usually greeted at the door as "Reverend," and if there has been any laxness in church relationships, the parishioner often immediately volunteers, "I have been intending to get back to church." Whether such comment indicates a guilt feeling or a strategic attempt to "beat the minister to the punch," it clearly indicates that he is seen as God's ambassador.

In every call the pastor should seek to expand the spiritual horizon of those on whom he calls. His presence should stimulate their interest and response to Christian faith and living. An attitude of understanding and expectance often expands spiritual horizons, as is evidenced in Jesus' relationship to Zacchaeus. There are times when religious and theological questions will and ought to be discussed on a call. This is not always necessary, however, nor does such discussion guarantee spiritual growth. It is also a mistake to believe that if scripture is read and prayer offered, the call is spiritual, and if not, it has been social. I once knew one minister who prepared four different "little services," as he called them, and if he could manipulate the conversation to the place where he could "give" one of them, he felt the call was "spiritual." Certainly, there will be many times in a pastoral call when prayer is appropriate, natural, and called for. There will be other times when that is not the case. The essential point is that every person should be made aware of the fact that the pastor called as God's ambassador and that his spiritual horizons should be expanded because the minister was there.

A fifth objective of a pastoral call is to establish a relationship that will serve as a bridge for more effective pastoral care in the future. There is no substitute for pastoral calling to establish the kind of relationship between pastor and people that will be a solid foundation for a future pastoral ministry. This is true because God's love is communicated through persons even more clearly than through words. In the face of death, tragedy, illness, or disappointment, there is little that can be said that can be of great help, but the presence of a pastor whose previous relationship has signified concern and spiritual depth can mean everything. Who the minister *is* counts far more at such times than what he says. For this reason, regular pastoral calling becomes essential. God's abiding love can be best communicated at a time of crisis through a person whose previous relationship has shown him to be both a man of God and a man of understanding concern. The personal relationship becomes the instrument through which God's healing love flows. Regular pastoral calling will open many opportunities for pastoral counseling. In the opening months of a new ministry, the largest part of one's counseling is likely to be initiated as a result of pastoral calling. When properly done, pastoral calling establishes the type of relationship that will encourage persons to seek out the pastor for counseling when in need of it. In a similar way, the relationship established in pastoral calling will better enable the pastor to guide persons into the various experiences within the life of the church that will be useful in the Christian maturing of each person.

3. What to Do on a Pastoral Call.

How shall I embark on a program of pastoral calling? This is a question often heard from the beginning pastor. This opening question is usually followed by: How much time should be spent in calling? How long should each call be? What do you do on a call? Only a lifetime of experience can really answer these questions, and then only for the minister involved. There is no one right answer. Let us content ourselves here with pointing the direction in which the beginning explorer might look for the answers.

Pastoral calling, like swimming, can only be learned by those willing to be involved in the experience. The first thing required of those who would learn the art of pastoral calling is to call. Make time in your daily schedule for calling from house to house. Unless this time is guarded carefully, it will be crowded out by other duties. Experience indicates that at least sixteen hours per week need to be reserved for calling in any parish. The time of day for calling must be geared to each particular community. It will usually be necessary to do both daytime and evening calling. One rural pastor in a dairy state made advance arrangements to call on farmers during the early morning milking period, going to the barn with the man, having breakfast with the family, and leading them in family devotions and a discussion of family devotional life. Regardless of when you call, the first step in pastoral calling is to determine to do so and to set aside the necessary time to meet your people in their homes.

Secondly, it is absolutely essential to know why you are engaged in pastoral calling. Remember the objectives of a pastoral call described above. If these objectives are understood and clearly kept in mind, they will serve as guideposts as to what to do and how to proceed during a call.

A third suggestion is to accept people as you find them. Do not register surprise at any circumstance encountered in calling. Unannounced calling will often bring people to the door in all kinds of dress and physical condition. The physical appearance of the person and house may be anything but the way they would have planned it for the minister's visit. The call may even interrupt a family argument or other highly charged emotional situation. The reaction of the pastor in the opening moment is crucial. Any sign of embarrassment, any evidence of a judgmental attitude or a rejection of the person can do real harm. An understanding attitude, a sense of humor, and a personal identification with the human situation of the moment may be all-important. Meet the person where he is, accept the situation, and move on from there. No planned opening should be attempted for any call, as every situation is different. From the moment the doorbell is rung, the call becomes a dynamic relationship of personal interaction, and the pastor ought to be prepared for such an encounter.

A fourth suggestion is to remember that the main concern of pastoral calling is not what you say but how you relate to the per-

143

son. The beginning pastor is often concerned with what to say to the point of believing that if he only had the words for every circumstance, pastoral calling would be easy. A student pastor will often remark, "If I only knew what to say, I wouldn't mind calling." Pastoral calling involves much more than accumulating a storehouse of the right things to say in all circumstances much like one might punch an I.B.M. machine for the answer to every question. Pastoral calling essentially is a relationship between two persons in a specific situation. The words exchanged are only one level on which the interaction is taking place. The eyes, tone of voice, facial expressions, attentiveness, interest or lack of it—all these are forms of interaction, too.

Fifth, be a good listener, and not with your ears only. Give your undivided attention to the person being called upon. Make a genuine attempt to understand what he really means by what he is saying. Be alert to implications that may not be obvious. Follow through on all leads and respond with questions at points where the meaning is not clear. The pastor must always resist the temptation to start talking when he should continue listening. Many a call gets off the track because the pastor breaks the train of thought. This will become evident if the pastor will take time occasionally to write up a verbatim report of some of his calls and then look at them objectively or, better yet, have another minister analyze them with him. Most calls would be improved if the minister listened more and talked less.

4. Values of Pastoral Calling.

Let me conclude this section by sharing some of the values I found in pastoral calling in my own ministry, listing them without comment.

1. It has enabled me to gain an intimate knowledge of persons and families and establish a personal relationship not possible in any other way.

2. Calling has introduced me to the world where people really live, in secular and spiritual realms alike.

3. Calling adds vitality to preaching. Through it, the areas of

need for preaching and the vocabulary that will communicate meaningfully to the congregation are indicated.

4. Many counseling opportunities arise in calling because the pastor is present when the need is acute, and many doors are opened for future counseling as well.

5. Bridges are built for a more helpful pastoral ministry in crisis situations that arise in the future.

6. There is an opportunity for God's spirit to work in a very personal way as the pastor deals with the individual parishioner at his level of need. (See Appendix A).

There are other areas of pastoral care that offer equally significant opportunities to establish redemptive interpersonal relationships. These are related to the opportunity to minister to persons at strategic moments in life, such as birth, Baptism, marriage, personal counseling, crisis situations, and death. We cannot here attempt to deal with the nature of the ministry to be performed in each of these situations.[9] Every minister needs to prepare himself adequately to relate to persons needing pastoral care for any reason. Such preparation should include clinical training as well as supervised field-work experience and seminary courses in the field of pastoral care. It must be remembered that, in times of tension, persons who are in genuine need of help are often more receptive to it than under normal circumstances. It is of extreme importance, therefore, that the pastor be equipped to meet their need. Pastoral care involves the pastor in intimate and trusted relationships that must be kept in strictest confidence, and the well-being of each person must be paramount at all times. This means that as a counselor, the pastor must recognize his own limitations and should not hesitate to make referrals when needed.

Redemptive interpersonal relationships are established between pastor and people in these varied experiences and contacts. They provide the matrix within which the church can become mature enough spiritually to reach out beyond itself and express God's love in relation to the needs of others, thus fulfilling its mission. When the love of God has been experienced, it can then be ex-expressed.

E. Establishing Redemptive Interpersonal Relationships Between Church Members

It is essential that all those within the fellowship of the church become aware of the fact that each person is a means through which the faith of others may be strengthened. As church members have contacts with each other, their lives should be mutually enriched and their understanding of Christian love enlarged. God speaks his clearest word to man through persons. Christian love personified speaks more clearly than the most excellent verbalization describing the nature of love. It is for this reason that personal example and contact become the most effective means of reaching the outsider. It is evident, therefore, that every minister need give serious attention to strengthening redemptive interpersonal relationships among the members of the church as well as between pastor and people. The church should provide the setting in which such relationships can take place. Opportunity must be given for members to not only worship and study together, but also to work and to have fellowship together and come to know and care about each other. The larger the local church becomes and the more scattered the membership, the more difficult the problem of real community and fellowship in the church becomes. An increasing trend toward impersonalism and mobility in society are heightening this sense of rootlessness and loneliness, making it all the more necessary for the church to provide deep and mutual concern among its members. People need to know one another, to work and serve together, to share their common hopes, fears, and faith.

For this reason, the church ought to provide many opportunities for persons to identify themselves with various small interest and service groups within its total life. Here persons may come to know one another personally and unite these service efforts around some aspect of the Christian faith of common interest. Church choirs, church school classes, women's, men's, and youth groups, special concerns for missions, evangelism, education, social concerns, stewardship and care of property, discussion, study and fellowship groups are examples commonly found in every church. These groups not only have tasks to do but also provide the opportunity

146

for redemptive personal relationships among the participating persons. One approach to increased personal involvement of *all* members in the life of the church is through a neighborhood family group plan, illustrated by the following case, as developed by a local evangelism committee.

THE NEIGHBORHOOD FAMILY GROUP PLAN

1. What is the purpose of a neighborhood family group plan?

In order that individual and family needs can be more effectively *discovered* and *met,* the church membership is divided into neighborhood geographic units of approximately ten families per unit to provide smaller groups within a church.

2. What situations might indicate that serious consideration should be given the neighborhood family group plan?

Lack of Real Fellowship: When members and families are not well acquainted with one another, real fellowship cannot be present. This becomes evident when there is no expression of personal concern and interest when crisis situations arise within other homes of the church.

Inactive Members: Persons out of touch with the active life of the church need more than an invitation to worship to revitalize their religious life. The church must discover who they are and why they are inactive and *continually* seek ways and means to revitalize their Christian commitment through personal contacts, tailoring the approach to each individual.

Limited Lay Participation in Leadership: To secure new leadership means having proper channels to discover abilities and stimulate interest in the life of the church. When lack of adequate leadership is a serious problem, it is likely that the church is unaware of leadership potential within the membership.

Discovering those needing pastoral care: It is not always easy for the pastor to know who is sick, facing a crisis, new in the community, or becoming disinterested in the church. Unless the pastor knows those who need pastoral care, he cannot reach them.

147

Administrative duties are too time consuming: If pastor and lay leadership are burdened down in "organizing" activities, something needs to be done both to simplify organizational routine and to enlist more people in carrying out the work of the church.

Inadequate knowledge of church program: If the membership is uninformed relative to local church affairs and denominational plans, an effective means of presentation and discussion of such matters could be the neighborhood family unit group.

All these needs and others would indicate that the membership and evangelism commission might profitably discuss the neighborhood family group plan and consider recommending it to the official board.

3. How would such a plan be initiated in a church? What would it involve?

Secure a large map: Divide the parish into groups of about ten families each on the basis of geography. A layman with a detailed knowledge of the community can and should do this work (mailman, tax assessor, taxi driver). Use map pins and small paper triangles with the family names written on them to identify the location of each family. Use narrow ribbon or yarn to mark off geographic divisions, so that these boundaries can be easily changed later.

Secure a leader: From each group of ten families select some person (or couple) with no other major church responsibility. One of the values of this plan is the growth of commitment and interest on the part of the leaders. The pastor, lay leader, and chairman of the membership and evangelism committee should confer in the selection of leaders. Personal calls should be made by the pastor and either the lay leader or chairman of the membership and evangelism committee to explain the plan and recruit leaders. The term of service should be for one year. Experience indicates renomination for two or three years is the probable maximum of effective service.

Call all leaders together: Have them discuss the needs and problems that led the official board to adopt the plan and the areas of concern in which they are willing to function this current year. These areas of concern might be selected from the suggestions below.

4. What are the possible uses of the neighborhood family group plan?

To build fellowship: Neighborhood group fellowship meetings could be held to help members get personally acquainted with neighbors who are fellow church members. One church discovered that, of the forty groups meeting by separate neighborhoods, there was no group in which any person could name every other person present. There could be individual group meetings or a combination of groups. These could be supper meetings, with discussion or program if desired.

To discuss the needs and program of the church: A real expression of how the church "feels" about any matter can quickly be discovered through simultaneous group meetings (a building project or to get ideas for long-range planning). Here is a real opportunity to explain and discuss the program of the church—local activities, conference program, general church plans. These ought to be treated separately, perhaps one each year.

To assist the pastor in getting acquainted with all the families of the church: As he meets with each group, the pastor can have contact with the whole church in a relatively short space of time. One pastor, with a willing wife, invited each neighborhood group into the parsonage once during the year. A cooperative woman's society provided refreshments, and the lay leader assumed responsibility for the program and fellowship activities for the evening, which included "truth-or-consequences" questions about the church. The consequences were learning interesting facts about some person in the group. Ninety percent of the membership attended these meetings. It is probably not an unrelated fact that church attendance increased over fifty percent that year.

To discover those in need of pastoral care: Group leaders could report illness, sorrow, achievements, inactivity, criticisms, and any other circumstance calling for pastoral care.

To welcome newcomers: Any new family moving into the neigh-

149

borhood could be welcomed and reported to the church office. The pastor could ask the group leader to have someone visit any new person expressing interest in the church and living in that neighborhood (see next item).

To assimilate new members: A fellowship friend from within the neighborhood family group could be assigned each new member joining the church. A welcome call could be made by the unit leader.

To save administrative and organizational time of other church groups: The division of the church membership in a card file of ten families to a geographic unit is very useful to many church groups desiring to contact the church membership (finance canvassers, spiritual life visitation, telephoning the congregation by the woman's society, etc.). The group leaders must not be used to make these calls. The organization concerned should make its own contacts, but the file, breaking down the church membership into small geographic units, can save them much time.

To assist the pastor in calling: The pastor can use the card file to call by neighborhood units and thus to do organized calling with a minimum of advance planning. The psychological effect of completing all the calls in a given unit may encourage him to complete more calls.

The purpose of these neighborhood groups is not to be ends in themselves or to establish life-changing depth relationships such as *koinonia* or discussion-action groups. Rather, their purpose is to acquaint persons within a given neighborhood with themselves and the regular church groups and programs with a view to ushering them into the mainstream of the life of the church. These neighborhood groups are conceived as catalysts; they are to activate their members without entering into the situation as competing groups that have become ends in themselves.

The effectiveness of such a family neighborhood group plan depends upon:

1. A clear understanding of it and a common acceptance of its desirability at the outset.

2. The selection of capable leaders for the groups.

3. The involvement of the leaders in discussing and determining the responsibilities they will assume.

4. Working the plan by the pastor and lay leader, but not overworking it. There must be some activity, but not too much. Probably two or three group meetings a year is adequate.

When carefully and properly initiated, such a plan can do much to strengthen personal relationships and Christian commitment within the life of the church.[10]

In an impersonal society and with the increase to two or more worship services on Sunday morning, any sense of real community and intimate personal relationships within the congregation is becoming more and more difficult. The neighborhood family plan provides an opportunity for those members of the church living in a neighborhood to come to know one another and to identify with another and to unite in a common loyalty to the church.

Redemptive interpersonal relationshps between members of the congregation occur on a depth level in various types of voluntary small *koinonia* or discussion groups. A detailed description and discussion of such groups will be given in the next chapter. Mention needs to be made of them here as they are the most effective means of producing change in persons and communicating the personal meaning of the gospel on a depth level available to the church. In any discussion of establishing redemptive interpersonal relationships between church members such small groups are of prime importance. In fact they are considered so significant they are being treated in a separate chapter.

One other area of creating redemptive interpersonal relationships is of such significance that it is also being discussed in a separate chapter. The equipping of laymen to give themselves in active service as a means of expressing their faith is of prime importance. Channels must be found for the expression of Christian action so necessary for the growth of the persons involved, for the expression of the service of love the church must render, and to reach in a mean-

151

ingful way our contemporary culture. Laymen have found that *serving* together through the church has proved to be a means of growth for themselves individually and that it has improved their relationships with one another. This concept will be developed in Chapter VIII.

■ ■ ■ Notes

1. Richard H. Edwards, *A Person-Minded Ministry* (Nashville: Cokesbury Press, 1940). A strong and comprehensive case is presented for keeping the person in central focus of one's ministry. This book still brings a needed emphasis in a day of "a program and organizational minded ministry."

2. Paul Johnson, *Psychology of Pastoral Care* (Nashville: Abingdon Press, 1953).

3. For adequate treatment of the dynamics of factors affecting the development of human personality, consult the following:

O. S. English and G. H. J. Pearson, *Emotional Problems of Living* (enlarged edition; New York: W. W. Norton Company, 1954).

Erik Erikson, *Childhood and Society* (New York: W. W. Norton Company, 1950).

Edward Glover, Psycho-analysis (London: John Bale Medical Publications, Ltd., 1939).

Karl A. Menninger, *The Human Mind* (3RD edition, corrected, enlarged, and rewritten; New York: Alfred A. Knopf, 1957).

——— *The Vital Balance* (New York: The Viking Press, 1963).

4. Howe, *Man's Need and God's Action.*

5. *Ibid.,* p. 75.

6. Clifford, *The Pastoral Calling,* pp. 34-35.

7. *Ibid.,* p. 76.

8. *Ibid.,* p. 79.

9. Those interested in guidance in these areas will find help in:

C. W. Brister, *Pastoral Care in the Church* (New York: Harper & Row, 1964).

Edgar N. Jackson, *Understanding Grief* (Nashville: Abingdon Press, 1957).

Paul E. Irion, *The Funeral and the Mourners* (Nashville, Abingdon Press, 1954).

Lindgren and Ellzey (eds.), *Field Education Manual.*

Carroll A. Wise, *Pastoral Counseling* (New York: Harper & Row, 1951).

10. For additional material on the neighborhood family group plan, see Clifford, *The Pastoral Calling,* Chapter 6.

CHAPTER VII

PROVIDE FOR THE CREATIVE FUNCTIONING OF SMALL GROUPS IN THE CHURCH

A. The Importance and Use of Small Groups in the Church

One evening a pastor remarked to his wife, "You know, . . . aside from pastoral calling and sermon preparation, almost my whole time is spent in getting ready for meetings or attending them." [1] This statement could be echoed by nearly every pastor. Likewise, many laymen spend much more of their time in group meetings in the church than in the weekly worship service or other congregational assemblies. If these group meetings are not fruitful, the church is wasting the time of pastor and members alike, besides missing a most significant opportunity.

Our modern civilization is so complex that nearly all organizations call for a breakdown into smaller working groups. This is true for example in the fields of industry, labor, government, and education. The church of our day is no exception. Even a small church is likely to have more than two dozen groups, such as:

A church board
An education committee
A stewardship and finance committee

153

A missions committee
A membership and evangelism committee
A christian social concerns committee
A worship committee
Trustees
From four to fourteen other special committees
From five to fifteen church school classes
Two or more choirs
A woman's society
Two or more circles of the above society
A junior high youth fellowship
A senior high youth fellowship
A young adult group
A men's group
One or more study and fellowship groups
Membership training classes

The larger the church becomes, the more numerous these various groups will be. Because of this inevitable pattern, the American pastor is being forced to ask how the various groups in the church can be made useful and creative. It is obvious that the pastor cannot be personally involved in leading each group, owing to the sheer number of meetings involved. The resulting need for strong lay leadership is good, since these groups should exist to enable persons to grow spiritually through their relationship to them, to give laymen an avenue for expressing their faith, and to further the mission of the church in various specific ways.

The pastor's role in relation to these many groups is twofold: first, to see that each group examines its reason for being and its place in the total life of the church, and, second, to see that leadership, training, and resource materials are available for the most creative functioning of each group, including the development and growth of their individual members. Paul Maves once put it this way, "Every minister is really a dean of a theological seminary. No minister can do all the teaching, counseling, preaching, administering, and fellowshipping that needs to be done in a church. He must rely upon individuals and groups within the church to assist in carrying out these functions." [2] The existence of many working groups in the church should be viewed as a way of giving concrete meaning to the theological concept of the priesthood of all believers.

The objectives of the various groups should be: (1) to provide a matrix of understanding and supportive Christian fellowship as a necessary atmosphere for personal growth; (2) to expose the individual member to the claims of the faith in a deep and personal way; (3) to enable persons of varying interests and abilities to find avenues through which they can personally serve Christ and the church; (4) to enable the church to extend its ministry to the world; and (5) to serve as a training ground for Christian decision-making in daily secular life. Not every group will fulfill all five objectives, but surely the existence of any group that ignores all of them ought to be questioned; and every church group ought to examine its reason for being periodically against these objectives. Church groups must do more than merely provide interesting activities that keep people busy carrying out some program.

Kenneth Benne of Boston University has suggested that small groups are essential to accomplishing four basic tasks.[3] These four categories indicate at once how vital it is for the church to be alert to any field of knowledge that will contribute toward improving the effectiveness of group functioning.

(1) Problem solving. The church is engaged in problem solving on many levels—personal, organizational, social, and above all, evangelical. Every group in the church has its own set of problems with which it must wrestle, as well as considering the problems confronting the church as a whole. If face-to-face groups have any essential contribution to make in problem solving, then the church needs to utilize such a resource and become familiar with the dynamics of effective group operation. In suggesting that small groups are basic for problem solving, the implication is that the leader *and* the group can reach a wiser decision than can either one without the resources of the other. The leader needs the insights of the group into the situation, including the attitudes of per-

sons involved, and the group needs the training, experience, and knowledge of the leader.

(2) Planning. This is a continuous activity within the life of the church, since all its groups are confronted with planning responsibilities. Benne suggests that face-to-face groups are basic for planning for several reasons. For one, the plans of a group must represent the thinking of the whole group, not just the thinking of the leader or a segment of the group. Moreover, since planning involves projecting from the known to the unknown, every conceivable insight and every possible obstacle needs to be considered in the planning process. This means that every member of the group must unreservedly share his thoughts if the best possible plan is to be evolved. Even industry has discovered that planning from the top can be improved by suggestions from the grass roots. Many a church program has been rendered ineffective because the group expected to carry it out was not involved at the planning stages.

(3) Producing change in persons. If Benne is right in stating that face-to-face groups are basic for personal change, then the church must be concerned with groups, for its very existence calls for changed persons. We have suggested earlier that personality is formed, deformed, and reformed in relationships with other persons. The small face-to-face groups with which any person identifies then becomes the matrix within which his life is shaped and influenced. Such groups may be either positive or negative in their impact, and their influence may be either conscious or unconscious. Alcoholics Anonymous is an example of a life-changing group deliberately seeking conscious positive change. The neighborhood bridge club is an example of a group unconscious of any atttempt to change persons and whose effect may be either positive or negative depending upon the persons and circumstances. The church should view its groups as consciously seeking to effect positive change and growth in those who participate in them. The church usually is most conscious of this opportunity in its "prayer groups," "study groups," and "*koinonia* groups," such as are described in detail in the writings of Robert Raines [4] and John Casteel,[5] but a similar potential also exists in boards, committees, and auxiliaries.

156

This fact implies that a knowledge of the dynamics of such groups ought to be a concern of the church.

(4) Providing personal stability. At first, this goal may appear to conflict with the previous goal of effecting change. Stability, however, does not mean to remain static, but to find an atmosphere and relationship to persons where one feels "at home" "wanted," "accepted" and where one is free to "be himself." Such security is needed and desired by all persons, and our mass society and impersonal culture have intensified the need for every person to find some group that provides it. Actually, personal stability contributes toward personal growth. In our cold, lonely, impersonal society, church groups can serve a real need by being a place of warm Christian fellowship in the full meaning of the term. The fact that many persons do not find such fellowship and stability in church groups may indicate a need for the church to be more concerned about the operation of its groups.

If the small groups in the church are to accomplish these four tasks, the church administrator must be aware of the dynamic factors involved in the functioning of groups and provide the required training for leaders and group members so that they can so function.

B. A Definition of Group Dynamics

If the groups of a church are to function creatively and effectively, it is necessary for the pastor as administrator to have a clear understanding of how groups behave and why. He can then work with the leaders of his church to help each group function in the best possible manner.

"Group dynamics" is a disturbing and provocative term for many pastors. It is often a misunderstood term. Those who hold it in disdain refer to it as "grope" dynamics, by which they imply it is a pooling of collective ignorance "which advocates 'groupthink' over individualism." [6] Those who enthusiastically hail it as a cure-all believe that all who have not "seen the light" are superficial and authoritarian. It is evident from such hostilities and stone-throwing that the terms needs to be carefully defined.

Malcolm and Hulda Knowles have suggested four ways in which this term "group dynamics" is properly used.[7] (1) "In its most basic sense, it is used to describe something that is happening in all groups at all times, whether anyone is aware of it or not. 'Group dynamics' used in this way refers to the complex forces that are acting upon every group throughout its existence which cause it to behave the way it does." (2) It is, therefore, properly described as a "field of study, . . . concerned with using scientific methods to determine why groups behave the way they do." (3) Group dynamics may, therefore, properly be referred to as a "body of basic knowledge about group behavior that has accumulated from past research." (4) Commonly, group dynamics is used to refer to "the use of knowledge about group process. In this sense, it is possible to speak of 'group dynamics principles,' . . . but never of 'the group dynamics method.' " It is our intention here to use the term primarily in the first and the fourth senses, hoping to encourage the church administrator to engage in further study of the field of group dynamics, as identified in the second and third points above.

The behavior of a group varies according to its leadership and membership. Groups with leaders who are overly concerned with "getting the task done" (raising money, planning a new building) usually minimize personal relationships within the group and tend to be authoritarian and insensitive to the needs and opinions of group members. Groups with leaders overly concerned with process and personal relationships tend to neglect the task or job responsibility and become such a *laissez-faire* group that they may fail in the achievement of their task. Groups with leaders evidencing balanced concern for achieving their task and for the interpersonal relationships and growth of their members have been labeled as "democratic groups" and usually are most effective in both task and personal growth achievement.[8] These descriptions of three types of groups serve to illustrate the fact that group dynamics is not a particular "method" of operating a group but rather an attempt to describe and understand the behavior of a group as it actually functions.

There are certain observations about group behavior that are particularly relevant to church groups. In terms of group behavior, church groups differ from other groups in their task goals but not in interpersonal relationships. Hence, all observations as to the behavior of persons in groups are as valid for church groups as any other. As we now enumerate certain observed principles relative to group behavior, it should be kept in mind that the more clearly these principles become known and understood by all members of a group (not just by the leader), the more likely the group will be able to function effectively in moving toward its task goal as well as toward the goal of personal growth of its members.

C. Principles of Group Dynamics

1. Every Person Needs to Be Made to Feel "at Home" in the Group.

No group can elicit the maximum creative response from its members unless every person feels truly at home in the group. Until each person feels he "belongs," is "accepted," and is "wanted" by other members of the group, he will not fully give of himself to the group. This involves a feeling of freedom to be oneself, to participate in any given moment or to remain uninvolved, a freedom to express opinions and doubts freely, to raise questions, or to propose some "far out" idea. Each person must feel that his presence is desired by the rest of the group, that his opinions are respected and needed, and that the other members of the group are concerned about him. Conversely, each member must convey to others his genuine concern for them, their needs, and their opinions.

Such an atmosphere is neither easily nor quickly created in any group but is necessary if every member is to make the maximum contribution of which he is capable. Unless each member feels at home in the group, he will feel unimportant to the group's success, his interest will wane, and he may drop out of the group. A concern for persons and what is happening to each one of them as a member of the group must be developed from the outset. Group members must, therefore, quickly come to know one another by name and to manifest an interest in important experiences and concerns of all other group members. Participation on a depth level is withheld until one feels the group really "accepts" him, and he feels his opinions

159

are respected and desired. The leader must, therefore, be sensitive to the "feeling tone" of the group from the outset and must seek to so sensitize all members of the group as soon as possible. Concern for moving toward the task goals must not be allowed to interfere with the establishing of an accepting atmosphere in which all members feel at home.

2. Group Consciousness of the Goals of the Group Is Essential.

Every group must have some task or concern to which it addresses itself. Its reason for being must be clear to all its members. An awareness of this concern will provide both cohesiveness and motivation to stimulate creative action. Herbert Thelen illustrates this principle clearly in a case study of the "block program" of neighborhood groups on the south side of Chicago, as they met to deal with their common problem of property deterioration in a racially changing neighborhood.[9] Their common concern for their property and neighborhood was linked to a growing respect for one another developed in their meetings, so that a creative solution emerged that would have appeared impossible at the outset.

It is not enough that every group have certain announced goals of which the leader is aware. All members of the group must know exactly what the group is trying to do and why. When such a common sense of purpose is absent, the group will get nowhere. I once attended a missions committee meeting that illustrated this perfectly. The chairman called the meeting because he had received a report blank for the annual meeting and he wanted help in preparing the report. The woman's society representative wanted the committee to sponsor a church-wide school of missions and came to the meeting with this as her prime concern. The church treasurer felt there would be a shortage of funds at the end of the year and he wanted to talk about how to raise money. Another man was eager to end the meeting in time for him to get home before a championship prize fight started. The pastor wanted the committee to take a long-range look at the church's missionary program and agree to meet regularly to do so. The chairman did nothing to help the group arrive at any common agenda or reason for meeting, so the five

160

members tried to move the committee in five directions at once. No one really listened to what anyone else said but repeated his own speech several times. As a result the group went home frustrated. Many cases like this one show the need for full agreement on the overall task of the group, as well as on the agenda for a particular meeting. The leader must help the group arrive at such an understanding before moving on to consider solutions and ways of action. There must be not only an agenda in the mind of the leader or on a mimeographed sheet of paper; the members of the group must really accept and agree upon the problems that are their common concerns.

Another implication of this principle is that a group needs to have a task or reason for being that is big enough to be challenging, a task of genuine concern to the individual members. Too many groups meet without a real reason for being; wasted time and personal frustration are the inevitable results of such occasions.

3. Growth of Persons and Achievement of Task Must Be Dual Concerns of Every Group.

It is important to combine the first two principles of the creative functioning of groups into one statement as an independent and separate observable principle. Every group must have a parallel concern for the growth of the individual persons who are members of the group and for the achievement of the task which the group has undertaken. These concerns must be held in continuous tension if any group is to function creatively. In addition to its functional task, every group has a responsibility toward every member to see that the process of interpersonal relationship is an enriching experience for each person. This point is particularly relevant for church groups. Persons grow and change through relationships, and the experience of being a part of one or more small groups in the church provides an opportunity to reach persons and minister to them in and through the process of the functioning of the group.

Concretely, the task goal of a stewardship and finance committee is to work out a program of stewardship education and a financial plan to raise sufficient funds to meet the budget of the church. While

161

pursuing this functional task, the group must also be alert to what is happening to the members of their group in the process. Are they becoming better stewards because of their relationship to the group? Is their concern for others (in their own group) deepening? It is possible for a group to become so task centered that it ignores its responsibility toward its own members. Such a task-centered concern can produce an autocratic approach which suppresses all opposition and rides roughshod over anyone who dares to raise questions or propose alternatives. Actually, such a procedure would stifle creativity and new ideas and impoverish the task accomplishment of the group in addition to its negative impact on the persons involved. On the other hand, it is quite possible for stewardship and finance committee members to become so involved with one another that the task is neglected by simply concurring to "do as we did last year." Such an approach robs the group of its creative potential.

The leader must help the group see that it will do its best work only when it is conscious of the parallel goals of the growth of persons and the achievement of its task and moves simultaneously in these two directions.

4. *Every Person Brings to Each New Group Many Impressions and Factors from Previous Groups of Which He Has Been a Member.*

Every group must reckon with the fact that persons are social by nature and that their response in the present group will be influenced by their participation in other groups—family, school, and voluntary associations of many kinds. Loyalty to one group will consciously or unconsciously alter behavior in another group. Paul Maves has suggested that remarks made in one group really are often made to an unseen "gallery of onlookers" from another group of which the person is also a member. I once knew a woman who reacted in official board meeting as though her fellow W. C. T. U. members were present to hear her remarks. A fear of what other groups will think of "our decision" is often influential in determining the behavior of group members. Political loyalties are sometimes revealed in a person's comments in a church group, and differences in political affiliation may even interfere with interpersonal relationships. This cross-fertilization of groups is one of the reasons the church has become so closely identified with its culture.

It is necessary to deal with these multiple loyalties in a creative, understanding manner. The group must become acquainted with the personal background of its members in order to be aware of the other group affiliations that will affect their behavior. Time utilized to know and understand each person in the group will not only contribute to better interpersonal relationships but will also contribute to task goals when "other group" influences come to the surface. When any group recognizes a situation for what it is, it is better equipped to deal with both the person and the issue involved. The quality of the interpersonal relations within the group will be crucial in dealing with this kind of problem.

It is well to remember that these "other group" affiliations have positive as well as negative influences. Many of the personal strengths and insights which a person brings to one group have come, at least in part, through association with other groups. For instance, a political leader may bring to a church board or committee specific information relative to some community situation that will be invaluable to the church group as it approaches the problem.

5. *"Hidden Agenda" Commonly Interferes with Group Functioning.*

Groups usually are working on what might be called "hidden agenda" as well as the "stated agenda" in their meetings. By this, we mean that there are things going on "under the table" into which the attention and energy of the group are being funneled by some of its members, though others may not be aware of it. The discussion may take the *form* of dealing with the "stated agenda" when in *substance* it is dealing with the "hidden agenda." For example, the verbal discussion may be about selecting curriculum material for the church school, but the real issue (about which not a word is spoken) may be a power struggle or personality clash between Mr. Jones and Mr. Smith. Hidden agenda confronts the group and its leader with one of their most difficult problems.

The sources of hidden agenda fall into three general areas: (1) personal needs or interests, (2) outside loyalties, and (3) interpersonal relationships. Since the first step in dealing with "hidden agenda" is diagnostic, let us deal with each of these areas briefly, beginning with the recognition of the personal needs of members as items of hidden agenda.

Very often a group is deflected from its stated agenda when one or more members (either consciously or unconsciously) interjects their personal needs as "hidden agenda." A desire to be recognized, to be a leader, or to grasp power may lead some persons to attempt to dominate the group. The personal insecurity of another member may interfere with the stated agenda as he seeks to avoid conflicts by pleading for some easy answer to a difficult problem. In another case, an intense interest in some cause or hobby may cause him to introduce irrelevant concerns into the discussion. Many other personal needs and interests may become sources of hidden agenda. The possibilities are as wide as the persons in the group.

A second source of hidden agenda is the subtle impact of the loyalty of group members to outside groups. This loyalty may be so strong that the member may see himself as "representing" the outside group—such as, the American Legion, the Temperance League, the Chamber of Commerce, a labor union, or a political party—while attending a church committee meeting. Every group leader needs to be alert to this common form of hidden agenda.

A third source of hidden agenda is the interpersonal relationships within the group. One person may be a dominating power figure in the church and in the community, and other members may fear the consequences of "crossing" him. Two persons of long-standing hostility may be fighting an old battle before the group in a power struggle for leadership or a point of view. Affection for an established leader may bring strong support, not because his ideas are sound but because he is well liked. Personal grudges and hostilities may also be very subtly and cleverly worked out in the group. All this consumes the time and energy of the group and interferes with progress in dealing with the stated agenda.

Assuming that hidden agenda factors are present in some degree in every group, how are they to be handled? Three suggestions will be offered, without developing them in detail. Each requires skill on the part of the group leader and sensitivity by the group members. First of all, over a period of time, the leader must seek to develop within the group an ability to recognize hidden agenda when it appears and to understand what it involves. It must be seen as normal for all groups and must be accepted in the light of a concern for personal growth and development of individual group members. In other words, up to a point it may serve a useful function. Secondly, the group must continually seek to operate in such an understanding atmosphere that members will be secure enough to be self-critical before the group, being able to admit to themselves and to others the basis of their behavior. This will enable them eventually to discuss the problem with other members of the group. Only when such an atmosphere of acceptance is developed can real personal growth take place and the hidden agenda be brought above the table. Finally, the group must recognize that *sometimes* an airing of feelings is essential before the group can proceed. The avoidance of a direct clash through hidden agenda proceedings is not always desirable. The situation may become such that all attempts to create an atmosphere of acceptance are to no avail and the tension can only be relieved when the whole group faces the issue squarely, by lifting the hidden agenda above the table and making it the stated agenda. Such a procedure is fraught with danger, and the skill and ability of the leader are very important in such situations, as is the general strength of the group. However, in certain situations and with skillful handling, it can be a helpful and healing experience. It is undesirable for a group to feel that things should always appear to be going smoothly and that conflicts are to be avoided at all cost. Sometimes, the only way to group health is to discuss directly the issues and tensions involved and to face up to them.

6. Certain Roles Must Be Performed in Every Group if It Is to Function Effectively.

If any group is to function in an effective manner, it must possess the skills, training, and tools to do the job at hand. This means that the group needs to be equipped with an understanding of what it is trying to do and the process required for success. There are certain task responsibilities that must be accepted by the group as well as certain attitudes and relationships that must be assumed by all members of the group. These are sometimes described as "Task Roles" and "Group Building Roles" that need be fulfilled in every group if it is to function properly. Briefly, these roles may be summarized as follows:

a. Task Roles (Functions that need to be performed in any group if it is to accomplish its task responsibility)

(1) *Clarifying*—reaching a common understanding of the task the group is trying to do, being sure that all members have a common understanding of what is being said, that everyone is talking about the same thing. Citing examples, illustrations, and implications to illuminate the meaning of what is being discussed.

(2) *Exploring*—seeking new ideas and ways of dealing with the problem at hand, looking at every possible alternative, calling for additional information, outside leaders or resources, discovering how others have handled similar concerns, or "brainstorming" the group to stimulate their creative imaginations.

(3) *Reacting*—involving the group in reacting to the acceptability and workability of the proposals under discussion, bringing to bear their experience and observations relative to the situation. Discovering how each member feels about the proposal and whether or not he feels it will be acceptable to others.

(4) *Coordinating*—trying to see how all ideas and suggestions fit together, seeking to find the relationships and implications of various comments, probing for some common denominator or consensus, discovering whether or not the group is moving in any particular direction.

(5) *Formulating*—clearly stating the implications of the discussion and crystalizing the ideas expressed into a proposed plan of action, moving the group toward adopting a program designed to move it toward its accepted functional task.

(6) *Evaluating*—checking the soundness of all ideas, testing all concepts against the facts and the reactions of the whole group, look-

ing squarely at all obstacles, setting up "feed back" to test the program while it is being put into operation and while it is being carried out.

b. Group Building Roles (Relational interpersonal processes required to keep the group vital and fruitful)

(1) *Encouraging*—creating a warm, friendly atmosphere, seeking to help every member feel at home in the group, aware that he is wanted and accepted by others, helping each member to "identify" with the group through interpersonal relationships and a common loyalty and interest in its task.

(2) *Involving*—securing the participation of all members by creating an atmosphere of receptivity and understanding, encouraging all members to express their real personal feelings, raise their doubts, and to share their creative insights, clearly communicating that the contributions of every member are essential if the group is to do the best work of which it is capable.

(3) *Gatekeeping*—guarding against the domination of some members, seeing that everyone has a chance to speak, seeking to maintain an atmosphere of respect that will prevent personal hostilities and bitterness, mediate and relieve tension so that all is done in Christian love.

(4) *Listening*—giving careful and full attention to what is being said, communicating that one is listening when others are talking by responding *to what was said* rather than raising a new subject when one speaks.

(5) *Diagnosing*— (recognizing the effect of interpersonal relationships on the group) , helping the group analyze just where it is, whether or not it is making progress and the contributing reasons, helping the group get back on the track when it has strayed away, dealing with hidden agenda, making the group aware of an important happening or insight that has transpired.

(6) *Expressing group feeling*—assisting the group to crystalize and recognize its feelings, encouraging individual members to express their own feelings and reactions to the handling of the task responsibility and to what has been happening to interpersonal relationships in the process.[10]

These task roles and group building roles need to be performed simultaneously and every member of the group must become sensitive enough to accept responsibility for fulfilling any role called for at any given moment. These are not functions to be performed by the group leader alone, nor can any specific role be assigned to any one member of the group. All roles must be the constant concern of each group member. Such group awareness must begin with the leader and will emerge gradually as the group functions under his guidance. A discussion of the strategic role of the leader and of his training for creative group work is, therefore, in order.

7. *The Group Leader Must Clearly Understand His Role in Relationship to the Group.*

The character and operation of any group will be greatly affected by the manner in which the leader conducts himself in relation to the group. This is a simple observable fact, experienced by nearly everyone who belongs to several groups or who has experienced a change of leadership in a group. Although the makeup of the group and the relationships and roles played by members of the group itself are of great importance, the role of the leader is a key one, influencing the response of the other members.

Early studies by Kurt Lewin document this conclusion.[11] These studies report the effect of different types of leadership on groups. The "authoritarian" leader sought to dominate and manipulate the group. The *"laissez-faire"* leader was completely passive and let the group drift where it would. The "democratic" leader helped the group define its situation and see its problem and then sought to involve them in wrestling with it, participating as a resource person, but holding the whole group responsible for decision-making. The results of Lewin's leadership study are very revealing. "Authoritarian" leadership evoked either a passive "rubber stamp" acceptance or hostile aggressive opposition. *"Laissez-faire"* leadership likewise proved frustrating and ineffective, both in accomplishing the task of the group and in providing good internal relationships. The performance of the "democratic leader" was superior in task achievement and personal relationships as well. Thomas Gordon discusses the meaning of democratic leadership in a helpful and detailed way.[12] His basic thesis is that the leader and the group can reach better conclusions than can either alone. Each needs the other to function most effectively. *The leader is responsible for creating conditions that will enable the group to do the best job of which it is capable.* The task concern and the decisions remain with the group itself. The leader seeks to enable each member to make the best contribution possible in dealing with the situation. The leader participates as a member of the group, using his skills, his knowledge, and his relationships with persons as resources to improve the functioning of the group. As a group member, he has a responsibility to participate in the group, but *not* to dominate or manipulate it. The following paragraphs will spell out more clearly the role of the effective group leader.

8. The Role of the Democratic Group Leader.

a. **He helps the group define its task and discover its needs.** The emphasis here is on the words "he helps the group." The leader cannot *tell* the group what its task and needs are. Though he may be aware of them, it is impossible to communicate to any group its task and needs by verbalization, mimeographed statements, manuals, and books. The leader's role is to involve the members of the group in a discussion and search to clarify their tasks, their reasons for being, and the procedures that will enable them to function satisfactorily. Genuine insight and understanding relative to the tasks and needs of the group will come only when the members of the group have explored and shared their personal feelings in an attempt to reach a common understanding of their task. In this process, the leader's first responsibility is to encourage the group members to contribute their insights and raise their questions, but he will also fulfill his secondary responsibility to share with the group his own insights in an appropriate nondomineering way at the right time.

b. **He seeks to relate persons within the group to one another and to encourage each to contribute his best to the group.** The leader will be sensitive at all times to the atmosphere of the group in regard to interpersonal relationships. He will seek to create an accepting atmosphere where each person will really be "listened to" when he speaks. Not only will the leader be understanding in his response to every member, but he will encourage other members to be also. The leader will use his own relationship with persons and his communication skills to establish stronger personal relationships within the group. He will be especially sensitive to any person who in any way evidences a feeling of not belonging to or not being accepted by the group. He will also be alert for any members whose personal needs are causing them to behave in such a manner that the group may reject them. Through his own understanding example, the leader will try to help the group come to understand such persons and in so meeting their personal needs, enable the group to function more effectively.

c. He is a resource person helping the group discover and mobilize resources for meeting its needs. A resourceful leader will possess basic knowledge in his field and will know where to turn for additional resources. This involves personal responsibility for advance preparation and study. Ignorance relative to the field of interest of the group is a definite hindrance to effective leadership. A resourceful leader must not only be skilled in working with groups but must also possess knowledge and skill in the task field in which he is exercising leadership. One of his responsibilities is acquainting the group with whatever resources are required to fulfilling its task. The leader should not see his task as that of telling the group what to do and how to do it. It is not his responsibility to make the decisions of the group. As a resource leader, he helps the group come to an understanding of its task, assists them in finding the necessary information and leadership to meet adequately their problem, and moves them toward decision and action. The leader needs to remember that he and the group, each contributing their best, can arrive at a better decision than can either alone. A good leader neither tries to dominate the group nor leaves it to flounder on its own.

d. He helps the group evaluate its work and consolidate its gains. Every group needs to look at itself occasionally to see where it is in relation to where it has been and where it is trying to go. The perspective of an honest evaluation is often a good tonic to improve future performance. The leader can help the group hold up a mirror to itself, both while it is working on a task and after the task is completed. The leader is not to see this as an opportunity for him to evaluate personally the group and thus "illuminate the group" with his own insights. Rather, he is to *help the group evaluate itself*. This will include a look at the progress made in regard to the task at hand and the reasons for success or failure. It will include a new look at the ultimate goal and at how to best proceed in the future. Through such a process of evaluation, the group will learn much about the roles of group members that contribute to an effective group.

e. **He assumes the responsibility of accepting personally the required roles of every other member of the group for its effective functioning.** The leader must always view himself as a member of the group. Being the leader, he has certain added responsibilities as outlined above, but these do not relieve him of any expectations required of other group members. It is important for the leader to remember that he must not violate or ignore his membership role responsibilities while functioning as a group leader.

D. Opportunities for Growth Through Committee Relationships

Being a member of a church committee is often seen as a routine duty, but it can be a challenging, exciting experience; and a good administrator will seek to make it so. The administrator's own attitude toward committees will be a determining factor. He may view committees as necessary cogs to keep the church machinery turning, or as *an avenue through which to minister to persons while enabling them to perform a useful Christian service.*

Many ministers have discovered that laymen often have their visions enlarged, their commitments deepened, and their personalities enriched while serving on a church committee. Early in my ministry, I was shocked to find the chairman of a missions committee who did not believe in missions. She acted as a fifth columnist seeking to sabotage every effort at missionary education or giving. My first impulse was to seek her removal as chairman. Another member of the committee was much wiser and suggested, "When you get to know her, you'll discover she is a great person. Somewhere, somehow, something got stuck in her craw in relation to missions. If we can get it out, nobody can or will do more for the cause of missions than she." The committee proceeded to listen to her objections to missions and to encourage her to be more specific in them. She began to read about particular mission fields so that she could intelligently object to the program. The discussions at the committee meetings kept growing more and more involved and specific. The entire committee became well informed on the subject as a result. Not only the information acquired, but also the relationship with the other committee members, who seriously listened to her and also talked back to her, began to work a change in her attitude toward missions after about eighteen months. This change was more than the reversal of a negative attitude toward missions. It also was evident in her new concern for others in all her personal relationships, including the members of the missions committee.

Small committees offer an opportunity to minister to persons and to effect personal change and growth, as well as to involve them in a significant experience of carrying out some aspect of the church's ministry. In short, *committees should be seen as a means of ministering to and through persons.* This *is* the work of the church. Such committee or group meetings are not to be seen as a necessary evil, to be tolerated so that one can get on with the real work of the church after the administrative chores are done. Properly conceived, a ministry to persons can and should be performed in the process of carrying out committee responsibilities. In the next chapter the principles enumerated here will be illustrated through a detailed description and analysis of the work of the nominating committee.

E. New Life Through Study and Fellowship Groups

In addition to encouraging personal growth through participation in boards and committees, many church administrators are welcoming the rise of special church groups for study, fellowship, and spiritual renewal. The existence of such groups within the larger fellowship of the church is not new. Jesus took the twelve apart from the multitude, and he had even more intimate fellowship with Peter, James, and John. The New Testament refers several times to the church meeting in homes—for instance, in the house of Aquila and Priscilla in Ephesus and in the house of Nympha in Colossae. Historically the spiritual power of such small groups in changing lives is well attested to by Spener's *collegia pietatis* and by the Wesleyan class meetings.

Renewal movements in the church today often are linked with some type of small group fellowship and study. Contemporary examples might include the "House Church" movement in England, the "Lay Academy" movement on the Continent, and the "Yokefellow" movement in America. Many types of small groups are to be found in the contemporary American church. Robert Raines describes the effect of the rise of small *"koinonia"* groups in his church.[13] In a volume edited by John Casteel, nine types of small groups operating in different church situations are described. In the introductory chapter, Casteel characterizes such personal groups as

a small number of persons, meeting face to face regularly for the purpose of the study of the Bible and of the Christian faith; for prayer; for the exchange of experiences, needs and insights; and for taking thought as to how they can best fulfill their calling as Christians to love and serve God and other people. . . .

Their purpose is to help members come into a primary personal relationship with God, with other persons, and with themselves.[14]

Such groups are not to be seen as ends in themselves, nor as "substitute churches," but rather as seeking to equip each member to participate more fully in the life of the church and to give himself to extending the church's ministry to the world.

1. Guidelines and Principles for Small Fellowship Groups.

The following observations are set forth out of the experience and research of the author as guidelines for those seeking to introduce such small groups into the life of the church.

a) No single mechanical pattern of operation can be imposed upon every group. Effective small groups must be dynamic and thus responsive to the unique circumstances and personal needs that call each into being. Fluidity rather than rigidity is called for.

b) Organizational and promotional *pressures* to form such groups or to involve persons in them are to be avoided and, if followed, will result in disappointing failures. The decision to enter into or to form such a group must be truly voluntary and represent genuine personal interest. The pastor, however, should be sensitive to signs of interest in such a group and should encourage such interest.

c) A common understanding of the basic purpose of each group and the responsibilities of each group member must be clearly worked out and understood at the outset. An opportunity to withdraw gracefully should be offered at this time to those not in full accord with the purpose and disciplines agreed upon in the group contract for membership.

d) Experience indicates that the most desirable size for such a group is from six to twelve members. Continuity and faithfulness of members are essential for an effective group.

e) A basic qualification for membership in such groups is a desire to grow. Casteel indicates several areas in which growth ought to take place.[15]

In self-understanding.

In an understanding and acceptance of other persons.

In understanding the Christian faith.

In a personal, experiential meeting of God.

In making responsible Christian decisions at work, in the home, and among people in society, church, and community.

In the capacity to give one's self in love in the service of God and of other persons.

In the capacity to continue growing.

f) The maturity and skill of the leader will be a determinative factor in the group's life, and leaders should be carefully selected and trained. (See the next section for a detailed outline of leadership training used at Skokie, Illinois.)

g) Each group will need to establish its own pattern and frequency of meeting. Usually, biweekly or weekly intervals are best. The format of each session and group will and should vary. Most groups have found the following ingredients desirable and necessary sometime during the course of their existence: Bible study, discussion of selected books, deep personal sharing of reactions, questions, and insights as to both personal concerns and matters of faith, prayer, and Holy Communion.

h) Mutual concern of the members for one another, and the full, free participation of all members are essential. The leader and the group members must constantly maintain an atmosphere of acceptance in the group.

i) All groups must be aware of certain dangers inherent in their very existence.

The temptation to become a "clique" or closed circle.

The temptation to spiritual pride, to see themselves as the "spiritual elite," as the "real church" within the larger "distorted church."

The possibility that the members of the small groups may "take over" most of the leadership positions of the church.

The possibility of becoming so involved in dealing with deep personal problems that damage may be done to a member of the group. Such church groups must *not* attempt group psychotherapy.

j) Every group need not go on forever uninterrupted. Any group may take a vacation period or decide to disband. For a group to discontinue does not mean failure. It may mean that the pressing needs which called it into existence have been met.

2. *A Case Study: Koinonia Groups at Skokie.*

Perhaps the best way to illustrate how small groups may be initiated and carried on in the church is to cite an example. The account which follows is given not as a workable pattern for other churches but as a concrete example of how one church went about establishing such groups. It is a first person account by the associate pastor who worked directly with the groups involved.[16]

KOINONIA GROUPS AT SKOKIE

In the fall of 1961 some of the most active members of Central Methodist Church, Skokie, Illinois, shared a conviction that there was not the vital, living, spiritual fellowship in their church which seems to have been present in the primitive church. In considering by what means this spiritual vitality might be recovered, it was decided that one possible source of such fellowship might be found in the creation of a small group movement in the church. Today (1963), there are nine of these groups meeting once every two weeks, led by members of the church. This end was accomplished by the following means:

The two ministers personally asked some twenty-five members of the church, known to be potentially those most interested in this approach, to meet together for eight consecutive Sunday evenings. We read through Robert Raines' book, *New Life in the Church*, trying to apply all that is said here to our own local situation. Accordingly, at the end of this eight-week period, we had a nucleus of twenty-five people who *felt strongly* that we should try the small group experiment in our local situation. From these twenty-five members, four couples were invited to come together with one of the ministers into a weekly leaders' training class. It was our intention from the beginning that these groups should and could have lay leaders, but we also realized that the quality of this leadership would be the most important single factor determining the success or failure of the experiment. Therefore, a definite leadership training program was carefully worked out.

This leaders' training group met weekly for the following fourteen weeks. In this training class, we had six distinct goals in mind.

a) Each leader was encouraged to contemplate his present religious experience and his present relationship to God. He thought about the various religious symbols with which he was familiar and attempted to comprehend their meaning to him, at an unconscious as well as conscious level.

b) There was then a teaching, or more formally intellectual, side to this leadership program. Here we tried to achieve a working outline of Christian theology, to have some working attitude to the question of the inspiration, authority, and interpretation of the Bible, to consider the likely sources of material for discussion in and presentation to the groups to be formed. The leaders also learned about Methodism, its history, doctrines, emphases, structure, ethos, etc.; and finally considered some of the implications of all the above for daily Christian living and for the solution of contemporary critical political and social questions.

c) Next, we come to the point where we were most concerned about the dynamic and functional aspects of the leader's role. First, we attempted to help each leader gain some general insights into his own personality structure—typical ways of feeling, behaving, relating, and responding. What were the dominant anxieties, fears, and personal concerns of each, and how did he deal with them?

d) We then tried to have each leader see himself in the context of a small group. To discover how well he was able to relate to people in the intense small group situation, to see himself as others in the group perceived him, to examine his own ability to accept other people, to hear and appreciate their feelings and concerns, not to be threatened by disagreement or doubt or personal criticism from others in the group, to ask himself to what degree he needs to be a manipulator of people—in a word, to what degree did he have a fundamental respect for human personality and for the feelings and concerns of other people, and to what extent did his own emotional needs prevent him from expressing and demonstrating this respect.

e) Then, each had to find an identity as a leader. That is, to find an inner security in his role. They seemed to achieve this in three ways: through their own religious experience, which meant they felt they had something to share and communicate; through having come to terms with their own feelings and personal needs for status, prestige, etc.; and through the assurance that they were being called by God to undertake this spiritual responsibility, and if God had called them, then he would enable them and would bless the entire enterprise.

f) Finally, the leaders, in the training class, worked through their

177

anxiety at being responsible for the handling of a group of people all relating to one another in a great variety of different and complicated ways. They worked through their fears about having to handle raw emotion and emotion-laden situations, considered the question as to when one should encourage or alternatively inhibit the free expression of feelings on the part of some member of the group, how to spot problem situations which required further and more expert handling, how to handle transference and counter-transference, in other words, how to comprehend and handle the dynamics emerging as a small group developed in the intensity of its cross-relationships.

When the leaders had been trained as best we knew how, we asked those ninety members of the church we considered the most likely to participate whether or not they would like to be in a small group. We found that fifty of the people who said "yes" really meant it, and accordingly we formed four groups and began to meet regularly.

As a consequence, some people have had very significant experiences. Mainly, three things appear to have happened.

a) Individuals have learned more about their faith and its implications for living. The creeds and symbols have come alive for them. Religious concepts are no longer intellectual ideas but have personal meaning involving daily decisions of life.

b) Individuals have found one situation where they could express their real inward feelings and yet be accepted; accordingly, they have developed as authentic selves.

c) Personalities have developed and grown spiritually and psychologically—if there is a difference—by entering into deep fully personal I-Thou relationships, both vertical and horizontal, within which they have found their true selfhood. For many, the idea of God has become a living reality found in and expressed through relationships.

3. What Small Groups Can Mean to the Life of a Church.

Clearly, one of the ways in which the contemporary church is finding renewal of spirit is in the small group movement. It is not the only way, but it is one way. Scores of churches will testify to what such groups can mean to the life of a congregation. For some persons, these groups have fulfilled an evangelistic function of effecting the change of a true conversion experience, and the spiritually dead have been brought to life. For others, these groups have resulted in a growth in Christian understanding beyond anything Christian education classes were able to do. A few have found an inner personal growth in self-insight and a self-understanding more profound than pastoral counseling often brings. Some inactive church members have had their love and loyalty for the church revived and have given themselves to the service of God and their fellow men. Some churches have reported that their small groups have been as a leavening influence, spreading increased vision and acceptance of Christian responsibility across the whole church. A deeper understanding of the Christian faith and the nature and mission of the church often has been a result. The power of the Holy Spirit has clearly used some groups as a means of making known God's power and continuing activity. Since this is so, the wise administrator will seek to provide for the creative functioning of small groups in the church as one of the guiding principles of his administration.

■ ■ ■ Notes

1. Paul Douglass, *The Group Workshop Way in the Church* (New York: Association Press, 1956), p. vii.

2. Paul Maves in a lecture at a Methodist pastors' school, 1957.

3. Kenneth Benne in a lecture at Garrett Theological Seminary, September, 1956.

4. Raines, *New Life in the Church.*

5. John Casteel, *Spiritual Renewal Through Personal Groups.*

6. Malcolm and Hulda Knowles, *Introduction to Group Dynamics* (New York: Association Press, 1959), p. 11.

7. *Ibid.*, pp. 11-14.

8. See Kurt Lewin, *Resolving Social Conflicts: Selected Papers on Group Dynamics* (New York: Harper & Row, 1948), for a full description of the authoritarian, *laissez-faire,* and democratic approach to leadership and its effect on the group itself.

9. Herbert A. Thelen, *Dynamics of Groups at Work* (Chicago: University of Chicago Press, 1954), pp. 1-30.

10. Detailed discussion of the various group roles may be found in Knowles and Knowles, *Introduction to Group Dynamics,* pp. 32-62; Douglass, *The Group Workshop Way in the Church,* pp. 108-23; and in the January, 1953, issue of *Adult Leadership.*

11. Kurt Lewin, *Resolving Social Conflicts: Selected Papers on Group Dynamics.* Only conclusions on experiments reported in detail are stated here. Consult the above volume for detailed accounts.

12. Thomas Gordon, *Group-Centered Leadership* (Boston: Houghton Mifflin Company, 1955).

13. Raines, *New Life in the Church.*

14. Casteel, *Spiritual Renewal Through Personal Groups,* p. 19.

15. *Ibid.,* p. 194.

16. Donald Williamson, associate pastor at Central Methodist Church, Skokie, Illinois, agreed to submit this account of this church's experience with groups after much urging by the author. Mr. Williamson was the staff person most closely associated with these groups.

■ ■ ■ CHAPTER VIII

EQUIP LAYMEN FOR LEADERSHIP
AND SERVICE IN THE CHURCH'S
MINISTRY TO THE WORLD

A. The Necessity and Significance of Lay Service and Witness

The work of the church is too vast for any minister or ministerial staff to attempt to accomplish. Furthermore, the very mission of the church requires the involvement of laymen, both for the sake of the mission and for the sake of the laymen themselves. In *The Purpose of the Church and Its Ministry,* H. Richard Niebuhr identifies a "new, emerging concept of the ministry," which focuses on the minister's role of equipping laymen to serve the church. In other words, "the church is becoming the minister and its 'minister' is its servant, directing it in its service." [1]

The wise church administrator will always remember that his responsibility is not to *do* the work of the church but to provide experiences that will *involve* the whole church in moving coherently and comprehensively toward an effective Christian witness. Sound church administration requires a recognition of the basic principle that laymen must be motivated and equipped to apply their talents to the life and work of the church. Over a quarter of a century ago, Albert Beavan wisely said, "The strength of a minister may be

181

measured not so much by the work he can do as by how much he can get others to do." [2] Many ministers fail here because they are unwilling to relinquish responsibilities to laymen. They insist on doing almost everything themselves, from being chairman of the church board to writing the publicity for the finance campaign, enlisting laymen only for such routine tasks as typing, mimeographing, and changing the bulletin board. A pastor with such a soloist's temperament merely obstructs the witness of his congregation. Instead, he should see his task as that of discovering, training, and applying the abilities of the lay members of the church toward a coordinated Christian witness.

The record of the New Testament church reveals that the entire Christian community has a mission to the world and that every member is called to active participation in it. The sharp division between clergy and laity that exists today is not evident in the New Testament. The "laos" of the New Testament included the whole church, and the mutual responsibility of *all* Christians toward the redemptive mission of the Christian fellowship was assumed.

In I Peter all believers are reminded of their responsibility to "declare the wonderful deeds of him who called you out of darkness into his marvelous light" (I Pet. 2:9). Every Christian is to view himself as a priest, one of God's own people, responsible for declaring to the world God's wonderful deeds. The writer to the Ephesians declares that Christ gave the church leaders (apostles, prophets, evangelists, pastors, and teachers) "for the equipment of the saints [Christians], for the work of the ministry, for building up the body of Christ [the church]" (Eph. 4:12). Every member should be a better servant of Christ because of the work of the leaders who should prepare all members to work together as a united redemptive Christian community. Paul's letter to the Corinthians illustrates this necessity for all Christians to unite their several talents in the work of Christ.

There are varieties of service, but the same Lord; and there are varieties of working, but it is the same God who inspires them all in every one. To each is given the manifestation of the Spirit for the common good. . . .

For just as the body is one and has many members, and all the members of the body, *though many, are one body, so it is with Christ.* . . .

Now *you* are the body of Christ and individually members of it (I Cor. 12:5-7, 12, 27. Italics mine.) .

In reading the New Testament, one cannot escape the conclusion that one of the chief responsibilities of the leaders of the church is the unified use of the gifts of all the members of the Christian community in making an effective witness for Christ. This goal seems always to have been difficult to achieve for several reasons. Some Christians felt their leadership ability and spiritual dedication were superior to that of their brethren and desired to be recognized as the "key" leaders. Other members appear not to have recognized their obligation to assume any responsibility. Still others became stumbling blocks to the brethren because of their unchristian living. Times have not changed greatly, and the church administrator today meets these same problems. Nevertheless, he is called to the same leadership responsibility to enable Christians to make a united witness in the world.

There is another reason why equipping laymen for service in the church is a basic principle of sound church administration. It is necessary for laymen to participate in the church's mission if they are to be truly Christian. To be Christian, by definition, means to be related in active love to all others who are "in Christ." It means also to extend the love of Christ to those presently outside the Christian fellowship. The administrator who fails to encourage full participation is, therefore, betraying his call by refusing to feed Christ's sheep. That is, he is withholding the means for his people's Christian growth through service to the church and the world.

Furthermore, at the practical level, the church simply cannot accomplish her mission of making known God's love to the world apart from lay service and witness. To put it bluntly, there is more teaching, shepherding, evangelizing, education, and worshiping to be done in a church than any minister can do. If the real work of the church is to get done, then laymen must assume responsibility for witness and service. Good church administration, genuinely concerned about the fulfillment of the mission of the church, must, therefore, include the equipment of laymen for leadership and service as one of its primary concerns.

Let it be clearly understood that *the clergyman has a necessary and unique place* within the life of the church, even though the church has a ministry to perform that requires all laymen to function as priests. Laity and clergy are mutually helpful to one another. The pastor, because he devotes all of his time to the inner workings of a congregation, can see the wholeness of the work of the church in a way that no other member can. His educational background provides an understanding of the scriptures, the faith, the church, of persons, and the required functional roles that enables him to guide and coordinate all activities of the church. His ordination sets him aside through the approval of the church to preach the word and administer the sacraments. The professional minister is a necessary coordinating leader of a local congregation, moving it toward an understanding of its unity of purpose, while seeking to make possible the effective witness of every member and the church as a whole.

B. Dimensions of the Lay Ministry

The dimensions of the lay ministry are threefold, involving a ministry to one another within the church, a strengthening of the church's witness as a Christian community, and an exerting of Christian influence on the world through the vocational and personal life. Let us examine each of these in turn.

1. Laymen Ought to Minister to One Another Within the Fellowship of the Church.

The New Testament is quite clear that Christians are to "bear one another's burdens" and strengthen one another's faith. Love for the brethren is an assumed attitude of every Christian. Care of the sick, the needy, the widows, and the orphans soon became

184

well-known outward and visible manifestations of Christian love in the early centuries. Unless there is such a sense of genuine fellowship and concern among those who abide in Christ, one of the distinctive marks of the church is missing. It is, therefore, the responsibility of laymen to minister to one another's needs, and it is the pastor's responsibility to encourage this kind of ministry in his congregation.

The pastor is, or ought to be, the best informed person in the congregation with respect to the personal needs within the church family. He should also know which members of the congregation are equipped to minister to each particular need, on the basis of their own past experience and Christian maturity. By bringing these factors together, a lay ministry of one member to another can be realized. No matter how effective pastoral care may be, it will be strengthened as it is coordinated with a lay ministry of those who care. In fact, such a lay ministry can create the matrix of a fellowship of acceptance and concern that may provide the only atmosphere in which spiritual healing can take place. Many attempts at pastoral care have been frustrated by the absence of such a lay ministry and fellowship.

Concretely, this may mean bringing persons in crisis into relationship with those who have passed through a similar crisis and who can bring newfound wholeness and maturity into the present situation. This may be helpful in different kinds of crises. For instance, women who have experienced a miscarriage can often reach out effectively to other women presently bearing that burden. Those who have faced the death of loved ones can render a healing ministry to those presently walking in the shadow of death. One person who had suffered severe economic loss became a real help to others facing varying degrees of economic crisis. Sober alcoholics are usually best able to help an active alcoholic. There is almost no end to the special ministries that can be performed by laymen for one another with careful guidance and selection by the pastor.

In every congregation, pastoral calling ought to be supplemented by lay visitation. This responsibility ought to start with the sick and shut-in and the aged. It ought to include visitation of the entire membership, visitors at the worship service, and prospective members. Such lay participation in calling not only will strengthen mutual concern and fellowship but will deepen and enrich the lives of those doing the calling. Such calling by laymen will need to be properly channeled. Laymen will need training and guidance for making certain kinds of calls. The proper supervision of lay calling will require that the pastor keep in touch with all such activities. There is, however, more calling needed in every congregation than the pastor can do. Therefore, he has a responsibility to provide the opportunity for laymen to experience this rewarding ministry and to render this needed service.

One of the most helpful lay ministries I have ever witnessed was carried out by six men in a men's club who provided the supportive atmosphere within which a paroled convict was reestablished in the community and in the church. The need for Christian friendship and acceptance is often the most vital ingredient for the redemption of the one in need. Unfortunately, all too often it is wholly missing from the life of the church.

Laymen often strengthen one another in their interpersonal relationships as they serve together in some church task. As they come to know one another through working as church visitors, as youth counselors, or as committee members, they can have a renewing and stimulating influence upon one another. As people work together for Christ, they often come to a new appreciation of each other, resulting in deepened commitment and enlarged understanding of the Christian faith.

Laymen often minister effectively to one another as they seek to explore the depths of the gospel through study and discusssion. Though the pastor may throw much light on the gospel through his preaching, he cannot become sufficiently personal to deal with the implications of the faith at the point of greatest need for every individual. Laymen need the opportunity to come together to explore deeply and thoroughly their own particular "pressure points" in relating Christianity to life as they find it. It is almost a universal

186

experience that when small groups of laymen do gather for such a purpose, an experience of real significance results. As they share common concerns and problems, raise their own questions about scripture and the teachings of the church, share their own failures and dreams and seek the light of Christ for their own and the world's needs, they render a mutual ministry to one another of almost immeasurable proportions. Is there a church that does not stand in need of such a lay ministry? One person describing the meaning of such an experience used these words:

I had not frankly and earnestly, or even casually, discussed religion with anyone for several years. Yet I found my initial reticence slowly disappearing in a gathering where everyone else had questions which they were willing to admit and for which they are sincerely trying to find the answers. I was impressed that there were others, persons I could respect, who cared about their religion, who were willing to share what they knew and was willing to admit what they did not know. Seeing how these people felt God had touched their lives and was still working in them, I began to see where I had also been touched and where God was working right now. I began to see that not all of my questions would be or even could be answered, but that I could live without answers. I felt I had seen through a glass darkly and was now beginning to see face to face. The words of the Bible began to have pertinence as never before, to become contemporary instead of distant. It became apparent that the experience of God had been true for other lay people and could be true in my life. An overwhelming and awesome thought.[3]

Here is a kind of ministry that only laymen can render to one another. Opportunity for participation in such a ministry ought to be a part of the life of every congregation.

2. Lay Service Should Strengthen the Church to Become a Redemptive Christian Community.

Building up the church is a legitimate concern of the pastor and a responsibility of laymen. The institution of the church has a ministry to perform in society, and to do so, it must be a strong, functioning institution. A weak church can never meet the needs of the world. Although institutional self-concern easily becomes a deadly temptation, only a strong functioning church (in a healthy sense) can really become a redemptive community in society. With the goal of achieving a redemptive purpose in mind, the church administrator gives his energies to building up the church. This is what H. Richard Niebuhr emphasizes as he delineates the meaning of his "new, emerging concept of the ministry," that of the "pastoral director." "His first function is that of building or 'edifying' the church; he is concerned in everything that he does to bring into being a people of God who as a Church will serve the purpose of the Church in the local community and in the world." [4]

If the church is to become in fact a people of God, a community through whom the love of God is to be made known to man in a redemptive way, it is obvious that lay participation in the life and work of the church must be widespread. Only a church in which laymen assume major responsibility for carrying the load can be adequate to today's demands. When Paul Maves says that every pastor should see himself as a dean of a theological seminary,[5] he means that the pastor must train the members of the Christian community for their mission. They will need training as Christian educators, evangelists, shepherds, stewards, youth workers, missionaries, social concerns workers, and as lay ministers of other kinds as well. It is the whole church that has a ministry to perform, and laymen need to be equipped for it.

Until a minister becomes overwhelmed by the tremendous number of responsibilities that laymen must assume if the church is to be strong enough to make any impact on the community, he will lack a proper appreciation and perspective of the importance of lay service in the church. A listing of services rendered by laymen in a Methodist church of 500 members is staggering. In planning a leadership recognition service, one pastor listed 568 different services being rendered by the members, not including special committees, various work projects, and church suppers. These responsibilities broke down as follows:

Administrative:

Official Board	35
Trustees	5
Nominating Committee	16
Pastoral Relations Committee	9
Other Committees	24

Worship:

Commission Members	12
Senior Choir	25
Youth Choir	20
Children's Choir	20
Ushers	16
Music Committee	4

Education:

Commission Members	16
Church School Teachers	42
Youth Counselors	14

Social Concerns:

Commission Members	12
Study Leaders	6

Missions:

Commission Members	12
Study Leaders	6
School of Missions Committees	22

Evangelism:

Commission Members	12
Fisherman's Visitors	12
Shepherd's Visitors	12
Neighborhood Family Unit Leaders	38
Koinonia Fellowship Leaders	10

Stewardship and Finance:

Commission Members	16
Annual Visitors	80
Auditors, Treasurer, etc.	8

Officers of Organizations:

Woman's Society (including circles)	28
Men's Group	6
Young Adults	6
Youth Fellowship	12
College Group	12

Such a list of lay services to the church makes it quite clear that no small responsibility of the church administrator is to discover and equip these laymen for their service of building up the church so that its witness may be an effective one.

One of the happy signs of our times is the fact that lay people appear to be accepting their ministries in many areas that were formerly viewed as the domain of the clergy alone. Laymen have long been identified with the church schools and with the financial leadership of Protestant congregations. Now, however, we see them sharing in the leadership of public worship, reaching out in bold new evangelistic efforts, witnessing to the Christian implications

of social issues, and ministering to the spiritual needs of their brethren in living rooms and by sick beds. Every pastor should rejoice
when such things happen in his congregation. He should be glad
when men and women are no longer content merely to dabble on
the fringes of the church's mission. He should encourage them to
explore the deepest dimensions of the faith and to undertake, as
part of *their* ministry, even the most difficult tasks to which Christ
calls his people. There should be no sense of competition between
pastor and people, only a sense of "varieties of service" and of
mutual encouragement.

*3. The Church Should Send Laymen Forth to Exert a Penetrating
Christian Influence on the World Through Their Vocational and
Personal Lives.*

The church exists not for its own sake but for the sake of the
world. "God so loved the world (not the church) that he gave his
only son." Bishop Ralph Alton is right when he declares, "The effectiveness of the church is not to be measured by what happens to
it as an institution, but by its impact on society." [6] The church's
ministry to the world takes two forms. One is the ministry to the
world rendered by and through the institution of the church, as
discussed above. The second is bringing to bear the light and the
leaven of the gospel upon the needs of the world by individual
Christians through their daily vocation and personal life in society.
It is to this aspect that we now give our attention.

The New Testament insists that disciples are called to follow
Christ on a full-time basis. Their influence is to penetrate the world,
as salt, leaven, or light exert their penetrating qualities. Whenever
and wherever a neighbor is in need, the Christian is to respond.
Each Christian is sent out into the world to live out his knowledge
that the Kingdom is at hand.

A very practical consideration also requires the vocational and
personal witness of every Christian all the time if an impact is to
be made on today's world. The simple fact is that the fundamental
life-changing decisions of society are not made by or in the church
today, but in government, business, education, science, labor

190

unions, and other secular groups. Issues of war and peace, economic well-being, freedom or slavery, educational and housing opportunities, and racial justice are not being decided in the church councils but in the various secular agencies of society. The church must do more than try to influence these decisions by its pronouncements and example, though it dare not do less. The only real hope for a penetrating Christian influence is through the Christian witness of laymen who in all vocational and personal decisions seek to make a Christian witness as businessmen, government officials, educators, scientists, or members of community groups.

This dimension of lay ministry is developed at length by Elton Trueblood in his book, *The Company of the Committed*.[7] Trueblood suggests that if one really wants to see the church at work, he might better follow the members in their daily round of living, instead of visiting a Sunday service.

What happens on Sunday is defensible only as a preparation for the daily ministry of the week which follows. . . .

If we were to take the idea of a militant company seriously, the church building would be primarily designed as a drill hall for the Christian task force. It would be a place where Christian ambassadors in common life would come together to be trained, to strengthen one another. . . . We may say that the Christian building should be a "launching pad," a place from which people engaged in secular life are *propelled*.[8]

This is a revolutionary concept for many pastors who are used to thinking of a church-centered universe where any church meeting is automatically assumed to be more important than any conflicting secular meeting. This concept forces the question of whether or not a Christian can make as valid (or even more significant) a witness as a member of a secular group than as a member of a church committee. One example will illutsrate the point. A certain church was planning a new educational building. The education committee had worked long and hard to define the goals of Christian education, to draw out their implications for teaching methodology, and to translate these findings into the size and type of rooms required for good Christian teaching. After many months of work, the night was at hand when the architect was to present his proposed drawings to the committee for its reaction. That evening the pastor was amazed to get a telephone call from his very loyal and capable church school superintendent indicating he could not attend the committee meeting at the church because it conflicted with a Y.M.C.A. board meeting. This call would probably have brought a rebuff from many pastors. The lay superintendent went on to explain that he thought this community meeting should take precedence over the church meeting, because he felt he could make a more important Christian witness there. That night the "Y" board was to decide on whether or not to open its swimming facilities to Negroes, and the superintendent felt that his vote for open swimming was a more Christian witness than he would make that night at the church committee meeting. Laymen have such opportunities to further the church's mission in many areas of daily life. The church needs to equip them to make such a witness wisely.

This dimension of lay witnessing will call for new and bold approaches. The church will need to expand the horizons of her self-image, and the pastor will need to enlarge his concept of his own role in many instances. Robert Raines suggests that

the one thing needful in the role of the clergyman for our time is that he prepare his people for their ministry in the church and in the world. *The chief task of the clergyman is to equip his people for their ministry.* All his work is to this end. The functions of preacher, prophet, pastor, priest, evangelist, counselor, and administrator find their proper places in the equipping ministry. The purpose of this ministry is that the people shall be trained and outfitted for their work in the church and in the world.[9]

Attempting to take seriously the dimension of lay witness in vocational life as a means of Christian penetration of society, Gordon Cosby writes,

The church might carry out its mission through small bands of people, just two or three or four or five, who would live out their lives in the midst of the world of business, the world of government, the world of mass media, the medical world, the educational world—out there where

192

they are making their tents, earning their living. Such little mission groups would be working at the problems of mass media, or on the issues relating to peace and prevention of war, or on race relations and housing, or with the poor. . . .

The congregation of the future will live under a common discipline. It will take seriously not just the gathering, but the going forth.[10]

Even though this is a long way from where the church now is, the church cannot ignore this dimension when considering where it ought to go.

We have seen the necessity of lay service and witnessing and examined the dimensions of such a lay ministry. We are now face-to-face with the very practical question of how laymen can be equipped for such Christian service.

C. How May Laymen Be Equipped for Christian Service?

We come now to the very concrete question of how lay witness and service can be developed. As might be expected, there is no simple answer to this question. However, as we examine the problem we discover three major lines of action. The first involves the broad area of imparting a growing Christian understanding and motivation to all persons related to the church. The second involves the discovery and utilization of laymen who will lead and train their fellow laymen in Christian service. The third is a concern for providing adequate training for the particular responsibilities given laymen. We will examine each of these in turn.

1. Provide a Personal, Growing Experience in Understanding the Meaning of the Christian Faith.

The *prime* need in equipping laymen for Christian service is neither recruiting nor training, important as these are. Since lay service is more than merely doing a job, the "equipment of the saints" must begin with opportunities for a growing personal experience of the Christian faith. Because everything one does must reflect one's understanding and acceptance of the gospel, Christian witness and service are really by-products of a deepening Christian commitment. Every church has a group of committed laymen who

193

can be counted on to respond to every authentic Christian cause, both personally and financially. They do not need to be "pressured" or "sold" on doing whatever particular task is at hand. They are sensitive to Christian responsibility and respond to all needs from their basic Christian commitment. Knowing what it means to be Christian, they seek to act accordingly. Every church has a few such persons. The question before us is how the whole membership can become similarly committed.

By listening to the comments of the committed, one may discover how the gospel can be made equally meaningful to others. One group of such persons in discussing why they were committed to the Christian faith and were involved in serving the church continuously gave the following reasons:

"It all began with my activity and involvement in the high school program as a teen-ager, and I have been actively working for the church ever since."

"I was raised in a home where all our time and energy beyond our daily work were spent in serving the church in some way."

"My personal commitment to Christ simply called for some meaningful expression through my relationship with the church."

"A feeling of being needed by the church was conveyed to me by my pastor, and I have been answering some Christian need ever since."

"I am serving in the church because I responded to a particular minister who aroused me from being a slumbering, inactive member. He had so much to offer and gave such effective leadership that I wanted to get in and help him, and I am still at it three ministers later."

"My beliefs motivated and impelled me to act upon them or give them up."

"The influence of a friend, a loyal layman, led me to venture into one service project, and that experience led me to another, and so it has gone down through the years."

"I do what I can as a Christian because of a deep personal satisfaction I have found in helping persons in a significant way."

"I came to life in my church relationship when my first child

194

was born and I was awakened to a new sense of my parental responsibility. I needed the church's help with my child, and in turn I felt obligated to strengthen my church."

As I listened to this group evaluation and later interviewed other active laymen, it became clear that motivation for Christian witness and service comes from many and varied sources. Every aspect of the life of the church has its part to play. This means that the best way to equip and motivate laymen for Christian service is to expose them to the total life of a church, where there is a clear understanding of purpose and mission, where a real attempt is being made to carry out this purpose and mission in the church's program. Extended personal exposure to enthusiastic, committed laymen and ministers challenges others to join them in service.

Whenever the gospel becomes meaningful in the life of an individual, the foundation for Christian witness and service has been laid. This is the first and most fundamental step in equipping laymen for Christian service. This is the desired common result of preaching, worship, Christian education, membership training, committee and auxiliary work, small group discussions, and pastoral care. In short, everything that goes on in the church ought to contribute toward the end of enabling and motivating laymen to give themselves in Christian service. The church must not be content to fill the pews on Sunday and the various meeting rooms on week nights. Its object is to become a working, witnessing community reaching out to serve the world. "To be an equipping minister will require skill, knowledge, and a great sensitivity. In this sense the minister ought to be a "professional," one who has a special ability in performing that kind of ministry which helps other people to perform their ministry, whatever it may be." [11] Only a minister who sees his role in this light will be able to coordinate all that goes on in the life of the church to contribute toward this end.

2. Discover and Utilize the Best Possible Lay Leadership.

The importance of placing qualified laymen in positions of leadership in the church can hardly be overemphasized. Unless its leaders are persons who understand the purpose and mission of the church, the church's real goals and objectives will never be realized. It is also important to place qualified laymen in positions of leadership in the church whose ability, commitment, and personality will stimulate other laymen to work with them. The task of the church is so great that every leader needs to be able to enlist the active help of many other laymen to carry out the activities and program of his group. Hence, the problem of discovering and utilizing the best possible lay leadership ought to be a fundamental concern of every church administrator.

Often the real leadership potential of a church lies dormant and unused. The central question is precisely how such leadership can be discovered, awakened, and put to work. The church needs to be constantly seeking to discover the approaches that will assist it in unearthing buried talent as well as awakening those with known abilities to accept leadership responsibility. The responsibility for this important work rests on the nominating committee of a local church. Therefore, the nominating committee is one of the most important committees in the local church. It not only selects the laymen who are to serve as leaders of the congregation, it also determines (at least recommends) the actual jobs that need to be done. This committee's matching of persons to responsibilities largely determines the effectiveness of the work that actually will be done. For these reasons the work of the nominating committee will be examined in detail. The following account will necessarily reflect the writer's experience in The Methodist Church, but the approach described is valid in any church.

THE COMPOSITION AND STRUCTURE OF THE NOMINATING COMMITTEE

The nominating committee is commonly composed of three to five members, although experience indicates that a larger committee (perhaps nine laymen plus the pastor) is better. It is also best to elect members to a three-year term, with three new members being elected each year and no one being eligible for reelection. Such a procedure provides for both continuity and a fresh point of view annually. The larger committee will provide for a better knowledge both of persons and positions than a smaller committee. A ten-member group can operate freely and creatively as a small group. It is our intention here to so detail the operation of this committee as to illustrate how the principles of groups, as discussed in chapter seven, can operate in this small administrative task group.

It is important that care be taken in the selection of the membership of the nominating committee. It is also strongly recommended that an annual church conference (congregational meeting) be authorized as the place of all church elections.[12] The election of church officers by the congregation stimulates interest. Before receiving nominations from the floor for the nominating committee, the crucial responsibilities of this committee should be clearly outlined to all present. Qualifications for the committee should include a comprehensive knowledge of the work and tasks of the church as well as a broad acquaintance with the leadership abilities of church members. It is also wise to ask for twice the number of nominees needed. This will prevent the closing of nominations and the acceptance of the first persons named who may be "top of the head" suggestions and not necessarily the best qualified persons.

Traditionally, the nominating committee has been conceived of as having an annual responsibility of selecting church officers and has met once or twice near the end of the church year to discharge its responsibilities. Often, the meeting has consisted in going over last year's list of officers and scratching off names of those who have died, moved away, resigned, or otherwise have been disqualified. The committee then received verbal nominations for replacements, arranged for some kind of notification to the new nominees (often by mail or telephone), and authorized the publishing of a new list of officers. That such procedures are inadequate is attested to by the inactivity of the majority of those thus nominated and quantity of potential leadership that remains unused in every congregation. A radical change in the operational procedures of the nominating committee is called for if the committee is to function effectively. It needs to take a new look at the implications of its task and responsibility. It needs to be aware of the fact that its responsibilities are too great to be met in one or two meetings a year. Meetings ought to begin in October or November to be ready for a spring election. The following is a description of a procedure believed to be far superior to the usual operation of this committee.

AN APPROACH TO THE CREATIVE AND EFFECTIVE. FUNCTIONING OF A NOMINATING COMMITTEE

The description presented here grew largely out of the experience of the writer and one or two of his ministerial colleagues. Some of the work sheets presented are adaptations. Such forms will be identified as they appear. It is hoped that this material will have the virtue of being born and tested in the fires of experience, and will be a concrete illustration of principles previously set forth.

The Opening Session

The first session of the nominating committee ought to be held at least six months before the election meeting. The purpose of the first session is to seek to involve the entire committee in a free and open discussion of their own understanding of what the concerns of a nominating committee should be. After the selection of a secretary, the pastor (or whoever is chairman of this group) should make a very brief opening statement. This opening statement should point out the importance of lay service in the church, both in enabling the church to fulfill its mission and in being a means of growth for participating laymen. He might then suggest that there are many, many problems related to lay service and leadership in the church and that this group is called upon to think them through and make recommendations concerning them. He may then point out that the group is concerned with particular local leadership needs that must be identified and fulfilled, and that the task demands the insights and contributions of every member of the group. From the outset, all members of the group are urged to share whatever thoughts or questions come to their minds.

The pastor should then invite the group to share their ideas of what the responsibilities and concerns of a nominating committee

198

ought to be, what policies ought to guide their decisions, and how the work of the committee might be improved over previous years. The pastor should then involve all members in a "brainstorming" session where every idea about the work of an effective nominating committee should be suggested and listed for later consideration. The pastor should go to the blackboard and write down the suggestions as they come from the group. The secretary should keep a permanent record of them in the minutes. Such a list might be headed "A Work Analysis of the Nominating Committee." The following is a list of concerns actually evolving from one local church committee discussion.

Work Analysis of the Nominating Committee [13]

To recommend for election the names of committee chairmen and members and all other officers of the church.

To replace ineffective members and fill vacancies created by death and moving away.

To determine what jobs are to be filled and make a job analysis of each one.

To discover the best qualified person for each position.

To make a personnel survey to discover the leadership interests and abilities of church members and assemble the results for ready reference in choosing persons for vacant positions.

To make a leadership study of the entire membership covering the number of jobs held, length of service, age, sex, and distance they live from the church.

To see that all age groups are represented in the church's leadership.

To work promising new members into the membership of church committees.

To nominate a proportionate number of women and young people to positions of leadership.

To spread the leadership responsibilities so that no one person has too many jobs. (Perhaps limiting the maximum number any one person may hold or the length of time a person may hold any one office would be advisable.)

To encourage every member to feel a personal responsibility to serve the church.

To exalt the position and role of laymen in the work of the church.

To see that leaders are trained in churchmanship and in the knowledge of their specific task.

Usually, the nominating committee is amazed both at the insights present in the group and at the magnitude of the task before it. As a result of such a free and open discussion by the committee members, they begin to *feel* the scope of their task, as well as the resources available to deal with it. Since it is *their own* work analysis, they will be likely to accept it as both valid and relevant. Such an opening session almost invariably involves all members of the group in the discussion at some point, and thus a feeling of "belonging" and being a part of the group will be experienced. This is a very important result of a first meeting. It is also likely that an interest in the work of the nominating committee as a worthwhile task has been stimulated. In short, this first session should help the committee grasp the scope and significance of its work, relate them to one another around a common task, and thus motivate them to further functioning. Other working groups of the church might well follow this same approach in their opening meetings or in seeking to revive a non-functioning committee.

In its second session the nominating committee might well begin to discuss in detail the meaning and implications of the items listed in its first session. This process may have to be continued into other sessions, as well. Whenever an idea is accepted the committee will want to make plans for following it through, including assigning responsibility for its completion. Whenever the task of evaluating all ideas is completed and assignments have been made, the committee is ready to work out an order of procedure for future meetings. One committee decided on the following list of questions to be considered at future meetings as the "pegs" on which it would hang the various study and research assignments.

1. What jobs are needed in our church? (A job analysis of church

jobs, with simplification and elimination of duplication was the motive.)

2. What are the qualities of Christian leadership desired in laymen serving the church?

3. How can the nominating committee become aware of the leadership potential within the church? (Report of talent survey, leadership study, etc.)

4. What nominating procedures within the committee will assure the selection of the most qualified persons?

5. How can the committee best secure the consent to serve of those being nominated?

6. What can the nominating committee do to insure a proper training program for those accepting leadership responsibilities? The approach to handling each of these questions will be considered in some detail as a means of illustrating the functioning of this crucial committee.

What jobs are needed in the life of the church? The answer to this question is an inescapable one for a nominating committee. This question implies a prior consideration of why the church exists, since it is impossible to evaluate the validity of any job apart from measuring it against its contribution to the purpose and task of the church. This basic consideration requires both study and discussion on the part of the entire committee. The depth and seriousness with which this exploration is pursued will determine the effectiveness of this committee. The nominating committee with a clear-cut concept of what the church is will find itself in a strong position to move the local church from where it is to where it ought to be. The proper guidelines for practical decisions are anchored here.

After examining the purpose of the church, the task of determining the needed job responsibilities begins by becoming familiar with certain given factors. Every denomination requires a certain structure and the creation of specified offices and committees. In some instances, there are options to be exercised by the local congregation as to size or possible combinations of responsibilities. These need to be carefully considered, especially by the small church seeking to simplify its structure. A list of offices and committees now operating needs to be examined carefully since it may have omitted some required offices or provided for overlapping and duplicating committees. All nominations should be functional; that is, the committee or office should have *necessary* work to do. No committee should be renamed simply because it existed last year. One church renominated its "Farm and Home Committee" for more than ten years after the last farmer had left the church. Committees with similar or overlapping duties are often found in the realm of the care of church property. Some churches wonder why the trustees never meet, and yet they set up separate committees on "insurance," "parsonage," "janitor supplies," and "remodeling" or "building." With nearly all their responsibilities for church property parceled out to independent committees, what reason do the trustees have for meeting? Before nominating any person for a particular job, every job and committee in the church ought to be carefully studied by the nominating committee to understand both its significance and the details involved in carrying out its task. All this needs to be done in an atmosphere of free exchange of ideas, with decisions reached by consensus. One group developed the form below as a guide to discussion and as a means of recording its decisions relative to each job or committee in the church.[14]

Job Analysis

Position or committee _____

Leadership and/or members necessary _____

_____

What is the purpose of this job? _____

_____

Where does it fit into the total purpose and program of the church? _____

_____

_____

What other tasks are related to it? _____

_____

What are the chief duties of the chairman? _____

_____

How much time would be involved in doing the task well?
Chairman? _____

Committee members? _____

Should this job be eliminated, or combined with some other
job? _____

_____

Should its program be expanded? _____

What new responsibilities or concerns should be added? _____

_____

_____

What is the recommended tenure?
Chairman _____

Members _____

Why _____

Final recommendation for leadership?

Date _____

Only when the nominating committee has thus evaluated every committee and job in the church will it have a sufficient understanding of the work of the church to be able to select leaders to carry out these various responsibilities.

Before considering specific persons for various jobs, the committee might well ask, "What are the qualities of Christian leadership desired in laymen serving the church?" The answer to this question will again emerge from group discussion. The experience of spelling out their feelings about the qualities implied in Christian leadership will provide the necessary context for naming particular persons later on. Every nominating committee has to assume some standards for Christian leadership, even when they are unconscious or unspoken. It is much more helpful for a group to try to verbalize its feelings on this matter and to seek a common understanding from which to make personal nominations.

One group came up with this list of qualities required for Christian leadership:

Qualities Required for Christian Leadership [15]

Personal commitment to Jesus Christ

Love of Christ's church

A genuine love of people

The desire and ability to grow in understanding the Christian faith

The desire and ability to grow in one's relationships to people

The ability to work with others

Daily exemplification of Christian habits and ideals, including church attendance

Possess an outgoing, mature personality

One who is not easily discouraged

A person with the courage of his convictions

Possess talent in line with the proposed task

Possess a willingness to accept and carry out responsibility

Be a person who is respected in the church and community

The shared experience of discussing these qualities of Christian leadership is of greater value than the particular list of qualities any group may develop. The experience gives a common measuring rod to be applied to individuals when the time comes for suggesting names for jobs. This experience will raise the level of nominations made by the group.

We now come to the consideration of how the nominating committee can become aware of the leadership potential within the church. The committee needs first of all to become aware of the present leadership situation in the church. At this point the subcommittee appointed earlier to study church leadership should report its findings on the number of jobs presently held by each lay person in the church (including those with no responsibility), an analysis of the tenure of job holders, and a breakdown on leadership according to sex, age, and the distance of residence from the church. This information can be charted or graphed and put into the hands of each committee member. On the basis of this information, the nominating committee may want to recommend some policy guidelines relative to tenure of office, number of offices that may be held by one person, proper proportion of leadership positions to be distributed to each age group or the new members in the church, or some other item the study may reveal that needs attention.

The nominating committee still faces the question of how it can become aware of the leadership potential of particular persons in the church. How can it unveil the hidden potential in many members or motivate to active service the known abilities of the indifferent? The solution to this problem is not simple. Many means must be used to make the committee aware of the leadership capacities of all the people of the church. One resource is the pastor's knowledge of the interests and abilities of persons on the basis of his pastoral contacts with them. Another is the personal knowledge of each member of the nominating committee, each of whom has intimate knowledge of some persons not known to others. Further help may come from persons now working in church groups, who may know of persons interested in serving in that type of work. Then, too, there always are a few who tell their friends of their desire to serve in a particular way. Church members should be invited to pass along such information to the committee.

Even when all these methods are used, there are many persons about whom the committee has little or no information. Is there any comprehensive, systematic way of discovering the interests and abilities of all members of the church? This is a difficult task, but

205

not an impossible one. For instance, some form of "Stewardship of Service Indicator" may be developed and used effectively, even though one-hundred-percent response and accuracy of reporting are almost an impossibility. Such an instrument may be designed which lists all the task needs of the church, and each member is asked to indicate his degree of interest and willingness to serve in each category. Even in the smallest church, some unknown interests and abilities will be uncovered; and the larger the church, the more essential such an up-to-date instrument becomes. When a "Stewardship of Service Indicator" is to be used, best results usually are obtained when the nominating committee draws up an instrument tailor-made for the particular church, listing only existing service opportunities and needs. If a standard form is to be purchased, it should be chosen carefully with the local church needs in mind. The following form was drawn up and used in one of the writer's churches. Experience indicates there is value in recording varying degrees of interest in each task.

Stewardship of Talent Indicator

Name _____ Date _____

Address _____

Telephone number _____ Marital Status _____

Date of Birth _____ Occupation _____

Education: high school ___, college ___, other ___, field of study _____.

Instructions

Please check all revelant columns for each item. If you have no experience or interest in any item, leave all columns blank.

Previous experience: indicates you have served in this capacity in the past.

Currently active: indicates the responsibilities you are now filling.

Serve if needed: indicates areas in which you would be willing to serve currently if needed and the proper training provided.

Future service: indicates areas in which you have interest and in which you would consider serving at some future date.

Service Areas	Previous Experience	Currently Active	Serve If Needed	Future Interest
Worship				
Usher				
Greeter				
Arrange altar flowers				
Provide memorial flowers				
Communion steward				
Worship committee member				
Music committee				
Read scripture				
Conduct service				
Lay speaker				
Nursery attendant during worship				
Educational Work				
Teach:				
Nursery				
Kindergarten				
Primary				
Junior				
Junior High				
High School				
Adults				
Assistant teacher				
Substitute teacher				
Help with special programs				
Pianist				
Vacation church school				
Attend adult study groups				
Nursery school visitor				
Home department visitor				
Department superintendent				
General Church School superintendent				
Secretarial and clerical help				
Librarian				
Youth group counselor				
Junior high				
High school				
Older youth				
Boy Scout work				
Junior choir director				
Youth choir director				
Camp counselor				
Operate audio-visual equipment				

Service Areas	Previous Experience	Currently Active	Serve If Needed	Future Interest
Evangelism				
Visitation of prospective members				
Visitation of inactive members				
Member of spiritual renewal study or discussion group				
Serve as fellowship friend for members				
Neighborhood unit or zone leader				
Provide transportation to worship services				
Evangelism committee member				
Visit sick				
Visit shut-in				
Missions and Christian Outreach				
Participate in missions or social concerns group				
Lead missions or social concerns study group				
Work in projects for community betterment				
Missions committee member				
Christian social concerns				
Committee member				
Prepare mailings				
Keep literature rack up-to-date				
Read and select for distribution new printed materials in field				
Stewardship and Finance				
Visitor for finance campaign				
Stewardship and Finance Commission member				
Church treasurer				
Church financial secretary				
Director, every member canvass				
Trainer of visitors				

Service Areas	Previous Experience	Currently Active	Serve if Needed	Future Interest
Trustee				
Building committee member				
Tither				
Proportionate giver				
Music				
Adult choir				
Children's choir				
Youth choir				
Choir director				
Organist				
Pianist				
Music committee member				
Vocal soloist				
Fellowship song leader				
Play musical instrument (Name _____)				
Administrative Leadership				
Serve on Official Board				
Serve as commission chairman				
Lay leader				
Committee chairman (Name _____)				
Auditor				
Special service (Name_____)				
Clerical and Publicity				
Typing				
Mimeographing				
Full-time employment as church secretary				
Addressing, folding, mailing materials				
Telephoning				
Report church news to local paper				
Work on parish newspaper				
Make posters and announcements				
Printer				

Service Areas	Previous Experience	Currently Active	Serve if Needed	Future Interest
General				
Slide or movie projection				
Transportation				
Baby-sitting				
Assist with church suppers				
Paint or repair church property				
Cleaning				
Recreation leader				
Art work				
Photography				
Drama group				

One of the best printed Stewardship of Service Records is available from the Board of Lay Activities of The Methodist Church.[16] It is comprehensive in the tasks covered; it gathers useful personal information related to church service; it can be easily filed; and those checking an interest in any given task can easily be identified by an ingenious and simple punching device. The holes near the edge of the card are punched out to the edge when an interest in the task is indicated. By inserting a wire or ice pick into the holes, all cards not so punched will be lifted out and all those remaining in the file are those persons indicating an interest in the particular task. Twelve blank spaces are provided for the local church to insert its own special needs not covered in the standardized listing of tasks.

Administrative Assistant to Pastor
Church Business Administration
Finance Secretary
Church Secretary
Office Worker
Choir Director
Organist
Custodial Work
Food Service Supervising
Parish Visitor
Director of Religious Education
Youth Worker

VOLUNTEER CHURCH STAFF

Visit Non-Members
Sick Visitation
Join the Church
Zone leaders
Church Host and Hostess
Greeter
Church School Officer
Department Superintendent
Recreation Leader
Youth Camp Counselor
Weekday Church School
Vacation Church School
Adult Teaching
Senior High Teaching
Junior High Teaching
Junior Teaching
Primary Teaching
Kindergarten Teaching
Nursery Teaching
Nursery Home Visitor
Story Telling
Craft Teaching
Work with Senior High MYF
Work with Junior High MYF
Teaching Additional Sessions
Secretarial Work
General Office Work
Typing
Telephone Work
Library Work
Help with Mailing
Posters and Displays
Assist in Counting Offering
Mimeographing
Church Newsletter
Will do work at home
Use of home for meetings
Car for transportation
Nursery Attendant

VOLUNTEER SERVICE TASKS

Name of Church________
Name________
Tasks Assigned and Year________

VOLUNTEER SERVICE TASKS

VOLUNTEER SERVICE TASKS

Study Discussion Groups
Adult Choir
Youth Choir
Children's Choir name
Boy Choir name
Music Librarian
Choir Robing
Pianist
Other Musical Instrument
Usher
Song Leader
Assisting in Worship
Religious Drama
Religious Art
Flowers for Altar
Woman's Society of Christian Service
Wesleyan Service Guild
Methodist Men
Daily Prayer
Bible Study
Lead Devotions
Lay Speaking
Scout Leadership
Food Preparation
Kitchen Help
Dining Room Help

Financial Every Member Visitation
Projectionist
Publicity
Sound Technician
Church Photographer
Lawn Care
Carpentry
Painting
Electrical Work
Plumbing
Parking Attendant
Spring Clean-up
Custodial Work
Community Social Service

1. Name _____ Marital Status: S ☐ M ☐ W ☐ Date _____

2. Address _____ Telephone ⎰ Residence _____
                                                    ⎱ Business _____

3. Change of Address _____

4. Occupations _____

5. Educational Background: High School ☐ College ☐ Business School ☐ Other ☐ Major Subjects ☐

6. Hobbies _____

7. Member of Church ☐   Methodist Men ☐   WSCS ☐   MYF ☐

8. Your Age Group: Under 21 ☐   21-30 ☐   30-40 ☐   40-50 ☐   50-60 ☐   Over 60 ☐

9. Prior Church Experience _____

10. _____

11. _____

12. Church Leadership Training Received and Dates _____

13. _____

14. _____

15. Comments _____

_____

_____

_____

_____

The manner in which a Stewardship of Service Indicator is presented to the membership will have much to do with how honestly and completely it is filled out. Experience indicates that it is unwise to mail this instrument to the membership or to distribute it at a Sunday service. Some form of personal distribution and personal conversation is essential. Three ways of presenting this form have proved almost equally effective. If the parish is divided into neighborhood family groups of about ten families in each geographic area, each group could meet in a home and discuss the whole area of lay service in the church, examine the specific instrument, and then take time to fill it out right there. Those not present are then later called on by the group leader. One church broadened the finance visitation to an authentic stewardship visitation, and the calling teams presented the Stewardship of Service Indicator in every home and received this pledge of time and talent before asking for the pledge of material substance. Such calling takes time, and visitors will be able to make only about half as many calls as usual, but it is very helpful and effective. A third procedure involves lay calling during Lent as a part of the Week of Dedication emphasis. The callers left the Stewardship of Service Indicator and asked that it be filled in and brought to the dedication service at the church to be placed on the altar as a symbolic dedication of the congregation to God. The original callers called back to pick up those not brought to the service. Some form of personal presentation and conversation about the Stewardship of Service Indicator are absolutely essential for satisfactory results.

The information gained in an initial Stewardship of Service survey must be kept up-to-date. All new members should be asked to fill in the instrument as a part of their membership training. As new information is discovered about any member, his card will need to be revised. The responsibility of keeping the file current should be assigned to one person, a member of the nominating committee.

A brief word needs to be said about cataloging and applying the information received. A master card should be prepared for each job category, listing all persons who indicated interest in that area of service. In this way, the names of all persons available for any given area of service can be seen at a glance. It needs to be kept in mind that the Stewardship of Service Indicator will be used as only one means of discovering capable persons for church leadership, and should be used in conjunction with other sources of information, as previously discussed.

When the nominating committee has clearly in mind the needed tasks, the qualifications for leadership, and the interests and abilities of the membership, it is ready to set up the procedures of nomination that will assure the selection of the most qualified person for each position. Discussion of nominating procedures should precede the making of any nominations. The whole group should give its attention to this important matter. Frequently, it has been the practice to simply receive verbal nominations by committee members for each position as it is being considered. A discussion of this nomination method by the group will usually reveal some of its serious handicaps. The method tends to stifle the consideration of more than one or two names for any position as it makes additional nominations appear derogatory of the first nomination or of the person making the nomination. Such a procedure also gives the advantage to the persons on the nominating committee who think and/or speak quickly but not always wisely. Under this procedure, the pastor often is tempted to speak up quickly before nominations are closed and thus tends to dominate the committee, or else he may withhold nominations because he does not want to appear to question the nominations submitted by laymen.

Some nominating committees have wrestled with this question and have developed the following approach. A written list of possible nominees for a position is secured by a secret ballot of every committee member and is placed before the committee for discussion before nominations are finalized. For example, if the leader needed is a chairman of the education committee, the first step would be for every member of the nominating committee to write down on a blank card the names of three persons he believes to be the best qualified. This is not a vote for nomination but a method of securing the individual creative thinking of every member of the group. A list of all the names appearing on any card is placed on a blackboard and discussed by the nominating committee. This allows the pastor, as well as every lay person, to get his suggestion before the group without appearing competitive with suggestions of other group members. After full discussion, the committee then selects their first three choices for the office. By selecting three persons, a preference order is already established in case the first choice cannot serve. It needs to be stressed continually that all evaluations of persons within this committee are strictly confidential and must not be discussed outside the committee. One committee prepared a work sheet to be used in this process of selecting the three most qualified persons for each office.

Personnel Analysis [17]

Position to be filled _____

Who are the three most qualified persons in the church for this position? _____

_____

Which of these three is now occupied with other responsibilities?

_____

Which of the two remaining has more of the qualities needed for this task? _____

Does he work well with a committee? _____

Is he inclined to dominate and "do it all himself"? _____

Has he the faculty of sharing responsibility? _____

Are his interests and experience in line with this work? _____

Is he cooperative? _____

Does he do a piece of work thoroughly? _____

What is his record in doing church work? _____

_____

Is he resourceful and imaginative? _____

Does he have a reasonably pleasing personality? _____

Is his temperament even? _____

Date _____

Experience indicates that it is wise to give first attention to nominating the individual church officers and the chairmen of all committees. This gives first attention to placing the most qualified leaders in positions of greatest responsibility. It also places in office those persons best able to enlist others in the task at hand.

Members of the several committees also should be named from written suggestions by all members of the nominating committee. From the total number of persons suggested, the desired number should be selected for nomination. Often committees will have both *ex officio* members and members to be nominated at large. The following work sheet developed by one Methodist church is a very good example of a helpful working tool for nominating commission members.

The Commission on Membership and Evangelism
(See ¶¶ 220-223 of the *Doctrines and Discipline of The Methodist Church.*)

Duties

To seek out the unsaved and the unchurched in the community, and to exercise all diligence that they may be led into a saving knowledge of Jesus Christ and into the fellowship of the church. . . . To seek out the inactive and negligent members of the local church, and to use all laudable means to restore them to active participation in the church's life and fellowship.

To lead the local church in the **Period of Spiritual Enrichment**, . . . to promote attendance upon the public worship of God, to arrange for the visitation of strangers, . . . to initiate . . . prayer groups . . . and retreats, to encourage private and family worship, . . . to distribute evangelistic and devotional literature. . . .

To promote organized visitation evangelism, . . . to encourage such groups as The Twelve, the Fisherman's Club, . . . to take a religious census of the community, . . . to assist the pastor . . . in training classes for church membership, . . . [and] assimilating new members, . . . to review the membership rolls of the church.

Membership	Suggested Nominees	Committee Nomination
Chairman	————	————
The following persons are named *ex officio* members by the *Discipline:*		
Pastor		————
Minister of evangelism		————
Church lay leader		————
Membership secretary		————
Secretary of spiritual life of the Woman's Society of Christian Service		————
Membership cultivation superintendent of the church school		————
Representative of Methodist Men		————
Chairman of Christian witness of the Methodist Youth Fellowship		————
Such members of the District Committee on Evangelism as have membership in the local church		————
Representatives from the other commissions (if they are not otherwise represented)		————
Not fewer than six members elected at large	————	————
	————	
	————	————
	————	
	————	
	————	————
	————	
	————	
	————	————
	————	
	————	
	————	————
	————	
	————	
	————	————

One final word is called for regarding procedures. In The Methodist Church it is customary to present a single slate of officers from the nominating committee with the privilege and invitation for nominations from the floor of the electing body. One practical reason for not presenting a double slate is that few churches, if any, can afford to have half their qualified leadership idle during the year. Except in cases of chairmen and individual offices, nominations from the floor can be added to most committees without withdrawing other names. Obviously, great importance is attached to the work of the nominating committee, and for this reason it has been treated in detail here.

When the nominating committee has agreed upon a slate of candidates, it must still secure their consent to serve if elected. If this is not done, persons may be elected who are unwilling to serve, and the work of the church will suffer. Too often contact is made with the nominees by mail, telephone, or mimeographed list. The only effective contact is a personal, face-to-face visit. To allow time for such contacts, nominations should be completed one month before elections. The following plan of contacting nominees has proved effective. The pastor and secretary of the nominating committee call together on all individually nominated church officers and chairmen of committees. The callers should explain in detail the procedures of the nominating committee in arriving at its final choices and should outline the duties and requirements of the office under consideration. When this is done, there will be a high degree of acceptance of responsibility. The proposed new chairman should then team up with some member of the nominating committee to call on the other nominees of the committee involved. This not only assures a high degree of acceptance but also enables the new chairman to get acquainted with the members of the committee and builds a helpful bond in beginning the work of the new year.

The final question before the nominating committee is what can be done to insure a proper training program for those called to responsibility. It is certainly unfair to place members in positions of leadership without offering help in equipping them for their task. Although such training is not the direct responsibility of the nomi-

218

nating committee, it does have an obligation to those it has recruited to see that training is offered. Let the following four brief suggestions suffice here. The nominating committee can:

1. Talk with all officers and chairmen, when getting their consent to serve, about the importance of training for themselves and their group.

2. Request the church Board to establish a training program adequate to the needs, including the required budgetary support.

3. Give a list of previous training opportunities to new officers as suggestive to what might be done in the future.

4. Volunteer to assist the pastor in planning a church officers' retreat.

The educational values of this approach to the work of the nominating committee can hardly be overestimated. Their understanding of the real nature and mission of the church and their exposure to the many facets of the work of the local church provide a depth of understanding that will make them better Christians and churchmen wherever they are for years to come. One layman said to me, "This experience has given me a pastor's-eye view of the church." By this he meant that he had seen the church in a comprehensive context rather than from the vantage point of a layman acquainted with a few areas of the church's life. The experience of serving on the nominating committee should be one of personal growth for the members, as well as furnishing an opportunity to serve the church in performing an important task.

3. Train Laymen to Fulfill the Responsibilities Given Them.

The training of laymen for the responsibilities of the Christian service they have been given is an inescapable responsibility. The training itself may be either offered by the local church or be made available to the local church by an outside agency. Usually, a church will want to make use of both types of training.

Every church will offer certain regular study opportunities to laymen, with a view to increasing their understanding of the Christian faith. This should be seen as training for Christian service and witness which should be an outgrowth of one's understanding of his faith. Such study opportunities might include adult church school classes, fellowship-discussion *koinonia* groups, and short-term courses (six to thirteen weeks) on the Bible or Christian beliefs offered semiannually by the pastor. Other, more specific training courses should build upon this foundation, and those assuming leadership positions in the church should be urged to avail themselves of these opportunities to enlarge their understanding of the Christian faith. More than likely those previously participating in such courses will be moved to get into some form of leadership responsibility as a result.

Experience indicates the wisdom of planning an annual spiritual life retreat for all officers, chairmen, and presidents of organizations in the congregation. Such retreats often run from Saturday afternoon through Sunday afternoon. The purposes of such a retreat are to deepen the Christian commitment of each person, to help all leaders arrive at a common understanding of the goals and objectives of the church, and to come to know one another personally. The work of each individual group or committee must be seen in the light of the whole mission of the church. Through sharing in a deepened personal commitment and a united purpose for the church, each person will return better equipped and motivated to lead his own group. Such a retreat should consist primarily of study and discussion of carefully selected Biblical passages, with periods for worship, prayer, and silent meditation. Another important aspect of such a retreat is the opportunity for the various laymen assuming leadership roles to get acquainted with one another as persons, as well as come to an appreciation of the spiritual sensitivity and insights of their brethren. Such a retreat will do much to motivate and inspire individual leaders to more fruitful leadership.

Beyond this, there must be some specialized training opportunities for specific tasks. These will vary from year to year, depending on the needs. Usually, the education committee will offer training for teaching in the several age groups in the church school. Particular tasks, such as visitation evangelism and the every member canvass, will require specific training periods for those participating. There will be years when large numbers of new committee members or other circumstances will call for specialized training for nearly any church group. This might include ushers, the pastoral relations committee, the parsonage committee, the committees on worship, evangelism, education, stewardship, missions, social concerns, or even the trustees. Such training usually is of a short-term nature and is focused on concrete needs of the group involved. All chairmen ought to be alert to the need and type of training called for by their particular group. It may be possible to coordinate all such specific training into a church-wide training school. When possible, there is much to be said for such an approach.

In contrast to the special training sessions, it is often possible to plan for in-service training opportunities for laymen. Such training takes place in the regular performance of duty and in the regular meetings of the group. Such training has the advantage of not calling for additional meeting times and also necessarily requires that the training be relevant, since it takes place in an actual working situation. The training of church school teachers through their use as assistant teachers and as members of a teaching team is an example of this type of training. The use of an experienced chief usher on a given Sunday morning offers a real opportunity for in-service training for less experienced ushers. Although advance training is needed for ushers, there are some things that will be learned only in the process of ushering. Very rewarding experiences are possible through brief training periods at regular church board meetings. For instance, a twelve-minute period in each board meeting may be used to present the work of some committee of the board or to bring information on some aspect of the church at large. It is a helpful experience for both the board and the committee chairman to have to outline to the board the objectives of his committee in twelve minutes. Sometimes, charts may be prepared to present important information in graphic and interesting form. Occasionally, a filmstrip may be shown, either for inspiration or for stimulation. One board divided itself into small groups to discuss assigned questions. The author's experience has been that if careful preparation and imagination are used, and if the brief time limit is observed, such in-service training will do much to lift the understanding of the board over a period of months.

Another approach to training laymen for service is that of personal guidance. Although time consuming, it usually is effective and sometimes necessary. A new church school teacher may need the personal attention of an experienced person to help prepare a lesson, observe the teaching session, and evaluate the experience. A commission chairman may need several personal conversations with the pastor or an experienced layman to gain an understanding of how he is to function as a leader. The time involved would prevent the application of this type in-service training on a wide scale by the pastor, but it has a greater range of usefulness when laymen work with one another.

Leadership training in the local church should include individual reading and study. This should be encouraged by making regular suggestions for reading to the church membership through the parish paper, bulletin announcements, occasional book reviews, and the use of the church library where one exists. Conversations during pastoral calls often can focus personal attention on the areas of interest or need of the parishioner. Surely every church officer should be supplied with the manuals, periodicals, and leadership material available in his field from the denomination, and should be carefully introduced to their content.

There often are excellent opportunities for training beyond the local church level. The quality and availability of such training will determine the type and amount of training a local church should attempt on its own. By and large, the closer to home the training center is, the more likely local people are to respond to it.

Community training may be offered on an ecumenical basis through the Council of Churches or the ministerial association. In some communities, these offerings are extensive and their leadership is of much higher quality than any one congregation could provide. Sometimes, two or three congregations of similar background will pool their resources to set up a common training school. For the small church with limited teaching resources for a leadership school, such an arrangement may be very helpful.

Many denominations hold leadership schools on a district or regional basis. Often a dozen or more nearby churches set up a common "churchmanship school" as one such venture was called. This particular school met on a college campus on six successive Sundays and offered classes for the following groups:

Committee on education
Committee on stewardship and finance
Committee on membership and evangelism
Committee on social concerns
Committee on missions
Committee on worship
Trustees
The lay leader
Pastoral relations committee
The building committee
Church music committee
Parsonage committee
Ushers
Audio-visual committee
Classes for workers with each age group in the church school (nursery, kindergarten, primary, junior, junior high, high school, adult)

No local church could offer as extensive a school. The leadership was drawn from the pastoral and lay leadership of all the churches involved. In many of these classes, there is real value in laymen being exposed to laymen of other congregations dealing with problems similar to their own. The exchange of ideas enlarges the vision of all. Any group of churches could set up a less pretentious leadership school and deal with those problems that are of present concern to them. The wise congregation will look beyond itself for leadership training opportunities.

Until recently little attention was given to training laymen for their daily witness to society in their vocational and secular life. The church's attention had been focused on training laymen to carry out the program of the church. A growing understanding of the mission of the church and of the meaning of the laity has brought into focus once again the importance of the church's witness to the world. Laymen have been saying recently that they desperately want and need help for their task of witnessing to the world. They are currently banding together in various kinds of small groups all over the world to train and equip themselves for their rediscovered mission. The Scriptures are being seriously and diligently studied; the meaning of discipleship is being explored; and the question of what it means to be a Christian in particular situations and vocations is being analyzed. Lawyers, doctors, editors, government officials, teachers, housewives, laborers, employers, and others are seriously searching for what is involved in being a Christian disciple in their specific vocational situation and are reaching out individually and collectively for a strength beyond their own to be able to make the required witness.

■ ■ ■ Notes

1. Niebuhr, *The Purpose of the Church and Its Ministry*, p. 83.

2. Albert Beaven, *The Local Church* (New York: The Abingdon Press, 1937), p. 166.

3. Raines, *New Life in the Church*, p. 90. Used by permission.

4. Niebuhr, *The Purpose of the Church and Its Ministry*, p. 82.

5. Paul Maves in an address to the Wisconsin Area Pastors' School, August, 1957.

6. Bishop Ralph Alton in an address to the East Wisconsin Conference of The Methodist Church, May, 1961.

7. Trueblood, *The Company of the Committed.*

8. *Ibid.*, pp. 72-73.

9. Raines, *New Life in the Church*, p. 141. Used by permission.

10. Gordon Cosby, "Church Renewal," in *The Christian Advocate*, September 12, 1963, p. 8. Used by permission.

11. Thomas J. Mullen, *The Renewal of the Ministry* (Nashville: Abingdon Press, 1963).

12. This option of holding an annual church conference (congregational meeting of all members eighteen years of age and over) instead of a Fourth Quarterly Conference is available to every local church if authorized by a previous Quarterly Conference, under paragraphs 197 and 198 of the *Doctrines and Discipline of The Methodist Church, 1964.*

13. Based on *Better Leaders for Your Church* by Weldon Crossland (Nashville: Abingdon Press, 1955) , pp. 25-26.

14. *Ibid.,* based on p. 37.

15. *Ibid.,* based on p. 22.

16. By permission of the General Board of Lay Activities of The Methodist Church.

17. *Better Leaders for Your Church,* based on p. 38.

CHAPTER IX

STRENGTHEN THE CHURCH
BY COORDINATED,
COMPREHENSIVE PLANNING

A. The Necessity and Value of Comprehensive Planning

Sound church administration requires comprehensive, coordinated planning. The church can only achieve its purpose when every segment of it is seen as a part of a larger whole with a single mission. Since the church is the "Body of Christ," all its members and working groups must be united in making a common witness. Our definition of church administration stated earlier includes "moving in a coherent and comprehensive manner toward providing such experiences as will enable the church to utilize all her resources . . . in the fulfillment of its mission." There must be a mutual supportiveness in all activities if the church is to achieve its mission of making known God's love. This will not take place apart from skillfully coordinated and comprehensive planning.

It is easily observed that most churches do not engage in such systematic long-range planning. Perhaps this is one reason why the church has not been able to reach and change society more effectively. Many local churches operate on hand-to-mouth planning. They consider the pressing problems of the moment at each board meeting without placing them in proper perspective in relationship to either past or future. The result is that expediency of the shallowest kind determines most decisions. Furthermore, the aim of relating current problems to past experiences or future responsibilities is often complicated by short-term pastorates. A rapid turnover of pastoral leadership works against the development of a long-range point of view on the part of laymen and ministers alike. Too often a church sets out to do only what can be completed during the present pastorate rather than seriously preparing for the needs of the more distant future. This lack of long-range perspective applies to denominations, also. The lack of coherent strategy in locating and relocating churches in the inner city in recent years is a case in point. The overabundance of very small rural churches likewise illustrates the same point. In spite of its importance, careful planning is often conspicuous by its absence in the church. Since this is so often the case, a discussion of the necessity and value of comprehensive planning seems in order.

1. A Unified Purpose Can Be Achieved Only When All Segments of the Life of the Church See Themselves as a Part of a Larger Whole with a Single Goal.

Since the mission of the church is making known God's love, some way must be found to bring a common understanding of this goal to all church groups so that their existence and activities contribute to this end. Far too often the various groups in the church see themselves as independent entities with their own reason for being. It is not uncommon for such groups to get lost in the lesser goals of their own activities and concerns and even to lose their sense of relationship to the congregation.

When any group goes its own way, it is unhealthy for both the group and the church. An independent woman's society for instance may set up a program, budget, and way of operation separate from the church and all its other organizations. It may involve many women in its activities and yet be useless or even harmful with respect to the mission of the church. The same can be said of youth groups, men's clubs, young adults, the church school, and all other groups, including the church board, trustees, and standing commit-

227

tees. Apart from the contribution to purpose, the existence of regular meetings, many activities, and growing memberships mean nothing. Unless some kind of careful, coordinated planning takes place, a church may even find that each of its groups has mounted its own horse and is riding off in a different direction, literally tearing the church apart.

A common understanding of purpose requires that careful attention be given to coordinated planning in the life of the church. It is essential for the whole church to understand what it should be trying to do. Careful plans then need to be made so that the energy of every group and committee is spent in moving toward the same goal, each performing a necessary function in support of the others. Careful, comprehensive planning leads a church to set up goals, to face the question of what a church ought to be, and to define *its* responsibilities in its own particular setting. Having defined administration as providing the means for fulfilling the purpose of the group it serves, we see that it is evident that such coordinated planning is an inescapable concern of the church administrator.

2. Isolated Individual Decisions and Commitments Often Influence Future Plans, Even When They Are Not Intended to Do So.

Today's decisions often limit tomorrow's actions, even when the decisions are not made with a view to their future effect. Many a church building has been remodeled extensively without looking at the long-range needs of congregation or community. Questions of relocation, merger with another church, or the need for new facilities are too often decided without consideration of how the present decision may hamper or burden the work of the congregation in the future.

One church voted to lock its lounge and kitchen to its youth, even on their regular meeting nights and for special events. This move "protected" the church property, but the inadequate facilities available for youth meetings clearly conveyed to the youth the lack of understanding and concern for them by the church. Not only did the youth program decline and die out at the time, but in later years there were many hostile and bitter young parents in the community who had been part of that rejected youth group.

The most difficult evangelistic task in the author's experience was created when a congregation had chosen to ignore for a quarter of a century a large area of low-income housing apartments in the community. The attitude had become strongly entrenched that only middle-income families were welcome in the church. When the church decided really to seek to minister to the people around it, its verbal invitations extended through calling fell on understandably deaf ears. An earlier decision to ignore the neighborhood complicated a later decision to try to serve it. Whether or not a church consciously makes long-range plans, its decisions of the moment have long-range implications. This being the case, a church needs to plan now with a view to moving the church toward what it ought to be in the future.

3. When Careful Planning Is Lacking, Groups in the Church Often Become Competitive with One Another and Duplicate One Another's Work.

Even when the various groups in the church may share a common understanding of purpose, their activities may be wasteful through duplication or even competition. Recently, one church discovered that four of its groups had independently planned a series of educational meetings involving adults in the church for the same month, two of them for the same evenings of the week. Such a concentration of adult study opportunities finds several adults having to choose between two or more groups to which they ought to go, and also finds these groups overlapping in their efforts to meet the need of adult study in the church. In other cases it might even be worse in that the competing activities offered may have no real relationship to the mission and purpose of the church, as for instance when a served public supper competes with the men's club movie on championship football. The church that does not plan carefully to avoid such shameful waste of time and energy is inviting chronic fatigue and frustration among its members. Many a church

229

is its own worst enemy as its groups compete for the loyalty, leadership, and energy of its church members.

4. *Without Coordinated Planning, Groups in the Church May Come to Feel They Are Ends in Themselves and Lose Their Sense of Perspective in Relation to the Church.*

Experience indicates that each church group tends to exalt its own importance and to become self-centered. Too often groups act as though the church exists to serve them rather than recognizing that they exist to serve the church. One custodian's committee felt that the whole church ought to revolve around the convenience of the janitor in terms of the setting of the time and place of meetings, the use of property, etc., and that this committee ought to be consulted on all such matters. A similar loss of perspective numbs the awareness of many groups toward the proper tasks and concerns of the congregation.

Every committee and organization in the church needs to see itself in relation to all other groups in the church and to the mission of the church. Only careful, coordinated planning involving every such group can provide the proper matrix for establishing a clear understanding of how each segment of the church may contribute to a unified effort toward a common goal.

5. *Long-range Planning Is Demanded by the Magnitude of the Church's Task.*

The church is called to communicate God's love to each new day and generation. This will not take place without careful attention being given to how the church can come alive and become meaningful in each given situation. The magnitude of this challenge calls for the best possible strategies the church can muster. The inescapable conclusion is that every congregation must plan its work intelligently and prayerfully.

The world's needs are too many and complex to be fulfilled in any one year or even in the next few years; therefore, a long-range view is demanded of the church. We live in a world of new nations and of increasing nationalism as well as in the world of the United Na-
230

tions seeking unity and peace. The whole area of human rights and dignity is being explored as to its meaning in the realm of politics, education, economics, race, and other social relationships. We live in a world of extremes politically and economically, where exploding tensions could result in nuclear annihilation. Our world is filled with lonely, confused people searching for some meaning in life. All this adds up to a mission so diverse and baffling that nothing short of a careful long-range, coordinated approach can possibly be adequate, either at local, denominational, or ecumenical levels.

For the reasons cited above, it seems clear that sound church administration must give attention to strengthening the church through coordinated, comprehensive planning as a means of harnessing the church's energy in an effective way as it seeks to fulfill its mission. Such planning usually will take place on three levels in the local church: long-range planning looking several years ahead, annual planning, and a continuous coordination of plans. Each of these areas will be examined in some detail.

B. An Approach to Long-range Planning in the Congregation

In my own ministry, few experiences have been more rewarding and beneficial to the church than engaging in serious, long-range planning. Such an experience requires a church to state its objectives and clarify its goals as it seeks to set forth what it believes a church ought to be in a particular community. These objectives provide a standard of measurement for proposed future actions and a perspective for separating the essential from the trivial. Perhaps most significantly of all, long-range planning provides the spark of motivation to replace an attitude of indifference or despair with one of hope, so that the congregation begins to move in a significant way toward becoming a real church. Long-range planning, then, becomes a means of renewal in the life of a congregation.

An actual case study of the long-range planning experience of a particular congregation will be reported and it will also serve as an illustration of the application of the five steps in the administrative process: recognition of need, planning, organizing, implementation, and evaluation. Every situation will need its own unique approach, and the example given is not intended as a "standard" approach. The basic concern is to be sufficiently specific to illustrate clearly one way to develop long-range plans. Possible alternatives will be suggested as each step is discussed.

1. How to Create a Recognition of the Need for Long-range Planning.

The church must first be made aware that there exists an area of concern that ought to claim its attention if it is really Christian. This concept of recognition of need is not to be confused with the manipulative idea that one begins by selling the church that it needs some particular program. For example, in the case at hand, the administrative process does not begin with a complete long-range program already worked out which the church is asked to vote upon and to carry out. Instead it begins with finding ways to awaken the church to the fact that it ought to be concerned about long-range planning. To attempt such planning before the need is commonly recognized is unsound.

How does a congregation become aware of the need to engage in long-range planning? This will vary from place to place, but in some way a church must be alerted to specific concerns and responsibilities that must be faced. A crisis situation of some kind may force a church to face its future whether it wants to or not. The church building may be destroyed by fire, and the question of rebuilding, relocating, or merging may force a hard, honest look at the future. Property may require a major expenditure for remodeling, and the questions of the future needs of the congregation may force a consideration of a new structure, moving to a different location, or uniting with another congregation. An expanding or shrinking population may cause a congregation to do serious long-range thinking. The changing character of the neighborhood surrounding the church may call forth a look ahead in the church's program. Neighborhoods change in racial or economic composition in the type of housing being erected, with the establishment of a college, or a new business district, or in other ways which might affect the future of a church and its program. A very practical problem such as a financial crisis may cause a local church to look not just at its momentary needs but also to seek to assess its future existence. Churches facing these and other crises can hardly escape the necessity to look ahead, to involve themselves in long-range planning.

Let us examine one church that was thrust into long-range planning because of a financial crisis. This church had historically been a "middle-upper-income" church and had for years depended upon large contributions of a few to meet the budget. These few aged and passed on. Finally, when one man died who had given 20 per cent of the previous year's budget, the church recognized a major crisis. At its next meeting the official board wisely realized that the problem was a bigger one than how to raise so many thousands of dollars by next June. It was quickly decided that the whole structure, ministry, and future of the church had to be examined with a view to determining whether the congregation had a future; if so what it ought to be doing in the next few years; and whether the needs and resources could be balanced. Two things were decided upon at that board meeting. A long-range planning committee of fourteen *ex-officio* members was set up and requested to function immediately. A second decision was to involve the entire membership in a series of neighborhood discussions to acquaint them with the situation and to ask each group to formulate a list of ideas which they thought would strengthen and challenge the church or about which they thought the church ought to be concerned.

When the families met in the thirty neighborhood groups, each group (about ten families) wrestled with the same question, "If our church were truly Christian, what should it be concerned about in the next ten years?" The groups were asked to dream out loud without out regard to financial and leadership limitations, as to what they conceived to be the Christian responsibility and ministry of their church in that community. A recorder was named for each group, and all the lists were then given to the long-range planning committee as resource material for its work. Everyone was astounded at the creative vision that was evident in the thinking of the people. Many of the suggestions did not find their way into the final plan, but nearly all the major items in the final plan were suggested in the group meetings. The most wonderful part of the experience, however, was not the ideas that came forth, but the spirit of unity and concern for the church that was evident in the lives of the people from that point on. They cared about the future of their church; they believed in it, even though it was in immediate financial trouble. From the beginning the long-range plan belonged to the congregation. Renewal was evident in increasing Sunday morning attendance, evangelistic visiting, leadership response, and financial giving long before the plan was even formulated. Participation in the planning had a beneficial effect almost at once.

The following list includes some of the neighborhood group suggestions that found their way into the final plan.

1. Give attention to deepening the spiritual life of the membership.
2. Offer multiple worship services to encourage attendance.
3. Establish a nursery to care for children during worship.
4. Find ways of reaching the surrounding neighborhood, especially the low-income housing area.
5. Establish a radio ministry beamed to the sick, shut-in, hospitals, institutions, and sanitariums in the area.
6. Reach the college youth and faculty. Establish a student program to minister to the campus two blocks away.
7. Establish a week-night youth center in the church basement.
8. Start a weekday nursery for children of working mothers.
9. Initiate regular lay visitation evangelism.
10. Establish a new adult church school class.
11. Find persons to take a recording of the worship service to shut-ins.
12. Hold a school of missions, and then establish a strong continuing missionary education program.
13. Study the feasibility of increasing the staff by adding a secretary, full-time custodian, and associate pastor or student worker.
14. Immediately remodel the chancel and repair the pipe organ or buy a new one.

15. Acquire adjacent properties for parking and expansion as they become available.

16. Add new church school facilities.

17. Secure needed items of church school equipment at once.

18. Have trustees do a complete property survey to see what items of repair are needed.

19. Tuck-point the stonework on the sanctuary.

20. Initiate a program of stewardship education and a sound financial plan for budgeting and fund raising.

The vision and insight represented in these suggestions started the long-range planning committee off with a sense of optimism and the knowledge that the congregation was behind it. The involvement of the congregation from the first, giving them a chance to recognize the need for long-range planning, is a key to understanding the remarkable way in which these plans were realized by the congregation, even surviving a change of pastors in the middle of them. In the administrative process, the principle of involving those concerned is as important as the steps in the process themselves.

There are other ways of arousing a church to recognize the need for long-range planning. Almost any board can be led to "dream out loud" about the kind of church they would like their church to become. Usually, an invitation to look at any area of the church life that needs improving, or to indicate any needs of persons or the community that ought to become the concern of the church, will bring a response. Once board members begin to share their insights, their vision, and their concerns about what a Christian church ought to be, the door to long-range planning is opened. If a board is very hesitant to express itself, there is another way to achieve the same end. After making a challenging statement on the nature and mission of the church to the entire board, the pastor may distribute paper and pencils and set aside fifteen minutes for everyone to write down his own answer to the question, "What I would like to see happen in this church in the next ten years." I once witnessed this procedure in a very apathetic congregation. When the unsigned papers were collected, and the statements read aloud and put on the blackboard by the secretary, everyone was amazed at the vision and farsightedness evidenced by the suggestions and discussed them freely. Immediately following such a session there is an opportunity to set up a long-range planning committee. The same procedure could be used in a series of neighborhood meetings and would involve an even larger segment of the congregation.

A study analysis of the current church situation is often another excellent springboard from which to launch long-range planning. Every congregation ought periodically to do a series of studies charting its past history in various aspects of its life. Ideally, such charts ought to be prepared and kept up-to-date by every congregation annually. In interpreting the meaning of the findings revealed in these studies, a church often is alerted to areas needing long-range attention, and this may launch the church into a total long-range planning program.

Studies of a local church should include an analysis of the following areas:

Membership (growth, age-sex pyramid, infant baptisms, geographic location, length of membership).

Leadership studies (age-sex distribution, number of positions, tenure of each office, distance from church, length of local church membership).

Sunday worship attendance (charted weekly from an accurate count by ushers).

Church school (membership, average attendance—total and by departments).

Missions (regular missionary giving, special projects, woman's society, and other groups, number of study or educational sessions each year).

Finances (history of giving—total, local, building, benevolences, per capita analysis, age-sex giving distribution, history of community income change, number and amount of pledges annually).

Community studies (population changes, school enrollment, neighborhood and housing changes, per capita income, community services).

When the facts for such studies are secured and transferred to

236

graphic line or bar charts, a church not only is able to see where it is and has been but can also recognize future trends. For many churches, a concern for comprehensive future planning arises out of such studies.

In more than one situation the existence of small discussion study groups has created an awareness of the need for a church to examine itself and its future. In one such instance a group had been studying Donald Miller's book, *Nature and Mission of the Church;* in another Robert Raines's book, *New Life in the Church,* proved to be equally stimulating. When even a small group of people catch a vision of the real mission of the church, they will begin to use this understanding as a yardstick against which to measure the work of the congregation. When the congregation is weighed in the balance and found wanting, there is fertile ground for a long look at how to effect the kind of change that is called for. A study group on the nature and mission of the church might well become the soil out of which an awareness of needed changes in the life of the congregation may spring.

A final suggestion for awakening a need for comprehensive planning roots in the experience of a pastor who began to discuss this question as he called on his parishioners in their homes, asking how they thought their church could better function as a Christian church in the community. He found not only that the people had ideas on the subject but that in many instances their insights were sharper than his own. A list of suggestions was compiled, and without identifying the source, a congregational meeting was held to discuss them. The gathering was divided into buzz sessions. Out of this process came a recognition that long-range planning was needed if the church were to rise to the challenge that was before it.

The first step in any approach to long-range planning is to awaken the local church to recognize a real need to engage in such a venture. Each church will arrive at this point of awareness by a different route, some of the most common avenues having been identified in this discussion. The important point is that the clearer and more widespread the recognition of need for long-range planning in the congregation, the sounder the planning is likely to be, and the surer it is to be carried out.

2. What Is Involved in Making Long-range Plans for a Congregation?

The second step in the administrative process is that of planning, in this case planning to plan. Who should be involved in a long-range planning in the local church? This is the first question to be settled before any planning can take place. The question is not as simple as might be supposed.

A small committee of three to five members is preferred by some pastors. There are certain values in a small committee that cannot be denied, one of which is efficiency in producing a completed set of long-range plans in the least possible time. Meetings can be scheduled more easily with smaller committees, and decisions can be reached more rapidly. A small committee is likely to be highly selective of people with vision who are willing to venture far beyond the general congregation. It is also likely that pastoral leadership can be more directly exerted in a small committee, although this may or may not be an advantage. There are, however, certain serious drawbacks of a small committee which seem considerably to outweigh the advantages. A small committee involves too few members of the congregation to gain the necessary representation of all viewpoints and attitudes. A realistic appraisal of congregational attitudes is important in long-range planning. A larger committee is likely to bring more insights and creative thinking into the situation because of the increased breadth of experience. In actual practice, a small committee often is composed of the pastors' ardent supporters, and the resulting plans are actually the pastor's. Such plans may be excellent when read in a mimeographed report, but may never be realized, owing to lack of general acceptance or to the pastor's moving.

Experience suggests the appointment of a large long-range planning committee of about fourteen *ex officio* members. The following personnel might well make up the committee: pastor, lay leader, chairmen of the committees on Christian education, missions, worship, membership and evangelism, stewardship and finance, and Christian social concerns, the chairman of the board, and the presidents of the trustees, woman's society, men's club, youth fellowship, and young adults. The values of such a large *ex officio* committee are many. Every major working area of the life of the church is represented. These persons bring a wealth and breadth of experience as well as creativity to the committeee. Such a group is likely to be a representative cross section of the basic points of view in the congregation required for realistic planning. A committee of this size is less likely to be dominated by the pastor, and its plans are more likely to become those of the congregation and thus actually carried out in the life of the church. With such a committee the congregation will be kept well informed as to what is going on, as every major church group is represented on it. Questions raised in other group meetings can be clarified by the planning committee representative from that group. In addition, he can bring back to the planning committee the feedback and reactions of the group to the proposals under discussion. This built-in "communication-information" factor of a large *ex officio* committee is of real importance. Every suggestion can be evaluated by the long-range planning committee from within, since some member of the committee is related to every group that will be seeking to carry out the suggestion. Thus the plans of a large *ex officio* committee are much more likely to be acceptable to the congregation, being regarded as the congregation's plans (rather than the pastor's or the committee's).

The decreased efficiency inherent in the larger committee is balanced by the fact that long-range planning ought never be hurried and should always be carried out with great care and thoroughness. The church described here took eighteen months to evolve final plans. Rarely can sound long-range planning be done in less than a year, and often it may involve two years of labor. Since all planning involves projecting from the known to the unknown, all studies involved must be accurately and thoroughly done, and all possible alternatives set forth and explored. The soundness of the plan evolved is of greater importance than developing a plan quickly.

If a church has entered into long-range planning after clearly sensing the need for it, then the planning committee is off to a good start, both in terms of attitude and of many concrete suggestions awaiting consideration and evaluation. Planning always involves moving from the known to the unknown, moving the church from where it is to where it ought to be. Planning, therefore, must logically include the following steps: studying the church's present situation (where it is), understanding the proper goal of the church (where it should go), and evolving plans for bridging the gap between the two.

First of all, the planning committee must secure full and accurate information on the present condition of the church and the community of which it is a part. If the studies on membership, leadership, attendance, church school, missions, finances, and the community, previously mentioned, have not been made then they should be made at this time. Complete instructions as to how to carry out such studies would be too detailed to include here. Most seminary graduates are trained to carry out such studies and can guide laymen in this activity. Guidance can be found in several standard works.[1] The author's experience is that the long-range planning committee should name subcommittees to prepare these studies. It is well to have every committee member serving on some subcommittee, naming the chairmen of the standing committees as chairmen of the study subcommittees, each supervising the study of his own area of church work.

The chairman of the membership and evangelism committee (a member of the long-range planning committee) would serve as chairman of the study subcommittee on analyzing the current and past church membership as to number, growth, age-sex division, and distance from the church. In addition, this subcommittee might well make the leadership studies involving gathering and charting information on number of leadership positions held, tenure of office of each officeholder, age-sex distribution, distance from the church, and length of local church membership. The laymen ought to gather the actual information necessary so that it is their study. Help may be needed in standardizing the graphing procedures. All the regular committee members should be involved in the study.

Likewise, the committee on Christian education ought to prepare the studies as to church school membership, average attendance, and analyze the information (past and present) by departments. The worship committee would secure the information as to the average attendance at the Sunday morning service over the past years. These figures should be based on an actual count by the ushers. The missions committee should undertake the study of regular missionary giving, special projects, giving of the woman's society, youth fellowship, and other groups, and the number of mission study educational sessions held each year. The group to gather the financial facts is the stewardship and finance committee. It would chart the history of congregational giving, both in terms of dollars and of per capita figures for local budget, building and remodeling, and benevolent causes. It will also need to chart the number and amount of pledges made annually and a current age-sex division, both of the number of givers in each bracket and the amount given to the budget from each. The changes in the income pattern of the community also will need to be recorded. Finally, the committee on Christian social concerns might well be assigned the needed community studies. These will vary from place to place, but would include such items as population changes, school enrollment, neighborhood and housing changes, and community services and needs.

These studies cannot be quickly done, and their accuracy is important both in understanding the present situation and projecting the future course of the church. Adequate guidance needs to be given to insure their accuracy. One of the values of such studies comes to the many laymen of the various committees who become involved at this point of gathering information and participating in the project. *The principle of involvement and participation is closely related to concern and commitment.* The more fully the congregation is involved in the process of planning, the more readily it is apt to respond to carry out the plans when completed.

Once the committee has determined the various studies to be made in relation to the local church, it ought to turn its attention to increasing its own understanding of the nature and mission of the Christian church. This study of the nature and mission of the

241

church by the committee can be going on while the various sub-committees are gathering data for their studies. The pastor is equipped by training and background to lead the long-range planning committee in this aspect of its work. The approach to such a study will vary from place to place. The experience must include studying the biblical concept of the church, reading and discussing one or more key contemporary writers on the subject,[2] and sharing fully the insights and questions of all the members of the group. Only a clear understanding of what the church ought to be can serve as an adequate standard of measurement for any proposed course of action in the local church. The committee's study of the nature and mission of the church is, therefore, a crucial factor in adequate long-range planning and must not be short-circuited. It is likely that six to nine months may be required to accomplish the subcommittees' local church studies and the study of the total committee of the nature and mission of the church. These two factors— an understanding of the local church situation and the nature and mission of the Christian church—are the two foundation stones on which long-range planning rests. Whenever the committee clearly understands where the church now is and where it ought to be, then, and only then, is it ready to try to bridge the gap by planning specific ways and means that will enable the church to move forward toward what it ought to be.

The long-range planning committee should then use every means to secure creative suggestions for enabling the local church to become truly Christian. In the situation previously referred to, a large number of concrete suggestions were made by the congregation through the neighborhood discussion groups. Before examining and evaluating them, the committee involved every other committee and organization in the church in self-examinataion in order to secure additional ideas. The long-range planning committee also added several ideas from its own discussions to complete the list of possible approaches for strengthening the church. After that, the process of careful evaluation was begun, in order to determine which ideas merited detailed study and consideration. It is at this point that the studies of the local situation and an understanding of what the Christian church ought to be come into focus as a plumb line against which specific suggestions are measured. Many suggestions will drop by the wayside as being trivial, irrelevant, unnecessary, impossible, or unchristian. At this time only the suggestions that are *clearly* unsuitable and undesirable are to be eliminated. The immediate goal is a list of ideas that have sufficient merit to warrant further investigation.

At this point it is desirable to assign the sifted list of ideas to the previously named six committees. In addition, all property items should go to the trustees, and all ideas related to church organizations to a subcommittee of all chairmen of such groups. Each group would be chaired by a member of the long-range planning committee, and all its members would belong to some subcommittee. It would be the responsibility of each subcommittee to examine each suggestion to discover what program or approach would be needed to carry out the idea and to determine how it would affect the life of the church. The lay or staff leadership required to carry out each idea must be calculated as well as the probable financial cost. Such an examination of each proposal will involve considerable investigation and discussion. Sufficient time must be allowed for each group to do its work thoroughly. If building and remodeling plans are involved, as they were in the previous illustration, outside professional persons may need to be called in for consultation, and, hence, requiring further time. It is important to try to envision all that is involved in each suggestion under consideration.

When all the information on the complete list of items is at hand, the long-range planning committee is then ready to evaluate those items to be recommended for inclusion in the final plan and to separate them from those items not to be included. The length of time to be covered by the long-range plan will need to be determined, and those items are to be approved that seem capable of execution within that period. When this point is reached, the long-range planning committee has completed the second step in the administrative process—that of planning what is to be done.

3. *Organizing to Enable Ideas to Become Realities.*

The third step is organization. This means to determine when, how, and by whom the developed plans will be carried out. Although the long-range plan must be divided into smaller units at this point, it is advisable not to make the breakdown too rigid. Personal experience has shown, for instance, that it is both theoretically and practically impossible to assign a numerical priority to every item in the plan. (The list in the church under discussion included thirty-eight items.) Neither is it possible to break a ten-year program into ten segments, deciding in advance just what must be completed each year. Too many unpredictable factors enter into the situation. Experience indicates it is better to group all approved items into three main priority groups (A, B, and C) without assigning a terminal date for each one. "A" priority simply indicates the most urgent concerns that ought to be begun or completed before attempting the "B" priority items, and that all "C" items in turn follow "B." Even here, absolutely rigid lines cannot be drawn. Special interests or resources may become available to accomplish some "C" priority item before all "A" items are completed. When this happens, it is well simply to rejoice and go ahead.

In our present case study, of the items listed in the long-range plan, the following priority assignment was given at the beginning of the ten-year period.

"A" Priority

Minister to the adjacent college campus

Deepen spiritual life of congregation

Multiple worship services

Reach surrounding neighborhood

Initiate lay visitation evangelism

Start new adult church school class

Hold a school of missions

Secure church school equipment

Strengthen the stewardship and financial program

"B" Priority

Provide nursery care during church worship

Tape worship service for shut-ins

Make extended property repairs

Add additional church school facilities

"C" Priority

Establish radio ministry

Establish week-night youth center

Establish day nursery for working mothers

Increase church staff

Remodel chancel and secure new pipe organ

Acquire adjacent property

Tuckpoint stone masonry

Several items were realized out of order of their priority because some individual or group became particularly interested in them. For example, in the "A" priority list it proved impossible to start a new adult class, to reach the surrounding neighborhood, or to hold a school of missions until late in the ten-year plan. On the other hand, in the "B" priority group, a child care nursery during the worship service was finished, equipped, and staffed in the first six months; and additional church school space was provided by the end of the first year, because of a large donation by an interested person and the volunteer labor of the men's club. In the "C" priority list the radio ministry, chancel remodeling, and increased church staff were achieved very early in the period. All this illustrates the fact that when a church lets its needs be known, various persons and groups may find a particular item that challenges them to assume responsibility toward its realization. The priority ratings are merely general guides for the united church effort.

Sound organizational procedures would suggest that the church hold an annual planning conference at the beginning of each year and make definite decisions at that time in the light of current circumstances as to what items in the long-range plan should be attempted that year. Any new needs of the congregation that have arisen can also be cared for. The long-range plan thus becomes a guide in keeping general goals and specific proposals before the church, while being flexible in terms of accepting relevant portions of it for action each year. Long-range plans ought to guide and challenge a congregation, rather than be a straitjacket from which there is no escape.

4. Implementation of the Plan in the Day-to-day Life of the Church.

The fourth step in the administrative process is putting flesh and blood into the plan and the organization, so that they come to life and are actually carried out. The long-range planning committee has no legislative power to implement its proposals. It is strictly a study-advisory committee, and its recommendations are to be presented to the proper church body or bodies for acceptance and implementation.

The completed plans of the long-range planning committee should be presented to the governing body of the congregation for discussion, amendment, and adoption, and for stating proper procedures to secure legislative consideration by the appropriate church groups. If a large planning committee has been at work for many months, and if the several studies have been referred to the various church committees and organizations as proposed here, the members of the church governing body will be familiar with the recommendations and the reasons for them. The more thoroughly the foregoing steps in the administrative process have been done, the easier and more effective the actual implementation will be.

It has been my experience that as soon as the church governing board adopts the long-range plan, it ought to be presented in detail to the entire congregation. To facilitate such a presentation, it is helpful to mimeograph or print the plan, listing the various items under the priority headings agreed upon. The actual presentation of the plan to the congregation, however, should be done in a manner that involves a face-to-face presentation and discussion of the plan. Only in such a manner can the questions it raises in the minds of the members be heard and dealt with so that what is being proposed is accurately communicated. This procedure also serves as an excellent gauge of congregational feelings about the plan. Since all

246

members of the congregation will be personally involved in giving time, leadership, and funds to carry out some phase of the plan, they must have a clear understanding of the whole plan at the outset.

In the present case the congregation was invited to meet again in neighborhood groups to discuss the completed plan with a member of the planning committee. In the course of two weeks, the whole congregation not only had been informed of the plans but had been involved in an intimate discussion of them. It is my judgment that the early completion of all items in the plan, in spite of a change in pastoral leadership, resulted largely from this involvement of the whole congregation, enabling them to participate gladly and sacrificially through the ensuing years. Another way of presenting the final plans to the congregation would be through a series of family night dinners at which time a portion of the congregation would discuss the plan together. It is important not simply to mail the plan to them without opportunity for face-to-face questioning and discussion.

How should the items in the long-range plan be voted into the actual life and program of the church so that they become realities? It would be unwise for the church governing body to adopt and initiate the total plan at once and thus commit every church board for the next ten years to every detail of it. The general adoption of it as long-range goals commits the church to it in principle but leaves to the board to appropriate year by year the particular portions it will undertake and to add other things required by changing circumstances.

Each year at its annual planning session the board should consider the items in the plan that ought to be undertaken that year. The items agreed upon should become part of the regular program of the church, and ways should be found to provide the required leadership and resources. In this way each item in the long-range plan actually is assigned by the board to the appropriate church group to be carried out in its regular program of work. Long-range planning becomes a means of adding the dimensions of depth of purpose, coherence, and comprehensiveness to all church groups and organizations, thus enabling the church more effectively to fulfill its mission.

5. *Evaluating the Plan to Keep It Current.*

The final step in the administrative process is evaluation. The other steps all fall into a chronological order (recognizing need, planning, organizing, and implementing), but the process of evaluation is involved in every step and must continue even beyond the project itself. All aspects of a long-range planning venture—goals, objectives, and approaches—must be evaluated. At every stage it is important to listen for reactions to every idea and to encourage honest evaluation of every concept. Sound conclusions will be reached only if there is a penetrating analysis of every suggested hypothesis. When the long-range planning committee submits its final proposal to the church for acceptance, it ought to be asking for frank evaluation of its work. Sound planning rests upon continuous evaluation. The annual planning sessions of the church board provide ideal opportunities for continuing evaluation of the long-range plan. The details of this annual evaluative procedure will be discussed in the next section.

The long-range planning committee itself should continue to meet at least annually, and oftener if circumstances require, to review the plan and the priority assignments and to analyze accomplishments and failures. It should also be sensitive to new needs and circumstances and should bring any recommended changes to the next annual planning session of the church board.

It is hoped that the foregoing discussion of long-range planning has shown the basic reasons why such an experience is important for sound church administration, as well as offering guidance for carrying out such a venture. If a church is concerned with fulfilling its nature and mission through the activities and experiences of its organizations and groups, it cannot ignore the needs for comprehensive, long-range planning as a basic principle of church administration.

C. The Place of Annual Planning in the Local Church

Most churches plan their programs and budgets a year in advance rather than operating on a month-to-month basis; every church ought to do so. Too often, however, what masquerades under the name of annual planning is actually only a calendar clearing of dates by all the church groups, each of which has worked out a year's program independently of the others. Although such calendar clearing does prevent various events from being scheduled on conflicting dates, it is not worthy of being called annual planning, since it lacks the following essential features:

A common understanding of goals and objectives by all groups.

A sense of perspective as to how each group fits into the whole (thus such planning fosters independence and self-sufficiency in the groups).

A coordinated and cooperative approach to one overarching basic program in the life of the church. (Duplication and competition among groups may result from independent planning.)

A sense of personal unity among all laymen involved in the several areas of the work of the church.

For these reasons, a coordinated approach to an annual planning session will be outlined here, in order to illustrate the meaning of comprehensive annual planning in the local church.

The spiritual life retreat for all chairmen and presidents of church groups, to deepen their commitment to Christ and their understanding of the Christian faith, should precede the annual planning session. The key leaders of the program of the church need to prepare themselves spiritually previous to leading the other officers of their groups in program planning. Such a retreat should be free from all program planning and should feature Bible study of selected passages, sharing of questions and insights relative to the Christian faith, and the opportunity for the leaders to get to know one another better. The schedule and activities for the retreat should be planned with these goals in mind. The spiritual preparation of the leaders is a necessary prerequisite for preparing the church program for the year.

As for the planning process itself, the following approach has proved effective. Since annual planning is a complex task, it should be obvious that more than one session will be required. The church should arrange at least two general meetings of all persons involved and several additional sessions by the separate groups involved. All members of the board, trustees, committees, and officers of all church organizations should be a part of the planning group. A date should be chosen when at least four full hours are available for the opening session, for instance, 3:30 to 8:30 P.M. on a Sunday. This allows for a two-hour session, an hour break for a fellowship meal, and a concluding two-hour work session. Obviously, a rural church would need to adapt the time schedule and might open with a noon potluck dinner and take a short break in the afternoon. At any rate, a large block of time must be made available. The following agenda has been used effectively by several churches.

(20 minutes) *Worship and Challenge*

A brief worship service centering on the theme of "The Nature of the church" or "The Meaning of Christian Commitment."

(20 minutes) *Listing of the Goals of a Christian Church by the Entire Group*

An attempt is made to focus the attention of the group on the mission of the church. Discussion should bring forth from the group various goals of a Christian church, and they should be itemized on a blackboard.

(10 minutes) *Report on Last Year's Goals*

The lay leader should briefly itemize the goals accepted for the previous year and indicate the areas of progress and of failure.

(10 minutes) *Priority Recommendations from the Long-range Planning Committee*

The items in the long-range plan that ought to be acted upon for the coming year should be listed, as well as any additions or revisions the committee desires to bring to the group.

(45 minutes) *Discussion by the Whole Group, Suggesting Particular Items Needing Consideration*

The entire group should be asked to contribute every suggestion it has as to how the local church can be improved in the coming year and to list the problems about which it ought to be concerned. The following questions usually evoke a response: What are the needs and concerns to which our church ought to give its attention? What problems ought to be dealt with? How can we do a better job? What are your dreams and hopes for our church this year? What suggestions for improving our church have you heard others make?

(15 minutes) *Outline Any Suggested Denominational Programs for the Current Year*

The lay member of the annual conference or the denominational body involved should outline briefly and clearly any proposed denominational plans involving the local church in the ensuing year. This is for information purposes only and will be referred to the concerned groups for discussion and recommendation later.

(60 minutes) *Intermission for Fellowship Meal; or*
(20 minutes) *Coffee Break*

Up to this point, the attempt has been to get before all board members and officers of the church a listing of goals and needs of the total church. By so doing, each group is exposed to the needs of the total church and will see its own small segment from the perspective of total needs. Apart from such exposure, church groups become very parochial. During the intermission, the secretary, the pastor and lay leader will need to make lists referring all suggestions made up to that point to the proper committee or organization for evaluation and discussion to follow the intermission.

(60 minutes) *Division into Groups to Discuss Particular Concerns*

All items mentioned should be referred to one or more of the subgroups and committees represented. They should add any additional concerns related to their particular responsibility. Each group should then seek to discover those suggestions that most urgently need its attention in the coming year and should work toward a tentative priority list to be completed in later separate meetings.

(50 minutes) *Reports from the Individual Group Meetings*

The final general session should hear reports of the separate group meetings as to what each one believes to be its most important needs and concerns in the coming year. These reports must be very brief, stating without elaboration the concerns for which programs will later be developed. It is important for every group to hear all reports, so that each may see itself in proper relationship to all other groups and the church as a whole. In addition, possible duplication and competition can be noted and worked out before the groups concerned meet again to finalize their plans.

This opening session will need to be followed with a series of separate meetings by each of the groups involved to plan in detail the program for the year and to meet the needs identified in the opening session. Detailed planning can only be done by the group involved, but it needs to be done in the light of common objectives and in relation to what all other groups are doing. It is for these reasons that the opening session described above is important. Such a session is important also, because suggestions from outside each group concerned are offered from the floor, and a broader base is established for the evaluation of every aspect of church life. Every group has a tendency to become ingrown and can, therefore, profit from other points of view.

The chairman or president of each group is responsible to see that its officers meet often enough to complete the details of the program for the year within thirty days (or before the next general meeting). For the auxiliary organizations these meetings should produce plans for the programs of the regular meetings and for any special projects they expect to undertake. For the committees, this stage means developing plans to strengthen areas of weakness or to initiate new areas of concern. Each group may find resources and suggestions for its planning from denominational periodicals or special publications. For example, the May issue each year of *The Methodist Story* is an annual program planning number, containing detailed program suggestions and other resource materials for each of the commissions.[3] An example of specific resource material available is a series of "Program Builder Worksheets" for each of the several groups, of which the one for the committee on education is included in Appendix B. During this period of planning by the separate groups, the chairmen need to meet together once to clear any conflicts or duplication of proposed programs or dates or to coordinate similar programs. Time spent in advance program building not only will result in better and more effective working groups but also will save much time and energy during the year that otherwise would be expended in an unplanned month-to-month operation.

At the next official board meeting, all chairmen and presidents of groups should come prepared to present outlines of their plans for the year (preferably mimeographed for distribution). At this time the church calendar should be cleared, and all known dates of activities entered on it. Any necessary adjustments can be referred back to the concerned groups. When such planning is done and each group in the church knows what it is going to try to do and what is being done in other groups as well, the church is much more likely to move forward with a sense of purpose and mission.

A word of personal testimony may be in order at this point. As a pastor I found great value in planning my preaching a year in advance, and in announcing the preaching schedule at the final session of annual church planning. Such an announcement symbolizes in a very concrete and appreciated manner the fact that the pastor-administrator is not asking his lay leadership to plan in advance without also disciplining himself to such planning of his own work. In so identifying himself with the laymen, an important bridge of understanding is built.

D. A Continual Coordination of Plans

Even when annual planning is carefully done, there is still a need to coordinate the work of the groups during the year. Plans may need to be changed, unforeseen circumstances arise, and new factors may enter the picture to call for adjustments of various kinds. As the year unfolds, there often are opportunities for cooperation and dovetailing of the work of the separate groups, if proper communication channels are open to deal with such situations as they arise. Thus, close cooperation of the various church groups is necessary not only when making plans but also in carrying them out.

One approach to such continual coordination is through the utilization of an executive cabinet. Such a cabinet may be composed of pastor, chairman of the board, lay leader, president of the trustees, and the chairmen of the committee of worship, missions, Christian education, membership and evangelism, Christian social concerns, and stewardship and finance. This cabinet might meet each month before the board meeting. Among its functions are educating all key leaders concerning the total church program by serving as a clearinghouse for reporting what is going on in each area of church life and keeping one another informed on major programs coming up, problems encountered, and changes in plans. The agenda for the board should be an outgrowth of the cabinet discussion. The pastor can use this cross section of leaders as a sounding board for new ideas and programs. It is an excellent advisory group in which initial discussions of proposed denominational programs for the local church can take place. By keeping every group in touch with the total program of the church, each one sees itself in proper perspective and relationship. Such a cabinet makes an additional contribution to the effectiveness of each group, in that the necessity to report to it and to discuss the work of his committee with this cabinet motivates the individual chairman to action in his own group. The executive cabinet, however, is primarily an open channel of communication through which unity and coherence is maintained in carrying out the planned program of the church.

■ ■ ■ Notes

1. Murray Leiffer, *The Effective City Church* (2nd revised edition; Nashville: Abingdon Press, 1961), and Herbert E. Stotts, *The Church Inventory Handbook* (Denver: Wesley Press, 1951). Other excellent materials are available from the headquarters of the various denominations.
2. Gustafson, *Treasure in Earthen Vessels.*
   Jenkins, *The Strangeness of the Church.*
   Miller, *The Nature and Mission of the Church.*
   Newbigin, *The Household of God.*
   Raines, *New Life in the Church.*
3. *The Methodist Story,* edited by Edwin Maynard, published by The Commission on Promotion and Cultivation of The Methodist Church.

CHAPTER X

UTILIZE ALL
AVAILABLE RESOURCES

A. The Importance of This Principle

Purposeful church administration calls for the utilization of all resources and personnel in a coherent and comprehensive manner in moving toward fulfilling the mission of the church. Up to this point we have explored the maximum use of resources and personnel within the congregation. We now turn to resources beyond the local church. No one congregation embodies all the knowledge and insight required to carry out its ministry in the most effective manner possible. Each one can profit from the experience of other churches with similar problems. If it does not use resources beyond its own membership, a congregation will often try to make a decision without understanding all of the aspects of the problem, or again, having accepted its responsibility in a certain situation, it may not have proper knowledge for carrying out its commitment. In either case a congregation is bound by the terms of its mission to seek all the help available, from whatever quarter it is offered. The concept of the church as a ministering community inevitably points a congregation beyond itself, as it seeks the means to fulfill its ministry. The church administrator must therefore be resourceful and imaginative enough to recognize and use any means that

255

will contribute to the church's proper task, at the same time guarding against any methods that conflict with or hinder that task.

Too many congregations not only fail to utilize the energy within their own memberships, but also stubbornly refuse to seek resources beyond their own doorstep, for fear of disrupting comfortable (and often ineffective) ways of doing things. One such ingrown church measured every idea by the question, Did we do this last year? The full impact of this point of view was felt one evening when a board member seriously made a motion "that this church never do anything in the future different from what it has done in the past." His solemn words caused the people to see the situation as it was; the members broke down in peals of laughter, even the man who had made the motion. They concluded that they had become more ingrown than they had realized. Every church needs to look beyond itself for new ideas and resources.

Local churches can learn from one another. Although the experiences and programs of one congregation cannot be encapsulated and released in another church with the same effect, much can be learned by sharing both positive and negative experiences. The present structure of the churches provides many opportunities for such sharing, and many more should be created. These opportunities range from informal meetings of churches in the same town or neighborhood to the formidable staffs of denominational and ecumenical boards. A wise pastor will expose himself and his people to the experience of other churches.

Although church administration has its own uniqueness derived from the mission of the church, it shares certain common concerns of administration with other fields. These outside agencies and disciplines offer many resources to local churches. Administrators should not be ignorant of these nonecclesiastical resources, nor slow in appropriating them wherever they are useful to the church's mission. For example, team teaching in secular education may have important implications for Christian education. Alcoholics Anonymous may be properly related to the church's ministry. The value of small groups for personal growth is presently of great interest to the church. Sociological studies, including the competent use of statistics, are invaluable in dealing with the church's mission in changing neighborhoods. Office management, industrial training techniques, psychological concepts, and insights from the arts all may have contributions to make. These are only a few illustrations of the fact that there are resources outside the church that can help further the church's mission.

The church administrator ought to see himself as a resource person, keeping abreast of developments in his denomination, in other denominations, and in allied secular fields. Such a role will entail considerable breadth in reading and in personal contacts. The pastor must continually seek more effective ways of serving this changing social and cultural situation. He must therefore be alert and teachable as well. He cannot, of course, be a skilled leader in all fields, but he must know where to go for the help that is needed.

B. Sharing Denominational Resources

Most denominations offer important resources to their constituent congregations to enrich and enhance their particular ministries to the world. Every minister ought to be acquainted with these sources of help, utilizing them in accordance with the special needs of his own congregation.

Most denominations produce an abundance of printed materials —books, periodicals, pamphlets, and tracts. Instead of becoming overwhelmed by the abundance, the administrator must select those items that will be genuinely helpful in his situation. Chairmen of the several church groups should be responsible for looking over the material in their own respective fields, presenting the most promising items to their committees for further consideration. A careful choice of a few really good pieces is to be preferred to indiscriminate distribution, whether the material is to be used by committees, in a literature rack, as a mailing piece, or a bulletin insert. Examples of useful printed material might include the periodicals published for ministers, officers, or the membership at large;[1] or the devotional guides that may provide a helpful tool for a spiritual life committee seeking to enrich the prayer life of the congregation.[2] Just as every church school is aware of the denominational material available to it, so other working groups should learn about the printed resources available to them.

Most denominations have a wide selection of audio-visual resources, often available to congregations at nominal cost. These include motion pictures, filmstrips, records, pictures, and turnover charts. Audio-visual materials are also available through interdenominational and public agencies (such as public libraries). Care should be taken, however, that each item is selected in relation *to the specific purpose for which it is to be used.* Reliable evaluations should be secured wherever possible; no film should be shown without its being previewed. An up-to-date listing of useful audio-visual materials is an important resource for the church administrator.

Leadership training opportunities of several kinds are offered to congregations by most denominations. The laboratory school for church school workers is a familiar example, combining training on a local church and regional basis. Often staff members of denominational boards travel extensively to bring help to local situations on a district or conference level. These boards provide training conferences in such fields as evangelism, missions, stewardship, and social concerns. Such training conferences can be of real help to the local church if they are well planned and the leadership is carefully chosen. Pastors should keep a careful watch over such ventures to see that the quality of training is kept high and relay their frank evaluations to the responsible ecclesiastical authorities. Since the quality of these denomination training efforts is potentially higher than any one congregation could provide, a serious responsibility rests upon the leaders who plan them. Few experiences are more disillusioning than to take local church leaders away from home to a training conferece that is not worth the trip.

In some denominations there are supervisory officials who may serve as resource persons to the congregations assigned to them. These men are often the nearest available help in time of need, and they are sometimes particularly well qualified by experience and familiarity with the local situation. These persons should also be able to direct the congregation to whatever resources are available

258

for dealing with the problem at hand. Their supervisory offices and their knowledge of the denomination may best be used in this manner.

Every denomination has a number of general boards that prepare local church programs for the whole denomination.[3] These programs are sometimes adopted by the denomination as a unit and at other times by the several regional governing bodies, such as conferences, synods, or districts. These denominational programs have been "sent down" to the congregations so often in recent years that many serious questions are being raised as to their validity and effectiveness. This is true in spite of the fact that the programs have usually dealt with such crucial areas of work as visitation evangelism, every member canvass, mission study and support, church extension, higher education, or specific study groups. In fact, resistance to such programs is not directed toward the problems they seek to deal with or even to the basic method outlined, but primarily toward the mechanics of implementing such programs. Some of the points of friction include requiring every church to begin at the same time and follow the same time schedule, insisting that the instructions be followed in every detail, injecting a competitive element by comparing results, evaluating the program's "success" by statistics, ignoring the welfare of the local church by requiring participation and the appearance of activity and progress, and ignoring the limited leadership resources of small congregations. Such denominational programs have become the symbol of ecclesiastical pressure and program-centered busyness, with ministers viewing them as stumbling blocks or as stepping-stones for the future professional advancement of pastors.

Furthermore, the results of the multitude of such programs in recent years is even more discouraging than the hostility they have engendered, even though most denominations have evaluated them as successful. Whatever statistical success can be demonstrated (and even this has not been very exciting), the fact is that an insufficient number of lives have been changed and communities have not been led nearer the mind of Christ. Churchman and secularist alike agree on the growing impotence of the church.[4] We have greased and turned ecclesiastical wheels, but we haven't gone anywhere. We have raised big budgets, but have not made Christian stewards. We have made many visits, but have produced few evangelists. Today's church is not effectively reaching the outsider.

In view of this dismaying situation, can a denominational program become a helpful and welcome resource, enabling the congregation to function more effectively? I believe the answer is yes—but only with a change of attitude on the part of denominations, pastors, and congregations.

In the first place congregations need help from denominational boards, in order to become aware of some of the problems they ought to be facing, to be exposed to new and more effective ways of doing things, and to gain knowledge of useful methods and techniques. Secondly, denominational boards are in an excellent position to offer such resources. Their staff members travel around the church and become acquainted with the pressing problems of congregations and with the common and uncommon ways of dealing with them. Nearly all denominational programs are born out of the painful pioneering struggles of real congregations grappling with real problems.

What, then, is the difficulty? It arises when the procedures developed in pioneering ventures are generalized and made mandatory for hundreds of congregations whose situations vary in hundreds of important particulars. The complaint heard most often is that all congregations are required to carry out the program simultaneously. It is hard to see that the few advantages of simultaneity come close to balancing the disadvantages of riding roughshod over the varieties of local circumstance. The denomination's real concern ought to be to involve, motivate, and inspire local churches to grapple with a problem *at the time it is a vital concern for them.* A board might well stand at the door with helpful resources and knock gently, rather than kicking the door down and saying, "Do this now!"

In addition to permitting flexibility of timing, the boards must recognize such points as the readiness of the congregation, its size and leadership potential, and its past experience in the same field of work. Such a recognition would require that more than one basic approach be offered and that alternatives be suggested in each step of the procedure. Programs designed for local churches should be similar to church school literature, with a variety of suggestions for presenting the material. Such suggestions are not made with the expectation that all of them will be used by any one teacher and certainly not by all teachers. In practice many congregations and pastors are in fact looking upon "mandatory" programs as optional resource materials and are adapting them to local needs, with or without the blessing of ecclesiastical authorities. Thus conceived, a denominational program is not a self-motivating, self-justifying entity, but a means to personal growth and a resource for furthering of the Christian mission.

The place of denominational programs is so prominent in the life of the church today that it may be useful to illustrate how good use can be made of them. First of all it is important to have lay representation at any meeting where such programs are first proposed, discussed, and decided upon. The minister and other congregational leaders ought to be involved in the decision-making group that determines the program. The free and frank reactions of all persons present should be *encouraged,* all questions being considered thoughtfully and honestly. If such decisions are railroaded through a group, the creative implementation of the program becomes extremely difficult. It is further to be hoped that all denominational programs for local churches will seek the approval of the governing unit of the churches involved before requiring participation.

Before introducing the program to a local church committee, the plan should be thoroughly discussed by the pastor, the lay representative to the group that determined the program, and the chairman of the appropriate local committee. The aim of these discussions is to clarify the understanding of these three persons concerning the program. The discussions will take into account such circumstances as whether the program deals with a problem recognized by the congregation, congregational attitudes toward denominational programs generally, past experience in the proposed area of work, possible conflicts with other plans already adopted, leadership and other resources required, and so on. On the basis of these discussions such matters will be decided as who will introduce the plan, how and when to introduce it, and other matters regarding the initial presentation.

When introducing any program, denominational or otherwise, sound administration requires the observance of the five basic steps in the administrative process (discussed in Chapter IV and illustrated at length in Chapter IX).

1. Securing a common *recognition of need.*
2. *Planning* carefully with the local situation in mind.
3. *Organizing* effectively.
4. *Stimulating and implementing* the plan through the organization.
5. *Evaluating the effectiveness* of the program, both during and following the experience.

It is important to remember to involve the pertinent committee at every step and as many of the congregation as is feasible at every point.

If any of these steps is bypassed, difficulty will come, and sooner or later it will be necessary to back up and move through the neglected step. In initiating denominational programs in the local church it is not uncommon to omit the first three steps altogether. The need is never discussed; the congregation has little to say about plans and organization. The plan and organization proposed from above is assumed to be adequate, and the congregation becomes involved only at the point of implementation (step 4). It is interesting to note that although the congregation has never heard of the steps in the administrative process, they are apt to force the committee to back up and at least limp through the steps, as such comments and questions as these arise from the congregation:

Why do we have to do this? (Need)
This proposal doesn't fit our small church. (Planning)
Somebody upstairs dreamed up this complicated setup. Can't we change it to fit our own needs? (Organization)
Our people will never respond to this. (Stimulating and implementing)

When such reactions as these go unacknowledged, a congregation will effectively sabotage a program (as when appointed leaders will not function) or else despiritedly go through the motions. A successful experience with a denominational program in a local church requires that *all five steps* in the administrative process be carried out *in the congregation.* By "successful experience" is meant a recognition that programs exist to awaken and change persons spiritually and not merely to produce immediate statistical results.

For illustrative purposes let us examine how a denominational program may be used creatively by a congregation. Since many denominations are actually involved in programs of visitation evangelism, such a program will provide a useful model. Most visitation programs to reach the unchurched involve the following elements.[5]

1. The effort is under the direction of the local evangelism committee, subject to approval by the board. Sometimes a special committee is set up within the evangelism committee.

2. Methods of securing the prospect list are spelled out, such as, conducting a religious census and examining the constituency list, church school rolls, women's society list, etc.

3. The number of required visitors is determined; visitors are recruited.

4. Visiting dates are determined, usually four to six evenings, often the same dates for all churches in a district.

5. A subcommittee on materials and supplies prepares the prospect cards and visitation assignments and secures all necessary materials for the visitors.

6. Training sessions for visitors are planned and carried out, usually in the form of supper meetings. Turnover charts are a common training device.

7. Visits are carried out, almost always by teams of two visitors. Usually decisions for Christ and the church are recorded on commitment cards.

8. Visitors meet at the end of each evening, in order to share results, which are often tabulated on a master sheet and telephoned to a district office for tabulation and comparison with other churches.

9. Sometimes the week of visitation is held in connection with a preaching or teaching mission, to be held during or following the visits.

10. Plans are made to make return visits to families not at home the first time.

11. Membership training classes are scheduled for those who make commitments and desire to unite with the church.

Assuming that some such program has been approved as the official program for every congregation for the second week in October, with training sessions for local church directors and committees to be held early in September, what is the best way for a congregation to approach this effort? As we have seen, such a detailed prescription of the timing is not an ideal situation, but this is the way in which most denominational programs are initiated. In such a case the pastor and congregation should neither rebelliously ignore the program nor automatically lock-step their way through every prescribed detail of it. Assuming that carrying the gospel to the unchurched is at the heart of the mission of every congregation, such a denominational program as this one ought to be regarded as a call to consider thoughtfully what evangelism means for each congregation at this time.

Step one is to examine and increase the *awareness of need* for evangelistic outreach by the congregation. This part of the process begins with the pastor and the two laymen most directly concerned, as previously discusseed. In this case, these persons will already have considered such matters as the need for this program at this time, the size and status of the constituency list, the congregation's attitude toward evangelism and toward visitation programs, and other related matters. Presentation to the evangelism committee will include a full discussion of all these matters, of the particular points where the congregations' evangelistic effort should be improved, of the fact that many other congregations are faced with the same problems (leading to a general concern by the denomination), and of the effectiveness and frequent use of visitation programs by other congregations.

As the committee recognizes the need for evangelistic outreach and the validity of the visitation approach, further discussion should center, not on the details of the proposed program, but on ways of awakening the entire congregation to this particular need. Suggestions may include presentation to the church board, discussion in such auxiliary groups as the women's society and the men's group, special study groups, discussion in neighborhood family groups, and a series of sermons on the need for leading others to Christ. In these and other ways the congregation at large should be awakened to its outreach responsibility. When this happens (not before), it is time to move to the second step in the process.

Planning should be undertaken with the intention to develop the best possible plan to meet the need that has been acknowledged. It is wise to encourage as much creative thinking as possible, for instance, by beginning with a "brainstorming" session of the evangelism committee, where every idea of every member is recorded for further consideration. This method could then be used also with the church board. Ideas should be solicited from other committees and auxiliary groups as well. The membership at large should also be invited to take part in this step by means of a loosely structured questionnaire or other device. (One congregation put a suggestion box in the narthex.)

As this step proceeds, some layman well acquainted with the denominational program will present it in detail to the committee and the board. The presentation should include an explanation of how the program was developed out of the needs and experience of other congregations, describing the manner of its adoption by the denominational body. In this presentation and afterward, it should be made clear that the responsibility of the congregation is to plan the most effective means of Christian witness possible and that the denominational plan may be modified by the suggestions of the members or that a substitute plan may be adopted. The evangelism committee, using all the sources of ideas just described, should feel free to present to the board for adoption the plan they believe will best do Christ's work in their community. They may recommend the denominational plan; they may propose a modified plan; they may move in another direction altogether. In any case the denominational plan will have

265

achieved its basic purpose of involving the congregation in facing up to its evangelistic responsibility, struggling with it, and doing something about it. Any church that goes through this process will have increased the spiritual vision of many members and will have developed a plan of action suitable to the church's mission in that community. If the denominational plan is adopted under these circumstances, it is likely to be carried out wholeheartedly. If another plan is developed, the wise denominational leader will encourage the experiment.

The third step in the administrative process is to develop an *organization* for carrying out the plan. Denominational suggestions for organization should now be examined and adapted to suit the congregational plan. Time schedule, structure of leadership, and details of method may all need to be altered according to local plans. All this can be done quite freely in the confidence that the congregation has developed a plan custom-tailored to the mission in its own community. Selecting leaders and visitors is an especially crucial matter in this type of program, since the Christian message to the community will finally be represented by two persons sitting in a neighbor's living room. Not everyone who is willing to "do some visiting" is a good visiting evangelist. Care must also be taken in the training of those persons who are selected. Training should be planned in detail according to the task at hand and the persons assigned to carry it out. Denominational training resources should be examined carefully, especially since they have been developed out of actual church situations by specialists in the field of evangelism. Nevertheless, the local committee cannot escape personal responsibility at this point, especially since some training materials offered by denominational boards have been woefully weak and shallow.

The fourth step in the administrative process is *stimulation and implementation*. The more thoroughly the preceding steps have been carried out, the more readily persons can be motivated to accept responsibility and actually carry it out. No church can properly begin a program with this step, in spite of a besetting temptation to do so. The chairmen of subcommittees will now begin to contact visitors and those responsible for the suppers, assignment cards, printed materials, mimeographing, and visitor training. The whole congregation must be well aware of the details of the venture. Careful plans for follow-up visits must be made. Additional workers will be needed for those visits and also to replace those who withdraw for reasons of illness or other unexpected circumstance. Provision must be made for adequate supervision of the effort. It is no small task to keep the assignment cards up-to-date for each evening. Some workers will forget to report back, some will get discouraged and will require help, a few may overstep the bounds of their assigned task. It is even possible that some changes in the plan will have to be made in the midst of the effort. The pastor and lay chairman should share this supervisory role.

If the congregation is generally following the denominational plan, help in motivation, stimulation, and training is usually available through district meetings. Often the enthusiasm and insights of workers from neighboring churches are as stimulating to local workers as is the outside leadership. Often these district meetings prove to be the positive turning point for many congregations. This is one of the real advantages of the denominational program approach.

The final step in the administrative process is *evaluation,* final not in time but only in order of discussion. Evaluation goes on throughout all of the other steps. Basic to any evaluation is determining the standards by which the program is to be judged and providing opportunities for exercising honest judgment. This program, like all others, must be judged by its contribution toward the church's mission of making known God's love to men. This applies not only to those who have been visited but also to those who participated in the program. In visitation evangelism there is a special temptation to evaluate only in terms of the statistics drawn from the commitment cards. Such a procedure falls far short of proper evaluation of spiritual realities and changed lives. Some of those "won" represent shallow and temporary victories. Some who refused to record a commitment may nevertheless have been deeply influenced. The effect of the program upon the workers is not recorded on the cards. At the conclusion of the effort, it is wise to evaluate every step of the program from a genuinely spiritual perspective. This final evaluation will be useful to any similar venture in the future. After some time has elapsed, it is good to evaluate the program again, when the lasting effects of the effort can be seen.

Regarding other types of denominational programs a similar approach should be taken to the one just described. Every congregation should feel free to accept as *its own* whatever program it decides to carry out. Whenever a denominational program serves as a stimulus to involve congregations in facing a basic concern—whether the denominational plan is adopted by every congregation or not—the purpose of the program has been achieved. An alert administrator will be aware of the program resources of his denomination, representing as they do the shared experience of other congregations, and will utilize them as the needs of his situation require.

C. Sharing Interdenominational and Ecumenical Resources

The effectiveness of the Christian witness to a community will nearly always be improved by taking an ecumenical view of the situation. This may come about as several congregations of different denominations come together for various kinds of training, either to enable each church to function more effectively or to prepare for a united or simultaneous program. Or it may come about as the churches take a look at the needs of the community and seek the best way to deal with them together. It is likely, in view of the current situation, that in the future local churches will have to rely more and more on such ecumenical resources as these.

It is clear that the Christian church as a whole and local churches in many communities are facing an acute crisis. In rural areas and in small towns there is an overabundance of small congregations of several denominations competing for a static or declining population, each struggling to hold on to a minister (*any* minister) in a time of diminishing ministerial supply. Often these churches are so small that they cannot have full-time pastors. Their small size and competitive attitude often prevent any significant impact on the community. The struggle of each one to stay alive as an institution leaves little energy for outreach. In the city the church is plagued by the same small church syndrome. Each congregation is too small to wrestle effectively with complex changing neighborhood problems by itself. Such churches are understaffed and must bear heavy financial responsibilities just to keep going. Although such churches are in the midst of the multitudes, they seem powerless to reach them. Even the suburban church, with its larger membership, staff, and financial resources, seems unable effectively to speak to the outsider or reach the insider on a deep level. Statistics indicate that church membership is increasing only half as rapidly as the population. Since 1960 church school enrollment has been decreasing in spite of rising public school enrollment. Parents no longer feel that Christian education is necessary for their children. With the cool response of most college students toward religion, the young parents of tomorrow will not be more favorably disposed toward Christian education than are the parents of today. All of these facts point to the need for the churches to face matters realistically and admit that they must find new and more effective resources to enable them to carry out their mission.

Every congregation can gain from and contribute to ecumenical efforts to improve the quality of the church's labors in the world. Let us look at some examples of fruitful cooperative ventures. To combat the almost universal spiritual illiteracy among professing Christians, lay institutes for studying the documents and experience of the church could be set up in many communities. Studies in the Bible, Christian beliefs, church history, and ethical implications of the gospel could be offered. Competent teachers could be found among the clergy and laity of the community, or funds could be secured to bring in qualified teachers from the outside. Such an effort is almost impossible for a small congregation alone, but quite feasible for several churches together. In addition, such an approach would be much more likely to appeal to the outsider.

The training of church school teachers is a perennial problem in most churches. Probably the poor quality of teaching in many church schools is an important cause of the decline in church school enrollment. Individual churches find it nearly impossible to offer helpful courses for their teachers, because of insufficient leadership. Presently

269

each denomination is seeking to solve this problem by gathering teachers from several churches of the same denomination for training conferences. This method, however, requires most of the teachers to travel some distance from home, resulting in poor responses. If all the resources for teacher training in one community were used, excellent training could be given right in the community, and many more teachers could be reached. The fact that each denomination uses different material works against such an effort, but the basic training courses could be given on such a basis (Bible, Christian beliefs, church history, how persons learn, understanding different age groups, and teaching methods). Such a training venture might lead to a union daily vacation Bible school in the community. Admittedly there is much prejudiced opposition to such an approach in many communities, but *the resources are there* for strengthening each church and for increasing the impact of all the churches upon the community.

The strength of the churches would be multiplied many times if all the churches in a community would come together in an effort to look at their community as it might appear through the eyes of Christ. Instead of each congregation seeking to minister to its segment of the community, let all the churches ask together, What are the community problems about which all Christians ought to be concerned? Then let them go on to ask, What is the best way to use the resources of all the churches in meeting those needs? Each denomination is interested in its own future, and certain laymen in every congregation and some ministers cannot see beyond the requirements of the survival of "our church." These obstacles to united concern are formidable. Perhaps the best answer to such vested interests is that unless some such step is taken in the next few years, the church may well approach institutional (as well as spiritual) death.

Churches would be amazed at their resources and potential impact if they would come together in any community and agree upon a united approach to community needs. A start has been made in this direction in some places. Comity committees are active in working out the location of new churches. Yoked fields, where one pastor serves two or more churches of different denominations, are becoming more common. Mergers of congregations of different denominations are taking place everywhere. The spirit of competition seems to be decreasing, and the needs of whole communities are being considered more seriously, resulting in united efforts in ministries to high school youth, older youth, college students, young adults, and other groups. A genuinely ecumenical meeting of minds can be a decisive factor in community decisions on crucial issues, such as, open housing and fair employment practices, restriction of liquor sales, establishment of hospitals, removing corrupt officials from office, elimination of slums, adequate and equal educational opportunities, and a host of other important matters.

State councils of churches often have important resources for local churches, with which every pastor ought to be acquainted. In some states staff persons are employed as resource leaders in various fields of concern. The state council usually has on file past studies of different kinds that may have helpful information relative to certain communities or problems. The services offered by state councils are so varied that it is difficult to discuss them in general terms. Sometimes laymen's retreats are sponsored by the state council, offering the combined benefits of excellent leadership and lay fellowship across denominational lines. State councils are also usually active in representing the churches in legislative matters related to moral issues and human rights.

The National and World Councils also have helpful resources for local churches. For example the monthly bulletins of the World Council on evangelism contain some of the best material available, both on the theological and the practical levels. Reports of pioneering efforts from all over the world are found there. The publication of the *Audio-Visual Resources Guide* by the National Council contains the most reliable evaluations available for religious audio-visual materials. Every congregation ought to consult this guide in selecting such materials, since it is more objective than any denominational or commercial publication. On questions of national import the National Council can often be of help to particular congregations. Persons who have taken stands on issues of conscience and religious conviction have frequently found help and support from

271

the National Council. The pastor and other congregational leaders should make these resources available to persons who need them. Presently the National Council is taking the lead in exploring the meaning of Christian stewardship by holding conferences, publishing material, and suggesting program approaches to interested congregations. The areas of help and the particular materials available will change from time to time, but the wise pastor will keep abreast of current offerings.

Whether we are aware of it or not, the era of denominations is passing. The man outside the church couldn't care less about the denominational divisions of Christianity; in fact they are a stumbling block to him. Furthermore, many church members do not demonstrate strong denominational loyalty as they transfer from one congregation to another. This is why a trend toward merging denominations is evident at the national level. Clearly the church needs to move beyond parochial denominational thinking as it views its ministry to the community. Although the way is admittedly a hard one to travel, the magnitude of the problems facing us is such that the church will have to choose between marshaling its ecumenical resources or becoming a quaint museum piece.

D. Relating Community Resources to the Church

The relationship of the church to the community and its resources must be seen within the context of the nature of the church and the role of the ministry, as set forth previously. The church is called into being by God to make known his love to all men. It is the task of the pastor to lead in enabling the whole congregation to perform its ministry to the world. Persons are the means through whom God's love is made known, and they are called to witness not only in and through the institutional church but through every personal, social, and vocational relationship. Likewise the minister is not to see himself as "serving the church" but as leading the congregation in serving the real needs of all persons in the community. Within this context, what is the relationship of the church to community resources?

A part of the church's concern is to involve its members in ex-

272

pressing and clarifying the gospel in the life of a community. This will require the church to be fully cognizant of the complex of groups and agencies that comprise the power structure of a community. It will cooperate with some of them, use the resources of others, and stand in judgment upon the practices of still others. The church administrator ought to be familiar with all the positive, serving resources of his community, becoming acquainted personally with those who are in charge of them. He should also know the problems of his community about which no one seems to be concerned.[6] The church should view community agencies as being available to meet the special needs of persons and should fully utilize their services to supplement the ministry of the church. They ought not to be seen as competitive or irrelevant but as enlarging the service that the church can render persons. Such agencies include schools, health and welfare departments, visiting nurses' associations, hospitals, convalescent homes, family service and child guidance agencies, mental health resources, police, courts, probation officers, doctors, city officials, and service clubs.

A minister arriving in a community should take an early opportunity to visit with the personnel of these agencies. He should be prepared to meet different attitudes on the part of these people, since their responses will be conditioned by past experiences with clergymen. Their responses will range from a warm welcome, to indifference or even hostility. Some clergymen may have condemned, ignored, or competed with certain agencies, thus engendering negative feelings. Some agency directors may be personally antagonistic to religion and to clergymen. Others will give ministers warm and even preferred treatment. One new minister reported that, acting on a suggestion from a seminary class, he began visiting community agencies. Most of the people had not been visited by a minister for so long that they were amazed and overjoyed. The visiting nurses' association reported that it was the first time in ten years that this had happened.

Every pastor will be ministering to persons who have been or ought to be related to one or more of these agencies. He should therefore acquaint himself with the exact services and limitations of each one, together with referral procedures. Such knowledge will enable him to be of help to his constituents and will prevent the church from duplicating community services which are adequately cared for. It will also enable the minister to recognize the gaps that need to be filled, giving the church a clue as to where it might focus its efforts to meet the most pressing needs of the community. There will be times when a congregation may align itself with one or more agencies in lifting the level of community life and awakening the people to urgent problems. At other times the church may need to stand in judgment upon existing agencies, when their policies and practices are unjust.

There are some general and direct ways in which the resources of community agencies may be used by the church. For one thing persons in the church who need available services should be encouraged to apply for them. Or again, information and studies useful to the congregation (as in preparing statements on issues or in planning programs) may be available through some of these groups. Personnel from community groups are sometimes available as teachers and resource persons for church study groups and other programs. Some groups offer films and pamphlets of various kinds. Too often a church overlooks these community resources, especially when it views itself as a self-contained institution and centers its efforts upon itself instead of seeking to carry out a mission to the community.

E. Keeping Abreast in Related Fields

Although every field of administration has its own uniqueness, derived from its particular purpose, each field also shares certain common concerns with other administrative fields. Therefore, the church administrator may adapt methods from other fields if they do not conflict with the church's purpose. Consequently, he must have some knowledge of certain related fields, keeping alert to resources that may be useful to the mission of his congregation.

For instance, there is certainly a business and financial aspect of the administration of the church. In our complex society the business procedures of the church demand increasing attention. Here is an area where the boundaries of successful financial methods and the implications of Christian stewardship may clash. Let it be unequivocally stated that the church cannot accept any program or procedure that violates the gospel. The ability to raise funds is not a sufficient criterion for accepting a financial plan. Christian stewardship must always be the plumb line against which all financial policies are measured in the church. There are, however, some helpful resources from the world of business and finance which meet the test.

In the realm of office management new procedures, techniques, and equipment to improve office efficiency are continually being developed. New filing systems are now available, for instance, that not only save filing time but also make the material more accessible. Improvements in copy reproducing techniques are another example. Technical advances in office management ought to be used by the church in accordance with the volume of work required of the office.

Industry has discovered the importance of in-service training of leaders, pioneering in demonstrating the necessity and effectiveness of such training and in developing training techniques. It is likely that the church has much to learn from industry at this point. Ministers are urgently requesting inservice training, and, although the church is experimenting along several lines, no acceptable answer has yet been found. In another area the church has benefitted from industrial pioneering in the small group process of communicating, expressing differences, and effecting change and growth.

Sad to relate, the business world has also been more farsighted in providing for the human needs of their employees than have the churches. Many lay workers in the church are still poorly paid, have little or no health insurance protection, and have inadequate vacation and retirement benefits. Some ministers are in the same unhappy condition. The church ought to treat its employees at least as humanely as many business firms do.

The field of education has many things to offer the church. Although Christian education has the unique goal of securing a growing commitment to the lordship of Christ, it has much in common with other forms of education, since all education deals with the problem of how persons learn. Advances in the psychological under-standing of the several age groups are as helpful to the church as to the public school. New and more effective teaching methods should always be welcome in the church. Such resources as audio-visual aids, team teaching, and new concepts in curriculum have already been appropriated. The time is not far off when the church will also embrace the methods of some public schools in fitting teaching ap-proaches to the ability and readiness of the students.

Psychology is another discipline with useful resources to offer the church. Any contribution to the understanding of persons ought to be welcomed by the church administrator. We have already dis-cussed certain basic psychological principles that have implications for church administration. Pastoral counseling and the broader field of pastoral care have taken on new dimensions in this century owing to increasing psychological knowledge. However, psychology, like business and education, must stand under the judgment of the gos-pel and must be contributory to the purpose of the church in order to be a useful servant. Although it must not be taken as the source or norm of Christian theology, it is a useful resource in the church's ministry to persons.

Sociology also has resources for strengthening the church's min-istry. As society becomes more complex and interdependent, it is increasingly important for the church to understand the culture with which it is seeking to communicate. Sociological studies can provide knowledge out of which the churches can more realistically develop means for carrying out their mission.

The potential contribution of the field of mass communications for enhancing the outreach of the church is so obvious as to be self-evident. Radio, television, magazines, and newspapers extend the impact of the church beyond its own membership in a way scarcely imaginable half a century ago. It is obvious that the church needs the technical help of the specialists in these fields in order to make the best use of the mass media. Here again, however, the means must not violate the end. Advertising techniques cannot properly be ap-plied to religion, since the gospel is not for sale. The Christian faith requires a response more durable and pervasive than that which induces people to buy deodorant. Nevertheless, mass communications offer a resource which the church cannot ignore and ought to utilize.

The church ought also to be sensitive to the interpretations of the arts relative to the mood of the times and to the place of religion in it. Good writers, dramatists, artists, and musicians are able to pick up the feelings and attitudes of the culture and express them in striking and honest fashion, thus providing Christians with a tool for understanding the world that they are called to serve. Artistic expressions may be true or false, good or bad, but they cannot, as a whole, be ignored. The church also ought to give more attention to the arts as mediums for communicating the gospel, mediums limited only by the artists' competence and the quality of their Christian experience.

These are only some of the fields from which the church can draw resources for her ministry. Certainly no pastor can or should attempt to become personally proficient in many fields. His role is that of a resource person, acquainted with each area enough to know where to go for competent help when it is needed. The administrator is a specialist only in clarifying the nature of the gospel and the church, so that he can guide the congregation in determining what resources from these various fields will actually contribute to the church's mission of making known God's love to all men.

F. Conclusion

Throughout this book we have approached the subject of church administration from the perspective of a person seeking to become an administrator. Since the goals of church administration are unequivocally predetermined by the work of Christ, the administrator must begin with a solid understanding of the purpose of the church as defined by the gospel. Out of this understanding certain basic concerns or principles are identified, claiming the attention of any church administrator who desires his work to be purposeful. By working with these principles the pastor *engages in a process* that will weld a disunited group of persons into an effective Christian congregation which reaches out to express God's love to the world.

Church administration must ever remain a dynamic process of

ministering to persons, even though it deals with a given gospel and predetermined goals. Since the gospel must be communicated meaningfully to each person and generation, and since persons are the indispensable mediums of such communication, there can be no once-for-all method for reaching everyone. Church administration therefore calls for dynamic interaction in accordance with the persons and circumstances involved in each situation. For that reason there must always be a polar tension within purposeful church administration, which is simultaneously *God-centered* (a given gospel) and *person-oriented* (for whom and through whom the gospel exists).

We have sought to spell out the meaning of this concept through defining purposeful church administration as "the involvement of the church in the discovery of her nature and mission, and in moving in a coherent and comprehensive manner toward providing such experiences as will enable the church to utilize all her resources and personnel in the fulfillment of her mission to make known God's love for all men." This definition will *become a reality* when the principles discussed here claim the attention of the church administrator and become operative in the life of any congregation in accordance with its own personal and corporate needs. A continuous concern for each principle in dynamic interaction with all others will mobilize any church to move from where it is toward where it ought to be.

■ ■ ■ Notes

1. For example, one denomination (Methodist) publishes:
The Christian Advocate, designed to deal primarily with matters of special interest to ministers.
The Methodist Story, designed to acquaint local church commission members with programs and resources available from each of the general church boards.
Together, designed to reach the total membership of the church with denominational and Christian concerns.
2. *The Upper Room,* published by the General Board of Evangelism of The Methodist Church is one example.
3. One denomination (Methodist) has the following general boards: Missions, Education, Evangelism, Lay Activities, Christian Social Concerns, Hospitals and Homes, and Pensions.

4. See the *New York Times,* April 19, 1962, for a report on the decline in enrollment in theological schools and the explanation that this implies that the church is irrelevant. Raines, *New Life in the Church,* p. 17, draws this same conclusion.

5. The program outlined here is similar to programs used in the following denominations: The Methodist Church, the American Baptist Convention, Lutheran Churches (some Synods), the Disciples of Christ, the Evangelical United Brethren.

6. The following sources will prove helpful in these areas:

Baker Brownnell, *The Human Community; Its Philosophy and Practice for a Time of Crisis* (New York: Harper & Brothers, 1950).

Frank Cuber and William F. Kenkel, *Social Stratification in the United States* (New York: Appleton-Century-Crofts, 1954).

Floyd Hunter, *Community Power Structure; A Study of Decision Makers* (Chapel Hill: University of North Carolina Press, 1953).

Leiffer, *The Effective City Church.*

Harvey Seifert, *The Church in Community Action* (New York: Abingdon-Cokesbury Press, 1952).

Rockwell C. Smith, *The Church in Our Town* (revised and enlarged edition; Nashville: Abingdon Press, 1955).

Roland Leslie Warren, *Studying Your Community* (New York: Russell Sage Foundation, 1955).

■■■Appendix A

A card found useful in pastoral calling by the writer is reproduced here. It provides a very brief introduction to each family. The larger the congregation, the more necessary it is to have some such family record.

(Side one)

Family Name_____ Parish Group_____
Address_____ Phone_____

Baptized	Ch. Member	Friend	Ch. Activities (See No. on back)
Mr.			
Mrs.			
Children's Birthdays			
Occupation of Father			
Mother?			
Dates Called On			

Additional Information on Back

(Side two)

1. Official Board
2. Commission or committee member
3. W. S. C. S.
4. Methodist Men
5. Young Adults
6. Church School
7. MYF
8. Choir
9. Teacher in Church School
10. Attends church worship regularly

■ ■ ■ Appendix B

The "Program Builder Work Sheet" reproduced here* is given as a specific example of material available from one denominational Board of Lay Activities (Methodist) to assist the local Commission on Education in detailed annual planning. Although this work sheet refers at times to Methodist organizations and publications, these materials are not essential to the full and creative use of this plan. This work sheet could serve as a guide for any local church committee on Christian education as it now stands, or it could be used to draft their own evaluation and plan tailored to their own particular needs.

* By permission of the General Board of Lay Activities of The Methodist Church, Evanston, Illinois.

	Check if planned for the new year			Money needed to do it
	Will start doing it	Now doing it well	Should do it better	
1. Winning Pupils to Christ and the Church Is any work currently being done in this area? Yes ☐ No ☐ Annual meeting of the Commission on Education with the Commission on Membership and Evangelism present to plan the details of the year's church school evangelistic program				
Annual school of evangelistic teaching				
Teachers and leaders informed and encouraged in their responsibility as personal evangelists				
Distribution and use of Teacher's Responsibility List				
Ordering and use of church school evangelistic literature				
Full use of the Easter season in church school evangelism				
2. Recruiting and Training Leaders Is any work currently being done in this area? Yes ☐ No ☐ Discovery and enlistment of needed teachers and workers				
Local church leadership training program				
City, subdistrict or district training program				
Sending leaders to conference and other training centers				
Encouraging youth and young adults to enter church vocations				
3. Lesson Materials and Teaching Procedures Is any work currently being done in this area? Yes ☐ No ☐ Adequate provision for space for classes and groups				
Adequate lesson and other material for all classes and groups				

284

	Check if planned for the new year			Money needed to do it
	Will start doing it	Now doing it well	Should do it better	
Leaflets, manuals and periodicals for all teachers and leaders				
Classroom supplies (paper, paste, crayon, etc.)				
Classroom equipment (furniture, chalkboards, etc.)				
Audio-visual equipment (projectors, speakers, etc.)				
Purchase and rental of audio-visuals (films, records, slides, etc.)				
Books for church school library				
4. Increasing Membership and Attendance Is any work currently being done in this area? Yes ☐ No ☐				
An active membership cultivation superintendent				
An understanding throughout church of importance of increasing church school membership and attendance				
Membership workers supplied with guidance literature				
Membership rolls and attendance records adequately maintained				
A continual search for prospective new members, with adequate follow-up				
Annual presentation to Commission by membership cultivation superintendent of comprehensive plan for membership and attendance increase throughout the whole church school				
5. Christian Stewardship and Giving Is any work currently being done in this area? Yes ☐ No ☐				
All pupils taught principles of Christian stewardship involving Christian use of money and support of church and other worthy causes				
Tithing emphasized as a minimum plan of proportionate giving				
Annual budget for church school				

	Check if planned for the new year			Money needed to do it
	Will start doing it	Now doing it well	Should do it better	
Promotion of personal giving to church budget and related causes				
Promotion and observance each fourth Sunday of World Service Sunday in the church school				
Annual observance of church school rally day with offering				
Promotion of Methodist Youth Fund				
Promotion of Children's Service Fund				
6. Missionary Education Is any work currently being done in this area? Yes ☐ No ☐				
Cooperative plans being followed for missionary education of children and youth				
Adequate use of mission study units, with particular reference to adults				
Special missionary programs in Methodist Sunday Evening Fellowship and as appropriate throughout the church school				
Cooperation with Commission on Missions in annual church-wide School of Missions				
Encouragement of adequate and systematic giving to missions				
7. Music in Christian Education Is any work currently being done in this area? Yes ☐ No ☐				
Supervision over the selection and use of music in church school				
Insuring that all groups have hymnbooks which meet good standards for sacred music				
The integration of children's and youth choirs into Christian education programs for children and youth				
Music supplies				
8. Christian Service and Social Concerns Is any work currently being done in this area? Yes ☐ No ☐				

	Check if planned for the new year			Money needed to do it
	Will start doing it	Now doing it well	Should do it better	
8. Christian service cont.				
An adequate program of Christian social service in the community appropriate to each age group				
Promotion of Christian interracial attitudes and activities				
Familiarity throughout the church school with the Methodist Social Creed				
Adequate emphasis upon abstinence from beverage alcohol, upon public and private morals, and upon world peace				
9. Family Life				
Is any work currently being done in this area? Yes ☐ No ☐				
Study groups in Christian marriage and homemaking for youth and adults				
Adequate guidance in the relationship of church and family				
Observance of National Family Week				
Application of family life guidance in *Discipline*				
10. Fellowship and Recreation				
Is any work currently being done in this area? Yes ☐ No ☐				
Cultivation of Christian fellowship throughout the school to aid in all work of Christian education				
Planning special recreation events, including outings, picnics, etc.				
Recreation equipment and supplies				
Interchurch recreational activities				
A. General Program, Organization and Administration				
Is any work currently being done in this area? Yes ☐ No ☐				
Adequate organization of Commission on Education				
Steps that should be taken in perfecting the organization of church				

	Check if planned for the new year			Money needed to do it
	Will start doing it	Now doing it well	Should do it better	
A. General program, cont.				
school, noting the four parts of a complete church school				
New classes and groups needed				
Keeping up to date on a study and analysis of the Christian education needs of the church to community				
Supplying all teachers and workers with the guidance booklets prepared by General Board of Education				
Understanding and use of the Methoodist Church School Record System				
Employment by the church of a minister or director of Christian education or educational assistant				
Employment of Secretary				
General furniture, equipment and supplies				
Observance of special days designated for the church school: World Service Sunday (every fourth Sunday), Church School Rally Day, Children's Day, Promotion Day, National Family Week, Christian Education Week				
Provision for celebration of appropriate events in the Christian calendar. Christmas, Easter, etc.				
Vacation church school				
Day camping				
Christian Adventure and Youth Activities Week				
Scholarships and delegate expenses to camps and conferences				
Commission, workers' conference, council and committee expense				
General promotion and publicity				
Miscellaneous items				
B. Christian Higher Education				
Is any work currently being done in this area? Yes ☐ No ☐				
Informing the church as a whole con-				

	Check if planned for the new year			Money needed to do it
	Will start doing it	Now doing it well	Should do it better	
B. Christian Higher Education, cont. cerning the significance of Christian Higher Education				
Informing the church and particularly youth and their parents concerning Wesley Foundation and institutions of higher education related to The Methodist Church				
Cultivation of the idea of financial support of these Methodist institutions, involving a specific item in the church budget				
Cooperation in the church observance of Race Relations Sunday, Methodist Student Day and Student Recognition Day				
C. Organizing and Sponsoring New Church Schools Is any work currently being done in this area? Yes ☐ No ☐ Securing guidance literature from the General Board of Education				
Promotion of an understanding of need for more church schools to serve an expanding population				
Review of territories within reach to determine if new church schools or outpost classes are needed				
Discussion with the district superintendent (whose approval is required) of plans for new church schools				
Enlisting the cooperation of youth and adult classes and individuals				
Enlisting the cooperating of the other commissions and the Official Board				

| | Check if planned for the new year | | | Money needed to do it |
	Will start doing it	Now doing it well	Should do it better	
Total estimated money needed to carry out this proposed program				$
Less estimated amount to be raised in the church school				
Remainder which must be secured from church budget				
Additional items not covered above:				
Summary of goals and objectives:				
Dates to be reserved for church school events:				

■■■ INDEX OF SUBJECTS AND AUTHORS

Abraham, 49
administration
achievement of purpose, 22-23,
60 ff.
as purposeful activity, 22
contemporary church, 15 ff.
increasing duties, 15-16
person-oriented, 64 ff., 68, 69,
121, 123, 135
program-centered, 21
qualifications for, 23 ff., 60 ff.
administrative process
evaluating, 30-31, 83-84, 243, 248,
267
dynamic interaction, 25, 71, 278
follow through, 79
involvement, 20, 63, 71-72, 74-75,
169, 181 ff., 198, 235, 241
organizing, 70, 78-80, 244-46, 266
planning, 75-78, 226-54
recognition of need, 19, 71-75,
232-38, 264
selection and use of personnel,
79, 80-83, 113-14, 238-39

administrative process—cont'd
steps of, 69-84
stimulating action and implementation of program, 80-83,
246-48, 266
supervision, 80, 82, 186
administrative process and denominational programs, 262 ff.
administering sacraments, 99-100
annual planning conference, 245
Alton, Bishop Ralph T., 190

baptism, 50, 55, 99-100, 131
Barnett, Albert E., 45, 46
basic beliefs, 35
Benne, Kenneth, 155
Best, Ernest, 48
Beavan, Albert, 181-82
Bible. See Scriptures
biblical record, 35
Blizzard, Samuel W., 15
"brainstorming," 199, 233, 265

Campbell, Roald, 23
Calvin, John, 35

Casteel, John, 134, 156, 173
centrality of worship, 94 ff., 101-2
change and growth of persons, 133-35, 156, 161 ff. *See* also personality dynamics
Christ
  authority of, 54
  head of church, 28, 44-47, 51
  origin of church, 45-46, 50
  revelation of God's love, 54
  the vine, 45
Christian faith, 26, 63, 73, 90, 94, 99, 193
church
  as living organism, 44 ff., 52-53
  as servant, 48, 49, 51, 52, 64
  community being redeemed, 57-58
  corporate interdependence, 47-48
  corporate unity, 47-48
  institutionalism, 17, 29, 49, 50, 64, 67, 68, 92-93, 268
  institutional structure, 48-49, 50, 65
  internal renewal, 52-53, 172 ff., 231, 234
church budget, 118. *See also* stewardship and finance
church, contemporary, 13, 15-21, 28 ff., 33, 34, 47, 62, 178-79, 226-27, 259-60, 268
church, definition of
  agent of God's love, 41, 48 ff., 51, 52, 60-61, 65, 66, 146-47, 183, 230
  body of Christ, 27, 43-53, 226
  bride of Christ, 44-45
  community of persons, 34, 54-55, 84

church, definition of—*cont'd*
  divine origin, 34-35, 39, 45-46
  fellowship of redemptive love, 41, 42, 48, 51, 53-58, 64, 69, 121 ff., 131, 134-35, 146-47, 187 ff.
  God's chosen community, 32 ff., 39-43, 65-66, 188
  New Testament church, 26-28, 32, 38 ff., 64-65, 70, 104, 173, 182, 183, 190
  witnessing community, 42-43, 49, 50, 56, 57, 62, 66, 121, 132, 181 ff.
church family nights, 75. *See also* neighborhood unit groups
church history, 33-35, 40, 46
church, local
  activities, 30-31, 61, 62, 66 ff., 133, 256
  administration, 15. *See also* purposeful church administration and administrative process
  attitudes, 20
  awareness of needs, 33-34, 71-75, 147, 232-38, 264
  circuit-charges, 20, 24
  coordinating activities, 78-80, 226-54
  effectiveness, standard of, 30-31, 62 ff., 66, 71, 83-84, 119, 126, 231
  goals, 28 ff., 30-31, 63, 84-86, 114-16, 146 ff., 195-96, 250
  ministering community, 48, 57, 61, 63, 64, 67, 84-85, 190, 195, 255, 268
  problems, 20-21, 123, 155, 268
  programs, 17, 76, 122, 226 ff.

church, local—*cont'd*
self-centered groups, 226-30, 255-56
study nature of self, 26 ff., 28 ff., 46-47, 63, 73-74, 83, 104 ff., 118-20, 201, 231 ff., 240 ff.
church membership
assimilate new members, 148, 150
inactive members, 147
meaning of, 100-2, 105-8
training for adults, 107-8, 134
training for youth, 105-7, 134
church, nature and mission of, 22 ff., 26-36, 38-58, 60, 62, 64, 66, 69, 89-90, 118, 122, 130, 190, 195-96, 227
church school, 110-20
Clifford, Paul, 139
committee meetings, 67, 196 ff.
committee interpersonal relationships, 113-15, 127-30, 160 ff., 171-72, 196 ff.
commitment
of congregation, 63, 73, 84, 104, 106, 111, 193-94, 220
of pastor, 47. *See also* pastor, qualifications of
community needs, 34, 230-31, 270-71
community of priests, 76. *See also* priesthood of all believers
community resources and the church, 272-74
community training courses, 222
communication
of gospel, 67 ff., 85, 90-91, 98, 121, 141 ff., 146, 194, 278
parishioner to pastor, 81, 109

communication—*cont'd*
pastor to parishioner, 67, 81, 82, 92, 121-52
persons to persons, 146-47, 228-29. *See also* relationships
two-way communication, 109
comprehensive planning, 226 ff.
annual planning, 247, 249-54
church renewal, 231, 234
church's task, 230
continual planning, 253
crises situation, 232
decisions, 228
duplication of activities, 229
evaluation of ideas, 243, 248
implementation, 246 ff.
involvement of congregation, 235, 241, 242
long-range perspective, 227
long-range planning, 231 ff.
making long-range plans, 238-43
necessity and value of, 226-27
organizing for action, 244 ff.
planning committee, 233, 238-39
recognition of need, 232-37
self-centered groups, 230
spiritual life retreat, 249 ff.
study analysis, 236
subcommittees, 240
understanding nature of the church, 241 ff.
unified goals, 227-28
concept of ministry, 28, 30, 33, 38 ff., 50-51, 89 ff., 104 ff.
consecrated imagination, 77, 221, 233, 242, 250
coordinating activities, 78 ff. *See also* comprehensive planning
cordination of planning, 253-54
corporate unity of church, 47-48

Cosby, Gordon, 192-93
covenant, 39, 42, 49
culture
  conflict with church, 29, 62, 63, 67
  impact on church, 16, 25, 28, 33, 70, 119, 130, 146, 153-54
cultural patterns, 26
Craig, Clarence Tucker, 43

decisions, 228-29, 261
democratic group leader, 168-72
denominational leadership training, 222 ff.
denominational programs evaluated, 259 ff.
denominational resources, 222, 257-68

ecumenical movement, 32
ecumenical resources, 268-72
education, Christian, 110-18
  goals and scope, 63, 110-11
  objectives of, 98, 114 ff., 131
  pastor's relation to, 111 ff. See also teaching ministry and pastor, as teacher
  structure for, 112-13
  teacher training, 117-18, 222 ff.
Edwards, Richard H., 122
emotional experiences, 127-29
ends and means, 30, 31, 35. See also purposeful church administration, goals
Erikson, Erik, 71
experienced relationships, 131. See also personality dynamics
evangelism, 56-57, 63, 67, 90, 106, 112 ff., 179, 216, 229, 263 ff.

evangelism committee, 265. See also evangelism
evaluation of church activities and programs, 30-31, 83 ff., 243, 248, 267
evaluation of denominational church programs, 259 ff.

family night groups, 247. See also neighborhood unit groups
fellowship
  meaning of, 54-56, 146, 157, 184-87
  origin of, 53-54, 56
  redemptive fellowship, 53 ff. See also redemptive interpersonal relationships
finance committee, 76, 161. See also stewardship and finance
Francis of Assisi, 47
Frankl, Viktor, 132

God
  calling of, 32-33, 40
  grace of, 40, 43
  love of, 40, 50, 54, 121
  revelation of, 44, 47, 52, 54, 65
Gordon, Thomas, 168-69
gospel, 25, 27, 34, 53, 67, 119, 195, 278
group dynamics, 157-71
  background of group members, 162-63
  definition of, 157-59
  goals of group, 155, 160-61
  group leader, 168-69
  growth of persons, 133-35, 161-62, 171-72
  hidden agenda, 163-65

group dynamics—*cont'd*
personal support, 159-60
principles of, 159 ff.
renewal of church, 172-73
roles of group, 165-68
role of group leader, 168-71
groups in the church, 153-79, 186 ff., 197 ff. *See also* koinonia groups, neighborhood unit groups, study and fellowship groups, and small groups in the church
group leader, 158, 162, 168-72
groups, principles for fellowship, 173-75
group roles, 165-68
growth through committee relationships, 171 ff.
Gustafson, James, 33

Holy Spirit, 34, 35, 48, 52, 53, 55, 179
Hosea, 41, 65
hostilities of the pastor, 125
house church, 173
Howe, Reuel, 131
Huss, John, 47
hymn-of-the-month program, 98

inactive church members, 147
incarnation, 54, 64, 65, 67, 126
initiative, 25. *See also* pastor, as leader and administrative process, recognition of need
institutional structure, 48-49, 50, 65, 67
institutionalism, 17, 29, 49, 50, 64, 67, 68, 92-93, 268
interdenominational resources, 268-72

Jenkins, Daniel, 53
Jeremiah, 41, 65
Job analysis, 201-3
Johnson, Paul, 122

Knowles, Malcolm and Hulda, 158
koinonia, 48, 53 ff., 56. *See also* fellowship
koinonia groups, 63, 67, 150-51, 153-79
koinonia groups, case study of Skokie, 176-78

"Lay Academy," 173
lay ministry, 184-93
mutual encouragement, 187, 190
pastor's responsibility, 185, 192
study and discussion, 186, 187
to the church, 185, 186, 187 ff.
to one another, 184, 186, 187
to the world, 190
lay visitation, 185-86, 263 ff.
lay witnessing, 85, 90, 102, 184-93, 213
leadership
group leaders, 135, 158 ff., 162 ff., 168-71
of pastor, 81, 94. *See also* pastor, as leader
potential, 196-219
qualifications of, 135, 159 ff., 183, 197 ff., 204 ff.
specialized training, 219-24
training laymen, 81, 102-4, 112, 176-78, 181-225, 249, 258
leadership responsibilities, 135, 168-71, 183. *See also* leadership, qualifications of
leadership talent file, 113, 206 ff.

Lewin, Kurt, 168
Lord's Supper, 50, 99-100
lordship of Christ, 47, 62. *See also* Christ
long-range planning, 231-248
Lovelace, Austin C. and William C. Rice, *Music and Worship in the Church*, 97
Luther, Martin, 35, 47, 53

Maves, Paul, 154, 162, 188
mergers of congregations, 270-71
Miller, Donald, 237
minister's time schedule, 13, 15, 17, 91-94, 136-37, 142-43, 153-54
mission of the church, 26-36, 38-58, 63. *See also* church, nature and mission
motivation for Christian witness, 195

National Council of Churches, 115, 271
neighborhood discussion groups, 233, 236. *See also* next listing and study and fellowship groups
neighborhood family group plan, 147-52
neighborhood unit groups, 74-76, 147-52, 160, 213, 247
Newbigin, Lesslie, 46
New Testament church, 38 ff., 26-28, 64-65, 104, 183, 190
Niebuhr, H. Richard, 16, 54, 85, 181, 188
Niles, D. T., 51
nominating committee
composition and structure, 196 ff.

nominating committee—*cont'd*
consent of nominees, 218
nominating procedures, 214
opening session, 198 ff.
operational procedures, 197, 214, 218
significance of, 200, 214
work analysis, 199 ff.

organizational process, 70, 78-80, 244-46, 266

pastor
as administrator, 15-21, 22 ff., 28, 60, 70, 71 ff., 80, 84-86, 110, 123-24, 124-27, 130, 255, 268
as agent of Christian faith, 90-94
as executive, 17 ff., 22, 255 ff.
as leader, 30, 75, 90, 112, 124-26, 154, 181, 227, 238, 257
as preacher, 98-99, 105. *See also* preaching
as symbol of Christian faith, 124
as teacher, 104 ff., 11-120, 193 ff. *See also* teaching ministry
called by God, 61, 204. *See also* pastor, qualifications of
image of, 16-18, 100-1
need for study, 18, 22-25, 46-47, 63, 91-94. *See also* above listing, qualifications
personal worship, 91
public relations, 17 ff.
qualifications of, 23, 63, 68, 90 ff., 94, 124-27, 145, 181-82, 192, 257
pastor as a mature person, 124 ff.
pastoral calling
need for, 63, 136-38, 185

pastoral calling—*cont'd*
  objectives, 102, 106, 132, 138-43, 237
  values of, 67-69, 144-45
  what to do, 142-45
pastoral care, 63, 67-69, 126, 127-29, 134, 141, 142-45, 147, 185
pastoral prayers, 97. *See also* worship
Paul, 26, 27, 47, 48, 54, 55
Pentecost, 42, 46, 107
person-oriented preaching, 67-68
personality development, 121 ff.
personality dynamics, 121 ff., 127-35, 139 ff., 156-57
personal goals, 132 ff.
personnel analysis, 215
person of the minister, 90-91. *See also* pastor, qualifications of
planned preaching, 253
planning
  annual planning, 249-53
  long-range planning, 233-43
  of programs for local church, 19-21, 69 ff., 156, 226-54
  priority needs, 244
  process of, 226-54
  study analysis, 236
  study for planning, 240 ff.
  resources, 252
planning committee, 233 ff.
polarity principle, 61, 69, 278
potential of lay leadership, 196-219
preaching, 51, 61, 63, 68, 92, 97, 98-99, 102, 105, 109, 124, 133, 253
priesthood of all believers, 49-50, 57, 76, 111, 182-83

principles for small fellowship groups, 174 ff.
programs
  initiated by local church, 19-21, 69 ff., 72
  initiated by outside agencies, 257 ff.
programs evaluated, 259 ff.
program planning, 226-54
public education, 24
public relations, 17, 18
purposeful church administration
  definition of, 21, 22 ff., 24-25, 31-32, 58, 60-87, 226, 277-78
  goals, 21, 30-31, 43, 44, 58, 63, 84-86, 227 ff.
  God-centered, 61 ff., 69, 221
  growth of persons, 156, 161-63
  pastor as administrator, 23, 60 ff., 130, 181-84, 192, 261 ff., 277. *See also* pastor, as administrator
  person-oriented, 64 ff., 68, 69, 121, 123, 135
  polarity principle, 61, 69, 278
  principles, 61 ff., 84-86, 89, 118-20, 181-84
  problems, 226 ff.
  standard of acceptability, 62 ff., 71

qualities of Christian leadership, 204 ff. *See also* leadership

Raines, Robert, 29, 134, 156, 173, 176, 192, 237
recognition of need, 71-75, 232-37
redemption, 53 ff., 57

redemptive interpersonal relationships, 19-21, 53 ff., 57, 69, 115, 121-52, 156, 171-79, 187 ff.

relationships
    group relationships, 129-30, 133-35
    interpersonal, 34, 42, 65, 67-69, 121-52, 161, 163 ff., 186
    language of, 68, 132
    man and God, 34, 40, 50, 53, 56, 63, 65, 95, 108, 115
    parishioner to pastor, 103-4
    pastor and youth, 107
    pastor to parishioner, 67 ff., 80, 82, 90, 111, 122 ff., 127-29, 134, 135-45, 273
    persons in relationship, 54, 57, 129-30
    person to person, 34, 53, 77, 85, 114-15, 122 ff., 146-47, 161

resources beyond local church, 222, 255 ff.

resources from secular fields
    arts, 277
    business, 274
    education, 275
    mass communication, 276
    office management, 275
    psychology, 276
    sociology, 276

retreats, 110, 220, 249 ff.

Richardson, Alan, 41, 48

sacraments, 50, 99-100

salvation, 47, 54

Second Isaiah, 41, 49, 65

servant
    church as, 48, 49, 52, 55, 64, 182-83

servant—cont'd
    pastor as, 138, 181

Scriptures, 26-27, 35, 39, 46, 64, 96-97

self-understanding, 124. See also personality dynamics

sermon, 96-99. See also preaching

Shaw, George Bernard, 126

small groups in the church
    change in persons, 156, 161 ff.
    contributions of, 186 ff.
    group dynamics, 153-79
    hidden agenda, 163 ff.
    importance and use, 153-57
    leadership, 158, 162
    objectives, 155
    pastor's role, 154
    personal stability, 157, 159
    planning, 156
    problem solving, 155
    procedures, 197 ff.

spiritual foundation for church administration, 89 ff.

state councils of churches
    resource leaders, 271
    laymen's retreats, 271

stewardship and finance, 24, 76, 90, 119, 130, 161-62

"Stewardship of Talent Indicator" 206 ff.
    distribution, 213
    use, 214

study and fellowship groups, 63, 90, 92, 108-10, 134-35, 146-52, 153-79, 186-87, 219, 237

study courses for laymen, 108 ff.

study of the Scriptures, 63 ff.

success image, 15-16

teaching ministry, 99, 104-20, 181 ff., 219 ff.

theology, 32-33

theological education, 91-92. *See also* pastor, qualifications of

Thelan, Herbert, 160

training church school teachers, 117-18, 269 ff.

training laymen, 81, 102-4, 112, 176-78, 181-225, 249, 258

Trueblood, Elton, 191

visitation evangelism, 185, 263 ff.

Walker, Daniel, 16

Wesley, John, 35, 47

World Council of Churches, 271

worship
function of church, 31, 42, 50, 61, 63, 89, 94-104, 118-20

leadership for worship, 96-101, 104, 189

music, 97-98

music committee, 97-98

resources, 96

worship committee, 102-4

■ ■ ■ INDEX OF SCRIPTURAL PASSAGES

Genesis

12:1-2 ....39, 42
13:14 49

Exodus

19:4-6 41
19:5-6a 40

Deuteronomy

7:7-8a 40

Isaiah

53 49
61 52

Amos

5:21 49
5:23-24 49

Matthew

16:18 50
20:27 51
23:11 51
26:29 42

Mark

2:27 65
10:44 51
14:24 42

Luke

4:18 52
22:20 42

John

13:35 55
14:9 54
15:4-5a 45

Acts

1:15 46
2:1 46
6:2-5a 50

Romans

1:11-12 55
8:35-39 56
10:9 44
16:14 55

I Corinthians

1:25	42
1:26-27	48
3:4	26
4:1	26
8	26-27
8:9	27
8:12	55
8:13	27
12	27, 43, 44, 47
12:3	44
12:4-7	48
12:5-7	182-83
12:12	182-83
12:21	48
12:27	182-83
13	27, 54

II Corinthians

13:14	55

Galatians

4:4	49
6:1	55
6:2	27

Ephesians

2:19	43, 55
2:19-22	45
4	43, 44
4:11-13	48
4:12	182
5:22-24	45

Colossians

4:15	55

Philippians

2:11	44

I Peter

2:2	57
2:5	57
2:9	57, 182
2:9 ff.	41

Revelation

1:6	41
5:10	41
20:6	41